Tuscaloosa
the tradition • the spirit • the vision

Produced in cooperation with
The Chamber of Commerce of West Alabama

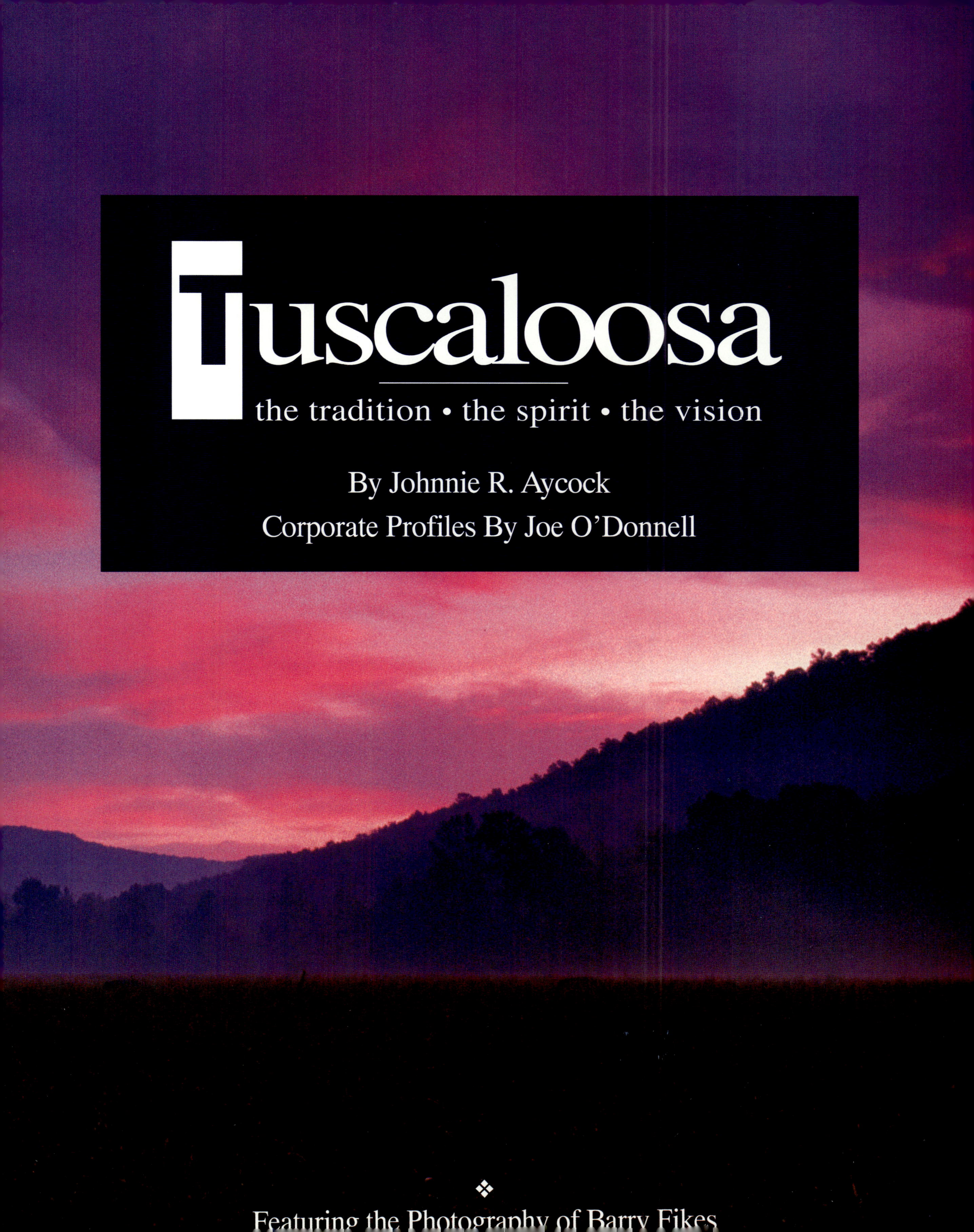

Tuscaloosa

the tradition • the spirit • the vision

By Johnnie R. Aycock

Corporate Profiles By Joe O'Donnell

❖

Featuring the Photography of Barry Fikes

Community Communications—Book Division
Publishers: Ronald P. Beers
James E. Turner

Staff for Tuscaloosa: The Tradition, The Spirit, The Vision
Publisher's Sales Associate: Bill Koons
Executive Editor: James E. Turner
Managing Editor: Mary Shaw Hughes
Design Director: Camille Leonard
Designers: Emily McClure and Katie Bradshaw
Photo Editors: Mary Shaw Hughes and Emily McClure
Production Assistant: Corinne Cau
Editorial Assistant: Robyn Putz
Proofreader: Opal Banish
Accounting Services: Sara Ann Turner
Printing Production: Frank Rosenberg/GSAmerica

Community Communications
A Division of LWT Communications Inc.

James E. Turner, Chairman of the Board
Ronald P. Beers, President
Daniel S. Chambliss, Vice President

Contents

Part One: The Tradition, The Spirit, The Vision

Foreword...page 8 ❖ Preface...page 10

Contents

Part Two: Tuscaloosa's Enterprises

Foreword

Cherished traditions—a quality, family environment—a winning spirit—an ideal home for business. All of these descriptive terms and more reflect the way I, and so many of our friends and neighbors, feel about Tuscaloosa.

And it is with a sense of pride, enthusiasm, and willingness to share our community that The Chamber of Commerce of West Alabama presents this first-of-its-kind book, *Tuscaloosa: The Tradition, The Spirit, The Vision*, to our community in recognition of Tuscaloosa's 175th anniversary as a community.

Within these beautiful pages, it is our sincere hope and desire that you will experience and feel the diverse, quality texture and healthy pulse of the Tuscaloosa-area community. The entire Tuscaloosa County and West Alabama region is a rich fabric of wonderful people, progressive partnerships, dynamic economic growth, and exciting opportunities. Within these pages, you will understand why our future is so very bright.

It's a magic time of renaissance in the Tuscaloosa-area community. Those of us who live here know and appreciate the warmth and friendliness of our people, respect our traditions and heritage, and recognize the opportunities for a prosperous future. Within these pages, we are proud to share a glimpse into the heart and soul of Tuscaloosa and the spirit of our people that provides new perspectives for lifelong residents and visitors alike.

This indeed was a challenging project for The Chamber and our community. However, our Board of Directors along with our progressive and generous corporate supporters believed that we had a wonderful opportunity to showcase our community's excellence, enhance our area's image, and contribute in a positive way to the spirit of Tuscaloosa.

On behalf of The Chamber's Board of Directors, who made the decision to publish this beautiful keepsake in honor and celebration of Tuscaloosa's 175th birthday, I am proud to present to you *Tuscaloosa: The Tradition, The Spirit, The Vision,* for it captures the essence of our community and our people.

Robert H. Shaw, Jr.
1994 Chairman
The Chamber of Commerce of West Alabama

Preface

None of us exist apart from each other or from the community we call home—and Tuscaloosa is indeed a special place to call home. Each morning, as the sun rises over the Black Warrior River and a new day dawns, I become even more grateful that our family chose Tuscaloosa as home and gave us the precious opportunity to become interconnected with so many marvelous friends and neighbors.

Tuscaloosa, like most communities, has its own unique personality that has developed over the years from our history and traditions, climate and topography, progress and setbacks. But most of all, Tuscaloosa's personality reflects the spirit of the people who live here. In our attempt to capture the spirit and personality of Tuscaloosa within these pages, I've gained a deep appreciation for just how marvelous our community is and its tremendous potential.

Whether all of us ultimately thrive and progress will be determined by our understanding of our interdependence on each other and our willingness to come together as unique diverse individuals and as a community to strengthen, nurture, and improve the lives of each other. It is through pride in our community, as visualized in the following pages, that in a small way, we can stimulate that sense of community.

We have attempted to bring to life, in words and pictures, the traditions, spirit, people, and qualities of the Tuscaloosa-area community. I sincerely hope we can capture your interest and pride in Tuscaloosa, your imagination, and more importantly, your commitment to help build an even greater community for the 21st century. Of course, in the final analysis, nothing can really take the place of experiencing Tuscaloosa yourself, which we encourage.

Please realize, however, in a book such as this that we've attempted to paint a broad picture of our community, and to include every dimension and detail is impossible. There are bound to be oversights and omissions, but we sincerely hope we've captured the essence of spirit and of a community that is very special.

The experience and involvement with this project has taught me several lessons and been filled with a mixture of emotions. I've learned that there is a great difference between writing and being a writer; and I've gained a great appreciation and respect for those true writers, who daily transform an idea or a vision into something real that touches our minds, hearts, and souls.

That mixture of emotions has included anxiety, inspiration, fear, and joy—but threaded throughout the process has been a thankful heart.

Thankful for the privilege my family and I have to call Tuscaloosa home and serve the area community with many of you. Thankful for the joy of encouraging, supportive friends, colleagues, and associates who made a difficult process somewhat easier and got me through the difficult times, again realizing we are interdependent on each other.

Finally, I want to share a few key special thank yous and acknowledgments that have made this challenging project a reality.

To The Chamber of Commerce of West Alabama's officers and Board of Directors for having the foresight and commitment to transform an idea into reality, thank you! And a special word of gratitude is due to Verta Barr and Jimmy Warren for your continued encouragement, support, and friendship, which played a key role in seeing me to the finish of the project.

To our generous corporate sponsors and subscribers, thank you for taking the risk to tell our community's story. Thank you for making this first-of-its-kind initiative possible. Thank you for transforming a dream into results that will have impact for years to come!

To Mary Hughes and Jim Turner of Community Communications, thank you for believing in Tuscaloosa and me personally. Thank you for your patience, cooperation, and persistence, and for never giving up on us. That extra bit of encouragement did make a difference!

To a totally dedicated and superior staff, you serve our community daily, often without your due recognition or the gratitude deserved. Your professionalism and dedication to building an even better community through The Chamber is appreciated. Especially to Brenda Bodie, Angela Nelson, and Cheryl Watts, thank you for the hours and hours of research, preparing material and keeping me from losing my direction, sense of purpose, and mind. You have made a significant contribution to the success of our project.

Finally, I'm blessed with a wonderful family who has provided a loving, encouraging environment and framework for me to serve and to hopefully grow. To my children, thank you and I love you; and to my wife, Miriam, whom I dedicate this book to, you have blessed my life with your grace, your kindness, and your love. Thank you for being you! ❖

Johnnie R. Aycock

Chapter

1

Introduction & History

Treasured Traditions, Community Reflections

A person standing at a certain vantage point along the banks of the Black Warrior, the grand old river that flows through the heart of Tuscalooosa, can see for miles in either direction. Turn one way and the eye follows the broad, smooth back of the river as it cuts through the trees and then pierces the darkening horizon. Turn the other way and there is the setting sun. Its dying orange

The simple beauty of the Black Warrior River is a reflection of Tuscaloosa tradition.

glow captured for a time in the smoothly flowing water, energizing the river with the light of a natural benediction breathtaking in its simple beauty.

A little closer to the water's edge, the reflectons become clear. The treetops, clouds, and sky are mirrored in the glassy river surface.

The best way to approach this book is to think of it, too, as a reflection. Look closely at the text and photographs and a community will come into focus. The tradition, the spirit, the vision of Tuscaloosa. A rising star of the New South.

Born in 1819 on the banks of the great Black Warrior River, Tuscaloosa is an exciting, unique community that reflects its history and cherishes its traditions, even as it moves forward with a proud vision of the future. Tradition and vision. At times, the two ancient and honored attributes of human society might seem polar opposites. But in Tuscaloosa, tradition and vision exist in a harmonic partnership that captivates the spirit of the people and enhances the very flavor of the community.

Consistently listed by various publications in the top third of America's most livable communities, Tuscaloosa has attracted major investment from around the globe. For most of the decade of the 1980s and midway into the 1990s, Tuscaloosa has been at the center stage of economic development in Alabama, leading the state with consistent new job development, economic growth, steady retail expansion, extensive upturns in real estate and construction, energy development, and aggressive, meaningful improvements in education from kindergarten to doctoral studies.

Even with a large metropolitan area's vast array of cultural, recreational, and economic pursuits, the small town atmosphere that still exists here makes living in Tuscaloosa very special.

The land that would become Tuscaloosa was home to native Americans for centuries. The region was a favorite hunting ground of the Creek and Choctaw Indians. According to early stories, these tribes once staged an Indian ball game to decide who would have the hunting rights to the area, in perhaps the precursor to the college football games that have so entranced 20th-century Tuscaloosans.

The intricate and advanced Indian culture of the Mississippian period flowered near Tuscaloosa in an area on the Tuscaloosa/Hale County line now known as Moundville. It was the ceremonial center of the region's

At historic Capitol Park, one can see the renovated foundation and site of Alabama's former State Capitol.

The Black Warrior River is still an important means of transporting goods in and around the area.

Native American culture. At one time, perhaps a century before the first coming of the white man, up to 10,000 Indians lived in villages surrounding Moundville.

The Native American roots run deep in this part of the country. The great Indian Chief Tuskaloosa lent his name to the city and county, as well as the Black Warrior River. In the language of the Choctaw and Creek Indians, the word "tuska" means warrior and "lusa" means black.

Hernando DeSoto and his Spanish soldiers first came to the part of the southeastern United States that would become Tuscaloosa in 1540. That same year, in the bloody battle of Mauvila, which took place about 100 miles to the south of the present-day city, Chief Tuskaloosa and more than 7,000 Indians were massacred by the Spaniards.

The first documented American explorers reached the Tuscaloosa area in 1810 and 1813, although there is evidence that the Black Warrior River was being used by some travelers as early as the 1770s. The area's first settlers arrived from South Carolina and Georgia in 1816; and on February 7, 1818, Tuscaloosa was created by an act of the Alabama Territorial Legislature.

According to one historical account, *Alabama Tales* by Drue Duke, "Tuscaloosa's first resident is believed to have been Thomas York, the founder of the town." Duke goes on to write, "as others followed, they were a mixed lot. One was a blacksmith who performed marriages; another was Joshua Holbert who brought the first farm wagon. Otis Dyer arrived as a surveyor and merchant, and a few years later was operating a ferry across the river between Tuscaloosa and Northport, originally known as Kentuck."

On December 13, 1819, with a population of about 600, Tuscaloosa was incorporated by the territorial legislature, one day before the state of Alabama was admitted to the Union.

In December, 1820, Newtown was incorporated. This "lower part of Tuskaloosa" was quickly subdivided and sold, and soon became the site of a courthouse, jail, hotel, and wharf. In 1825, Newtown was dissolved and merged with an expanding Tuscaloosa.

Tuscaloosa became Alabama's state capital in 1826, and what followed was a 20-year period of robust progress and diversification for Tuscaloosa. Agriculture and commerce expanded and prospered, the population of the young state capital grew, and a great deal of the community's cultural and social heritage was formed. The University of Alabama was established, which would have a profound impact on Tuscaloosa for years to come.

The U.S. Congress had set aside land in 1818 in the Alabama Territory for the support of, what was termed, a "seminary of learning." During the second session of Alabama's new General Assembly on December 18, 1820, that "seminary of learning" was officially established and named the University of the State of Alabama.

On April 12, 1831, Reverend Alva Woods, D.D., became the first president of The University of Alabama, with inauguration ceremonies held in Tuscaloosa's Christ Episcopal Church.

The University Club, originally built by James Dearing, served as the Governor's Mansion during the period that Tuscaloosa was the state capital.

Tuscaloosa's economy flourished during the two decades that the city served as the state capital. Many prominent structures were constructed, several of which still remain today as important reminders of the city's fascinating history. The Gorgas Home was the first structure built on the original University of Alabama campus. The University Club, originally built by James Dearing, served as the Governor's Mansion during the Capitol period. The Old Tavern served as a favorite "watering hole" for state legislators. And the renovated foundation still stands at the site of the original state capitol.

In 1846, the young, growing city received a devastating blow when the state capitol was moved to its present location in Montgomery. While the agricultural areas of Tuscaloosa County continued to prosper, commercial interests declined significantly because of the loss of the capital. The value of real estate plummeted, the population declined, and income dropped sharply.

But, as so often has happened throughout the years in Tuscaloosa, individual

Reverend Alva Woods was the first president of The University of Alabama. Photo courtesy of The University of Alabama Special Collections.

community and business leaders stepped forward to turn around the fortunes of the struggling community. Leaders such as Robert Jemison, Horace King, and others made their mark on Tuscaloosa.

A planter, lawyer, businessman, and politician, Jemison had an immeasurable impact on Tuscaloosa during this period. From his success in agriculture, Jemison expanded his business interests to include transportation, mining, lumber, brick, and numerous construction projects, providing local employment when the need was great.

It was Jemison's political leadership, along with the emotional encouragement of Mrs. Dorothea Dix, that steered the decision to locate the Alabama Insane Hospital, now Bryce Hospital, in Tuscaloosa—an accomplishment that was perhaps the stimulus largely responsible for Tuscaloosa's emergence from its economic hardships following the state capital move.

Another early Tuscaloosa leader who has become a symbol for civic responsibility was Horace King. Born a slave, King was a skillful and successful builder. Upon gaining his freedom, he became a very wealthy man and a successful legislator. King even constructed the first bridge across the Black Warrior River in 1835.

In the 1830s and 1840s, large water oaks, found in the vast forests of Alabama, were planted in abundance along the streets of Tuscaloosa. History records that Thomas Maxwell was the citizen that first gave Tuscaloosa its nickname of "The City of Oaks," which over time evolved into the "Druid City." Even after many of the oaks were removed later, Tuscaloosa retained its title as the "Druid City" in honor of those magnificent trees.

In the period from 1855 up to the Civil War, Tuscaloosa continued to grow as an important industrial and trade location. Factors that contributed to this progress in those early days were strategic

Tuscaloosa has been nicknamed "Druid City" in honor of the magnificent oak trees in the area.

location, abundant natural resources, a growing labor market with a strong work ethic, and an extensive water supply. Today, these are still critical elements in the community's economic growth.

There are several Civil War-era structures still in use that survive as reminders of the past. These include the President's Mansion at The University of Alabama; and the Robert Jemison home on Greensboro Avenue, which was completed during the Civil War and extensively renovated in 1993 and 1994 to become the Tuscaloosa Visitor's Center.

During the 1870s and 1880s, Tuscaloosa continued to flourish and industrialize. Transportation and utility systems grew, and several key developments took place that laid a foundation for today's prosperity and success.

For example, the first train came into Tuscaloosa in 1871, a new bridge was built connecting Northport and Tuscaloosa, and the Tuscaloosa Water Works was established in 1887. In 1871, the First National Bank of Tuskaloosa opened its doors on the corner of University Boulevard and 22nd Avenue, where The Chamber of Commerce of West Alabama stands today.

In 1876, the Southern Presbyterian Church, under the leadership and guidance of Reverend Charles Stillman, D.D., established a black educational facility in Tuscaloosa to train ministers. The institution was renamed Stillman Institute in 1895; and today, Stillman College continues to serve and play a key leadership role for all of Tuscaloosa.

Throughout the decade of the 1880s, the infrastructure of a modern city was laid. In 1885, the present public school system was established by a special act of the legislature, and later that decade a charter was granted to Southern Bell Telephone and Telegraph to serve Tuscaloosa. In 1886, the Tuscaloosa Railway Improvement Corporation applied for a charter to build, equip, and operate a street railway, gas works, water works, and electric power works in Tuscaloosa, asking for an exemption of municipal taxation for a 50-year period.

Today, the Black Warrior-Tombigbee River System, which connects to the Tenn-Tom Waterway, serves as a vital resource and transportation artery for the Tuscaloosa area, with a vast array of raw materials and goods being moved daily along the river. Continuing improvements over the past 80 years by the U.S. Corps of Engineers have significantly affected the river's development along with Tuscaloosa's prosperity and access to the world's markets.

While World War I did cause a short pause in Tuscaloosa's development, the 1920s saw the rapid expansion of the city. Voters approved a bond issue that led to the establishment of Druid City Hospital, and the Partlow State School added to Tuscaloosa's ties to the world of modern medicine.

In addition, an aggressive recruitment effort by the Tuscaloosa Chamber of Commerce convinced Alabama Power to open a center in Tuscaloosa in 1923. That coup was followed by the establishment of Gulf States Paper Corporation in 1929, which would become one of the community's most important corporate citizens for many years to come.

Gulf States founder, Herbert Westervelt, turned to Alabama, which basically had been ignored by the paper industry, when he decided to consolidate his extensive operations. He selected Tuscaloosa as the site for his headquarters because "it had everything: water, labor, natural resources, favorable transportation costs plus The University of Alabama and an enthusiastic welcome from

The Old Tavern served as a favorite "watering hole" for state legislators during the Capitol period.

the townspeople." It's interesting to note that same combination still works effectively more than 65 years later.

The University of Alabama also experienced significant growth during the 1920s under the leadership of Dr. George Denny. Enrollment increased to nearly 5,000, and facilities expanded through one of the most extensive building programs in the country. The university gained national prominence during this period as the "Capstone of Education," which directly contributed to the pride and spirit of the people of Tuscaloosa. Today, Dr. Denny's name appears on such key landmarks as the Denny Chimes and Bryant-Denny Stadium.

The Great Depression hit Tuscaloosa and Alabama hard; but, even in the midst of it and afterwards, the people of Tuscaloosa continued to exhibit courage and determination. Through federally created jobs, the people of Tuscaloosa built and expanded educational facilities, and completed several major construction projects including the Bama Theatre, City Hall, airport facilities, Oliver Lock & Dam, water reservoir, and Veterans Affairs Hospital additions. These were projects vitally important to getting Tuscaloosa back on its feet, yet to this day they continue to make an impact.

A sense of renewed vigor, expansion, and change bouyed Tuscaloosa's economy during the 1940s. Growth in the industrial sector took off during the war years. Construction, housing, and retail experienced substantial levels of growth. When the returning veterans came home from World War II, they returned to a growing city.

B.F. Goodrich Tire Company opened its doors in 1946 and with over 1,000 employees began producing tires. During that same period, Hunt Refining established its presence in Tuscaloosa with a new refinery. The coal and coke ovens at Holt were reopened and still other manufacturing firms, such as Central Foundry and Reichhold Chemical, were established.

World War II also changed agriculture in Tuscaloosa County. Emerging from a decade-long decline, farmers saw new demand and increased prices for their cotton, soybeans, meat products, and other produce. The good prices the fruit of their labors brought allowed the farms to diversify profitably. Farmers also began to, by necessity, turn to machinery to produce their products to replace the declining number of available farm workers.

Another outcome of the war was a healthy growth in population. During war years, Northington Hospital served thousands of returning veterans and wounded soldiers, many of whom elected to stay and live in Tuscaloosa. One such veteran was Al DuPont, who has served Tuscaloosa as mayor since 1982.

Population expanded rapidly between 1940 and 1950, accelerating residential growth and a postwar housing boom. New suburban shopping centers such as Leland Plaza, Parkview Center, and others began to dot the Tuscaloosa landscape during the 1950s. And manufacturing continued to grow as well. In 1952, J. Reese Phifer established a small operation that would grow into the world's largest producer of woven screen products, Phifer Wire Products.

The Bryant Museum, dedicated to Paul "Bear" Bryant, attracts visitors from all over the country.

The variety of architectural designs and styles capture the spirit of the people and enhance the flavor of the community.

School desegregation and the civil rights struggle also began in the early 1950s following a landmark Supreme Court case decision. In Tuscaloosa, Arthurine Lucy had applied for admission to The University of Alabama in 1952, and prepared to enter classes finally four years later on February 3, 1956. It was a difficult and tragic time for Tuscaloosa as law and order broke down.

In a series of editorials during early 1956, James Buford Boone, Sr., publisher of *The Tuscaloosa News*, shined the light of truth on the community's concerns with this breakdown of law and order. In that Pulitzer prize-winning editorial published on February 7, 1956, and entitled, "What A Price for Peace," Boone wrote: "When mobs start imposing their frenzied will on universities, we have a bad situation. But that is what has happened at The University of Alabama. And it is a development over which The University of Alabama, the people of this state, and the community should be deeply ashamed . . . and more than a little afraid."

"Our government's authority springs from the will of the people. But their wishes, if we are to be guided by democratic principles and processes, must be expressed by ballot at the polls, by action in the legislative halls, and finally by interpretation from the bench."

The struggle for freedom and civil rights continued in Tuscaloosa and the nation well into the 1960s and 1970s, with perhaps one of the most significant moments of the movement happening in Tuscaloosa in 1963.

On June 11, 1963, then Alabama Governor George Wallace staged his famous "stand in the schoolhouse door" at The University of Alabama in an attempt to keep Vivian Malone and James Hood from being admitted to school.

It was a trying and difficult time for all the citizens of Tuscaloosa, Alabama, and the nation as this "center stage" event became a symbol of misguided resistance that still casts a long shadow over us.

However, Dr. Culpepper Clark of The University of Alabama, and author of the book, *Stand in the Schoolhouse Door*, looks at the event today in a different light, which reflects the change that has taken place and continues to take place in human relations.

Dr. Clark emphasizes that June 11, 1963, should be remembered as a "defining moment when segregation was surrendered and change was achieved." He goes on to point out that Tuscaloosa was a "battleground for freedom," and urges citizens to "move beyond the image of resistance to an appreciation of our capacity to change and remember what has been accomplished at the university and in the community in human relations."

Indeed, the 1960s and 1970s were years of transition, change, moderate economic expansion, coupled with serious declines in Tuscaloosa's manufacturing base. The major events and developments of the decade period included the integration of the Tuscaloosa City Schools, the construction of Lake Tuscaloosa, the opening of Jim Walters Resources in Brookwood, the building of McFarland Mall, the improvement and expansion of the airport, the establishment of the Tuscaloosa County Industrial Development Authority, and the founding of the Northport Chamber of Commerce.

But the truly important developments in Tuscaloosa emerged from the bitter crucible that was the national local economy in the latter half of the 1970s. When things appeared at their bleakest, a new spirit of determination and community emerged in Tuscaloosa. As local banker Chuck Sittason describes it, "a new spirit of cooperation was formed and from that came the birth of the "Tuscaloosa team concept."

During the 1980s and 1990s, Tuscaloosa emerged as one of the premier communities in economic development, innovation, educational excellence, and public-private partnerships in the nation. The proof is in the results.

Tuscaloosa has become a significant player and competitor in the international marketplace and the arena of economic development. With the impetus of the nationally acclaimed "Rochester experience" in 1982-1983, which saved and enhanced a failing General Motors plant, the Tuscaloosa area sought out and won new corporate citizens for the area, including Mercedes-Benz, one of the world's leading corporations that selected Tuscaloosa as the site of their new American automotive corporate home and assembly plant.

Other key accomplishments in the 1980s contributed to the strength of the area and its leadership role in the region. University Mall was opened in 1980. The Tuscaloosa County Industrial Development Authority expanded its countywide initiatives. The Airport Industrial Park was established through a joint effort of local governing bodies and the private sector. And the Tuscaloosa and Northport Chambers of Commerce merged to create a more effective and viable regional organization, The Chamber of Commerce of West Alabama.

Furthermore, important and meaningful changes were achieved in the public arena during the 1980s as Tuscaloosa's three-man commission form of government, in place since 1911, was abandoned in favor of a more representative mayor-council form of government. This major change, which had been encouraged by leaders in the black community for years, opened a new era of inclusiveness in government.

On October 8, 1985, the new seven-member council took office, and Charles Steele, Jr. and John England, Jr. were inaugurated as the city's first black councilmen. Since that day, many other African-Americans have assumed key leadership roles throughout the area, a fitting tribute to the successes of the Civil Rights Movement and the vast changes in Tuscaloosa since the days of Arthurine Lucy.

As the 21st century approaches, Tuscaloosa is positioned as an exciting, rising star. But there is also a realization that, as a people, we face an exhilarating series of challenges and opportunities in economic growth, human relations, and the maintenance of our very special quality of life.

As Helmut Werner, chairman of the board of Mercedes-Benz AG, said on September 30, 1993, as he announced to the world that Tuscaloosa had been selected as the site of the company's first American automotive plant, "Tuscaloosa is the ideal place to create a home."

Over the years, the people who have called Tuscaloosa home have experienced the city's special sense of community. It is this unique spirit that is captured in the pages of this book—not in the facts and figures as much as in the reflections and images that convey the spirit of our people—that honor our treasured traditions—and that reflect the visions of a people excited about the future. ❖

Denny Chimes, a Tuscaloosa landmark, was named for Dr. George Denny who was the president of The University of Alabama during the 1920s.

Gulf States
Lopez Lumber Company
HYSTER

Chapter

2

The Economy

From Homegrown Business to the Global Marketplace

From homegrown businesses to the global marketplace, Tuscaloosa is built on and around abundant natural resources; a strong, diversified economic base; and our people, who are dedicated to a combination of old-fashioned work ethics and productivity coupled with a bold, energetic spirit of cooperation.

More than 100,000 permanent residents live in the Tuscaloosa-Northport

Gulf States Paper Corporation chose Tuscaloosa as the site for its headquarters because of the favorable transportation costs and natural resources.

metropolitan area, the economic hub of the West Alabama region. Strategically located, Tuscaloosa County—the second largest in area in Alabama—has a growing population of over 150,000 citizens in a metropolitan statistical area embracing 1,340 square miles.

The Appalachian Mountain range meets the broad coastal plain of Alabama in Tuscaloosa, with the Black Warrior River flowing right through the heart of the area. Because of our geography, Tuscaloosa is physically a diverse area, with hills and mountains to the north; flat, fertile land to the south; glistening lakes and rivers throughout; and an abundance of rich natural resources.

Tuscaloosa's marketplace is equally as diverse. It functions as the economic hub of West Alabama, serving over 300,000 people. Easily accessible to an array of major markets in the Sun Belt, the Tuscaloosa-Northport area is 50 miles southwest of Birmingham; Memphis, Atlanta, and Nashville are less than a half-day's drive away; and Mobile Bay, New Orleans, and the Gulf Coast are but a few hours to the south.

The cornerstones of Tuscaloosa's economy include major employers such as The University of Alabama; a variety of health care related centers such as DCH Regional Medical Center, Alabama's third-largest hospital; Northport Hospital-DCH; Veterans Affairs Medical Center; and Bryce Hospital and Partlow Development Center.

The growing manufacturing community produces compact discs, videotapes, tires, steel, coal, methane gas, wood and paper products, woven wire screen products, textiles and chemicals, tub and shower enclosures, roofing materials, automotive component parts, and automotive assembly beginning in 1997. With name manufacturers like Mercedes-Benz, JVC, Phifer Wire, Johnson Controls, Uniroyal-Goodrich/Michelin and many, many others calling the area home, Tuscaloosa attracts investment from some of the world's leading corporations and investors, and we sell our products worldwide.

The Tuscaloosa JVC plant manufactures video cassette tapes and compact discs for domestic and international markets.

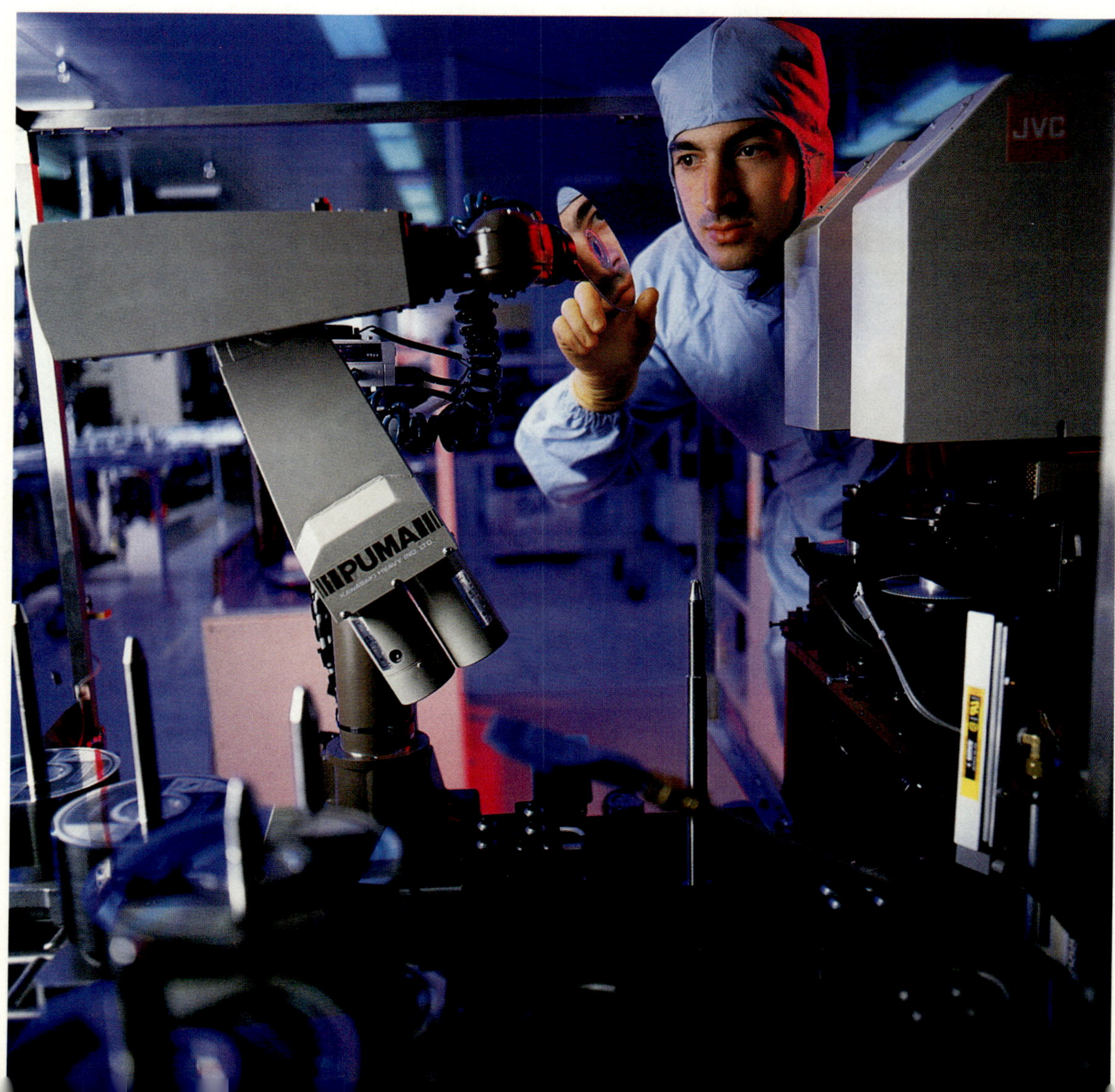

After months of analysis, Mercedes-Benz selected Tuscaloosa County as the site of their first automotive manufacturing and assembly plant in the United States.

Throughout Tuscaloosa's history, there has always been a driving spirit of optimism and a tradition of overcoming obstacles to build a quality community and prosperous economy. The community has always come together, primarily through private sector and business leadership, to meet challenges and lift the community to new heights.

A defining moment in the area's economic history happened in 1982. In the fall of 1982, 200 workers at the Rochester Products Plant in Tuscaloosa did not expect to have their jobs by the end of the year. The General Motors plant, which made replacement carburators for GM automobiles, was no longer profitable and the decision was made to close it.

The Tuscaloosa community, however, fought the closing. Civic and business leaders, under the leadership of Charles Land, who was serving as president of the Greater Tuscaloosa Chamber of Commerce and as chairman of the Tuscaloosa County Industrial Development Authority, aggressively put together an innovative plan for a University of Alabama-led partnership.

The University of Alabama, under the leadership and vision of then President Dr. Joab Thomas, went into a partnership with the UAW and General Motors to save the plant by creating an applied research facility—a "factory of the future." University faculty members, students, plant employees, GM, and UAW officials—all working side by side, met the challenge and created a profitable, state-of-the-art plant that set a pace for the community that is still evident. Today, the plant, now Harrison Division of General Motors is a major, prosperous employer.

"The Rochester Experience created a unique opportunity and model to test academic ideas in the real world and give students and faculty hands-on experience in several disciplines," according to Dr. Barry Mason, head of the original university team and today Dean of the School of Commerce and Business Administration at The University of Alabama. "You dream of having a laboratory to work on real world problems. It was a remarkable moment in our history as a community."

The cooperative initiatives between local government, business, and the university scored again in 1985 with the announcement of a $75 million high-tech, "mini-steel" mill. Tuscaloosa Steel, originally privately held and now a subsidiary of British Steel, was built on the original site of the Central Foundry, which had been closed just a few short years earlier. At the time, it was the first steel plant built from the ground up in the United States in almost 20 years.

This spirit of cooperation and community vision has fueled the economy of Tuscaloosa over the past decades, and it continues to enhance the community's competitive position. With the involvement of such institutions of higher education as The University of Alabama, Shelton State Community College, and Stillman College, businesses and industries in the area benefit from increased productivity, new technology applications, and technical training and innovation. It's a "win-win" scenario that's hard to beat.

Jack Warner, chairman of the board of Gulf States Paper Corporation, directs the company's vision from their beautiful corporate showplace in Tuscaloosa.

Tuscaloosa Steel was built on the original site of the Central Foundry through a cooperative initiative between local government, business, and the university.

A new sense of optimism, progress, and achievement grew in Tuscaloosa during the early 1980s. An industrial park was put in place through another partnership initiative of the cities of Tuscaloosa and Northport, Tuscaloosa County, private business, and the Industrial Development Authority. In 1984, Tuscaloosa led the state of Alabama with more than $150 million in new industrial capital investment, 57 percent of the entire state's total. Tuscaloosa was indeed on a roll and had become a significant economic competitor.

Charles Land, publisher of *The Tuscaloosa News*, points out that "in a three-year period, from 1982 through 1985, Tuscaloosa built an infrastructure of a fully developed industrial park, with substantial private and public funding, and committed community leadership. It was an important beginning, but our economic development effort will be a long-term proposition and will require patience and perseverance." How accurate that prediction has been.

On January 17, 1986, after a thorough selection process and national search, the Victor Company of Japan announced that JVC America would be located in Tuscaloosa to manufacture video cassette tapes for domestic and international markets. Later, a compact disc manufacturing facility was built alongside the tape plant.

Today, after more than $100 million in investment, the Tuscaloosa JVC plant, which employs more than 800 area residents, has become one of JVC's most productive facilities in the world. Ken Awakura, former executive vice president of JVC America and head of the operations for JVC's first seven years in Tuscaloosa, tells the story.

"Almost 15 years ago, JVC Japan sent a research team to find a location for a new factory that would manufacture videotapes, CDs, and computer disks. The team looked carefully at over 100 locations that met our basic needs. The number one reason we chose Tuscaloosa was the enthusiastic welcome of the local government and community. Tuscaloosa had the infrastructure a plant of this type would require, and our team valued the Southern hospitality of the people. In the end, many places met the basic requirements, but the human factor is what made the difference in Tuscaloosa."

Awakura, who was promoted to a high management position with JVC in Japan in late 1993, also pointed out that "Tuscaloosa has given us the support we needed to build a state-of-the-art factory. As a matter of fact, we have exceeded productivity of sister plants in Japan and Germany."

Ground was broken for yet another world-class facility in Tuscaloosa in April, 1989. Johnson Controls, a Fortune 200 company, invested $12 million initially in a 70,000-square-foot facility at the Airport Industrial Park to create a state-of-the-art injection molding operation to serve their vast number of automotive clients, including the Saturn Project. Johnson Controls is yet another chapter in the "Rochester Experience" of the early 1980s linking development of industry with the successful initiatives and applied research capabilities of higher education.

Throughout the decade of the 1980s and into the 1990s, Tuscaloosa has continued to attract new and expanding firms into the local economy—firms such as J.D. Cahill, Southfield Carton, and Hailiburton. New capital investment and job creation has been the result.

The early 1990s opened with the decision by Hanna Steel to build a highly technical and sophisticated facility in the Airport Industrial Park, joining a growing array of tenants in the park. A precision-driven manufacturing operation, the original 144,000-square-foot facility, with an announced expansion in 1994, produces tubular steel products that go into Murray bicycles, Lazy Boy recliners, and a host of other consumer goods.

Tuscaloosa's accessibility to the Black Warrior River and other modes of transportation have been key ingredients in Hanna's plans for expanding its markets and international trade capabilities. The company plans to establish its own dock facilities and canal directly from its site to the Black Warrior to handle its growing exports to Mexico, Panama, and other countries.

In November, 1992, Globe Manufacturing announced a $40 million investment in a 115,000-square-foot facility in Tuscaloosa. The city was selected over sites in North Carolina, Georgia, Ireland, and others for a highly technical process that will produce synthetic spandex fiber for use in textile and nonwoven applications. With employment of 150 persons, Globe has added another quality, world-class operation to Tuscaloosa's Airport Industrial Park.

For Tuscaloosa, September 30, 1993, was more than just a date on the calendar. It was one of those once-in-a-life-time moments when, as the song says, "stars fell on Alabama." And it was a special, three-pointed star that symbolized world-class quality.

Mercedes-Benz, one of the world's premiere corporations, whose tradition is synonymous with excellence, announced to the world that Tuscaloosa was the place they had chosen to call home.

After months of intensive, detailed analysis of at least 115 sites in 30 states, Mercedes-Benz selected Tuscaloosa County, specifically the small community of Vance, as the site of their first automotive manufacturing and assembly plant in the United States.

Helmut Werner, chairman and CEO of Mercedes-Benz AG, emphasized in making the announcement, "We were and are convinced that Mercedes Benz can produce world-class, quality products in Tuscaloosa County, Alabama, and we are convinced that we have chosen the right, long-term

Tuscaloosa is built on and around abundant natural resources.

partner for Mercedes Benz. Tuscaloosa County is the ideal place to create a home."

The million-square-foot facility will begin to produce a brand-new all-activity vehicle beginning in January, 1997, that will be sold domestically and worldwide from Mercedes' 966-acre site in Vance, 12 miles north of Tuscaloosa. The significance of the Mercedes-Benz project will be felt for years in Tuscaloosa through added value to the economy, job creation, and various intangible benefits that cannot be measured in dollars and cents alone.

Anthony Topazzi, chairman of the Industrial Development Authority and "point man" during the recruitment process, stated that "the decision by Mercedes-Benz is perhaps the most significant economic development initiative in the history of Tuscaloosa County and Alabama." He goes on to emphasize that "the ball is rolling and I look for big things ahead. There will be many other opportunities and announcements in the future. Our star is shining."

It is projected that over the next 20 years, the area's economy will be infused with over $6.4 billion in added value in terms of payrolls, benefits, and spending; and that the Tuscaloosa County retail market will expand by over $50 million annually. Job creation will accelerate in the manufacturing, supplier, distribution, and service sectors because of the international impact of Mercedes-Benz. In addition, Tuscaloosa will receive enormous advantages in world-class training, apprentice, and educational programs that will touch all of our citizens.

The vehicle to move Tuscaloosa and Alabama forward into an exciting, prosperous global economy has pulled up at the front door of the community, ready to accelerate our people into a "new age" of progress.

Tuscaloosa's thriving business climate and strong economy are actually the results of individual dreams that have been translated into results over the years and have provided a stable, diverse base that today's advancements are built upon.

Reese Phifer, born and raised in Tuscaloosa, got an idea in 1952, and started weaving aluminum wire into insect screening and selling it to window manufacturers and hardware stores in the South. Over the years, the little company grew, primarily because it produced a quality product at a fair price and assured good, timely delivery.

Today, the Phifer product line includes both aluminum and fiberglass insect screening, custom-drawn aluminum wire, Phifertex fabrics for use in outdoor furniture, as well as several products designed for sun control. The market area has also grown and Phifer products, produced in Tuscaloosa, are sold today in more than 100 countries throughout the world.

A family-owned and people-centered company, Phifer Wire has grown into the world's largest producer of aluminum and fiberglass insect screening. With over 1,200 employees, Phifer Wire Products has been a rock of stability and caring in Tuscaloosa, and has been consistently recognized for its commitment to the community; for its exceptional export business; and for its leadership role in the employment of the handicapped and disabled.

In 1941, James Harrison, Sr. and his wife, Elizabeth, purchased the Central Drug Store, a Tuscaloosa landmark since the 1920s. In 1955, Druid Drugs was purchased to give Jim Harrison, Jr., the oldest son and a recent pharmacy school graduate, a store to manage. Over the next few years, the Harrison family acquired a few more stores in Tuscaloosa as they became available, and the rest is history.

Today, Harco Drugs, Inc. is one of the largest employers in Tuscaloosa and Alabama with over 2,000 employees, and has been recognized at virtually every level of the retail drug industry for innovation, service, and achievement. Harco was honored as America's Number One Drug Chain in its category by "Drug Store News," in 1986; and in 1990, Jimmy Harrison, Jr. was named Chain

Harco Drugs, Inc., under the direction of Jim Harrison, Jr., is one of the largest employers in Tuscaloosa and Alabama.

Dreamland is famous for its delicious barbeque and proof that a small business can have a big impact.

Drug Retailer of the Decade by the trade publication "Chain Drug Review."

With its corporate headquarters and distribution center in Tuscaloosa, Harco also operates other independent divisions including Harco Totalcare, a home health care business that is now the largest supplier of durable equipment products in Alabama; and The Carport, a multistore auto parts business formed in 1983.

Our people have always been at the heart of the area's economic progress and stability, and perhaps no other major employer has been as consistent a symbol of that quality work force than the Uniroyal-Goodrich Tire Company, headquartered in Tuscaloosa since 1946.

Purchased by Michelin Tire Company in May, 1990, the employees of the plant have been faced with growing global competition in a fast-changing tire industry. Time after time, they have faced very difficult issues and industry changes; yet the workers have stepped forward to accept the challenge and make the tough decisions to ensure that the Uniroyal-Goodrich plant continues to provide job opportunities and meet world-class standards and productivity requirements.

The Uniroyal-Goodrich Tire Company in Tuscaloosa has become a symbol of partnership and progressive management-labor relations over the past years, and this has resulted in a manufacturer that continues to produce world-class radial passenger and light truck tires that are sold all across America and around the world.

The people of Uniroyal-Goodrich have demonstrated over and over again their commitment to quality, productivity, versatility, and capacity for change. It is an industry that has not only been a cornerstone of Tuscaloosa's economic foundation, but that can lead the community into the 21st century.

Along with the Uniroyal-Goodrich plant, Gulf States Paper Corporation always comes to mind when a person thinks about Tuscaloosa. For decades, the company and its chairman, Jack Warner, have touched virtually every area of community life.

From simple beginnings as early as 1884, Gulf States Paper has grown into one of the nation's largest privately held corporations. In 1929, Herbert Westervelt determined that Tuscaloosa was the best location for him to consolidate all of his firm's pulp production, papermaking, converting operations, and corporate headquarters. Today, Jack Warner, as chairman of the board, continues to influence and direct the company's vision from its beautiful national headquarters complex in Tuscaloosa.

Gulf States is a growing, diversified company with its roots and heart in Tuscaloosa and Alabama; and its company philosophy and motto "Quality Counts" is reflected in all of its operations, its service to its customers, and its commitment to the community.

Gulf States operates out of one of Alabama's corporate showplaces. Its headquarters is a regular stop on most visitor's itinerary with people from every state and over 60 foreign countries on the firm's visitor's book. With over 2,200 employees nationwide, headquarters staff work amid one of the most outstanding private collections of art, artifacts, and sculpture in the nation while enjoying an efficient business environment.

With over 2,000 employees, the Mining Division of Jim Walters Resources has been a major employer in the Tuscaloosa area since 1970, and today, the company serves customers around the world from our community.

Located at Brookwood in north Tuscaloosa County, the corporate offices, training center, supply facilities, and other departments support one of the country's largest and most productive mining operations. The Mining Division is the world's largest producer of Blue Creek coal, which is widely known for its quality and low sulphur content. Using longwall mining techniques along with new technologies and methods, Jim Walters

Uniroyal-Goodrich Tire Company has been a cornerstone of Tuscaloosa's economic foundation since 1946.

Resources mines to depths of 2,200 feet, which is the deepest vertical shaft coal mine in North America.

Continuing research, technology development, coal reserves, and new production standards and techniques keep the Mining Division as a major employer in Tuscaloosa County and a growing exporter of quality coal to world markets.

Industry is diversified in Tuscaloosa and provides an exciting and stable foundation to the area's economic prosperity. The wide range of manufacturers in the area often surprises most visitors. Increasingly, the scope of our manufacturing sector has taken on an expanding national as well as international flavor.

Other major employers in the manufacturing sector include such well-known names as Hunt Refining, which has been located in Tuscaloosa since 1946. With over 200 employees locally, Hunt's corporate offices in Tuscaloosa direct refining, marketing, and transportation operations nationally as a producer of gasoline, jet fuel, and other refinery products.

Then there is Coral Industries, the nation's largest producer of enclosed shower and tub units; Randall Publishing, a diversified company that includes publishing, awards, and the Overdrive Network, a nationwide radio system for the trucking industry among its services and products; and Peco Foods, a poultry processor with markets around the world.

Working in Tuscaloosa is still based on the old fashioned work ethic coupled with a bold new energy that makes for ultimate success and prosperity. And that entrepreneurial spirit spills over into the small business community, retail, and other economic segments of Tuscaloosa.

Retail trade in Tuscaloosa's MSA has continued to exhibit steady growth resulting in approximately $1.4 billion in retail sales in 1993. One of the exciting opportunities projected in association with the development of the Mercedes-Benz plant in Tuscaloosa County is that annual retail sales will increase by approximately $50 million each year, resulting in a rapid expansion in retail opportunities.

McFarland Mall, originally opened in 1969, went through a major renovation and expansion in 1993, while Tuscaloosa's largest mall, University Mall, opened in 1980. Along with the Bama Mall, these three major centers provide an effective draw to shoppers from throughout the West Alabama region. Coupled with 45 shopping centers, Downtown Tuscaloosa, and Downtown Northport, the Tuscaloosa area offers a broad mix of family-owned neighborhood stores, unique specialty shops, and shopping outlets to meet the needs of consumers.

Evidence of the community's diversified economy can be found in the fact that health care and related services is actually the largest employer in the Tuscaloosa market, outside the state governmental payrolls.

DCH Regional Medical Center accounts for over 3,200 employees, with approximately 2,500 employees combined at Bryce Hospital and Partlow Development Center; over 1,100 employees at the Veterans Affairs Medical Center; over 500 on the payroll at Northport Hospital-DCH; and a growing and substantial number of professional health care providers located at various outpatient and surgical centers.

As the "Capstone of Learning," Tuscaloosa also claims a significant employee base within the area's various educational institutions. Major employers include The University of Alabama, Shelton State Community College, Stillman College, the Tuscaloosa City and County school systems, and numerous private and church-related schools.

The community's financial industry also continues to be a strong and integral component of Tuscaloosa's economy and provides a broad base of business leadership. Six major banks, with over $1.5 billion in deposits as of mid-1993; 11 credit unions with over $400 million in assets; and two savings banks provide a wide variety of financial services in the Tuscaloosa area to meet the expanding needs of business, industry, construction, real estate, and a variety of personal needs.

As a major generator of jobs and economic activity, the small business community continues to be at the heart of Tuscaloosa's entrepreneurial spirit.

Northport contractor Roland Pugh can attest to the fact that the Tuscaloosa-Northport metropolitan area is a growing, diversified community with a solid economic base.

Johnson Controls, a Fortune 200 company, built a state-of-the-art injection molding operation at the Tuscaloosa Airport Industrial Park.

Support for business development is provided on a broad and effective basis. The Chamber of Commerce of West Alabama has an active, ongoing program and support services for small business development and existing industries and businesses. Along with the Tuscaloosa County Industrial Development Authority, opportunities are available to assist with strategic planning, site development, training, retention and expansion assistance, and other business development initiatives.

A myriad of additional resources are in place throughout the community to ensure prosperous and growing small businesses. Among the active business partners in the community are the Alabama International Trade Center, the Small Business Development Center, Small Business Institute, and the Center for Economic and Business Research, all located at The University of Alabama and active as community partners.

In addition, Tuscaloosa has an active and effective Service Corps of Retired Executives, known as SCORE, that provides consistent support and counseling for small businesses, new and existing. Shelton State Community College is also a source of training and support for small business development, along with the innovative work of Stillman College's Disadvantaged Business Enterprise Program, which has obtained proven results for minority business assistance.

With growing support and nurturing, Tuscaloosa's minority business development continues to accelerate and present new, growing opportunities for investment and job creation. Actually, minority business owners and leadership have been part of the Tuscaloosa area's development since the mid-1860s, but there are new initiatives in place creating diversified opportunities.

As Luanne Baker, local businesswoman and assistant director of Stillman College's Disadvantaged Business Enterprise Program, points out, "minority business development in Tuscaloosa is poised to experience unprecedented growth. By utilizing the principles that have been developed and practiced in the past by our minority business community, and by taking advantage of new trends and our community's favorable business climate, Tuscaloosa is on the cusp of realizing great economic gains by minority-owned and women-owned businesses."

The ongoing programs and support services from groups such as Stillman's DBE program, the Chamber of Commerce, the African-American Business Association, and others are making a positive impact. For example, one of the unique initiatives of the Disadvantaged Business Enterprise Program is the process used to designate minority businesses, especially in the construction industries, and plug them into governmental transportation projects and the bid processes. It works wonders.

Charles Storey, a local real estate broker and business leader, emphasizes that "Tuscaloosa has the kind of business spirit that understands that our whole community is maximized when all our citizens feel that they are a part of this winning economic machine we call Tuscaloosa." And that winning economic machine is diversified and innovative.

One of the newest, promising industries in recent years has been the businesses and services that have sprung up to cater to retirees. According to Bill Mackey, who retired to Tuscaloosa after a successful military career, "Tuscaloosa is the best-kept secret in the nation."

An active retiree recruitment program is under way in Tuscaloosa to give away that secret, and the community has become, in recent years, a prime location for retiring

Tuscaloosa area retailers offer the community a wide range of shopping experiences from family-owned stores and specialty shops to shopping outlets and malls.

Tuscaloosa County supports some of the country's largest and most productive mining operations and is a growing exporter of quality coal to world markets.

annually, according to the Convention Bureau, and Tuscaloosa benefits from major attractions such as the state-of-the-art Paul Bryant Museum and Conference Center, University of Alabama sporting events, Heritage Week, Kentuck Arts Festival, Sakura Festival, Cityfest, and a host of other events.

Tuscaloosa is a growing, exciting, and diversified community with a solid economic base. During a four-year period, from 1989 through 1993, over $426 million in new commercial and residential construction took place in Tuscaloosa with another estimated $100 million in the Northport area.

couples. With an average net worth of at least $225,000, and a significant level of annual spendable income, retirees are cutting new economic paths for Tuscaloosa.

Four key factors that retirees look for before selecting a community include educational opportunities, cultural activities, medical facilities, and recreation. As Judy Wilhite, a leading community advocate for retiree recruitment, underscores, "Tuscaloosa has all of these factors in abundance."

The diversity of Tuscaloosa's economy can also be seen in a prosperous, growing hospitality industry. With over 2,000 rooms, Tuscaloosa lodging facilities continue to grow along with an expansion in the number and a variety of restaurants in the area.

According to the Tuscaloosa Convention and Visitor's Bureau, housed in the historic Jemison House and Visitor's Center, meetings and convention activities continue to grow with over 700 conferences and meetings held in Tuscaloosa in 1993.

The visitor industry impact on the Tuscaloosa economy exceeds $30 million

Barry Mason, dean of the College of Commerce and Business Administration at The University of Alabama, sums it up well. "At the depth of hard, challenging times as well as the height of success, Tuscaloosa understands and believes that business and industry don't come to sites . . . they come to solid communities that offer an environment for quality living."

"It's a fairly simple formula," Mason adds. "Start first with what's good for the community and its people, then add the specific elements to provide a climate for economic growth and productivity, and then blend in a 'can-do' attitude among the community's leaders."

In Tuscaloosa, that formula works; and because of it, Tuscaloosa has become the ideal home for business. ❖

OUTPATI

DCH Regional Medical Center offers the Tuscaloosa area up-to-date diagnostic, medical, and surgical services.

Chapter

3

Health Care

Technology and Caring are the Heart of the Matter

Tuscaloosa cares for the health and well-being of all its citizens with an extraordinary depth and breadth of health care services for a community of its size. In fact, Tuscaloosa can boast of a more comprehensive range of medical and health care services than can be found in any area of comparable size and population in the South.

The DCH Healthcare Authority, a community-owned health care

system, serves the Tuscaloosa area. The system includes DCH Regional Medical Center, the third-largest hospital in Alabama. As the referral medical center for 10 counties, DCH offers the community almost every diagnostic, medical, or surgical service available.

In addition to the Medical Center, DCH Healthcare Authority includes Northport Hospital-DCH, a 150-bed community hospital, and the DCH Rehabilitation Pavilion, a 150-bed rehab hospital.

The area is also served by a privately owned radiology clinic, outpatient surgical center, family health care centers, and a host of other health-related offices and clinics. Three institutions operated by the Alabama Department of Mental Health and a

Veterans Administration Medical Center add to the strong health care presence in Tuscaloosa.

Longtime physician Dr. Jerre White has seen the growth in numbers and quality with his own eyes. "Having practiced in Tuscaloosa for over 32 years, I have seen the medical community grow from about 50 physicians to over 300 today. The growth of our private hospitals with the multiple medical disciplines that are available has been extremely gratifying," Dr. White says.

Jill Stokely Webster, a registered nurse and former president of the Alabama State Nurses Association, agrees. "Tuscaloosa's health care systems offer the health care professional

Many laser surgery options are available at Northport Hospital-DCH.

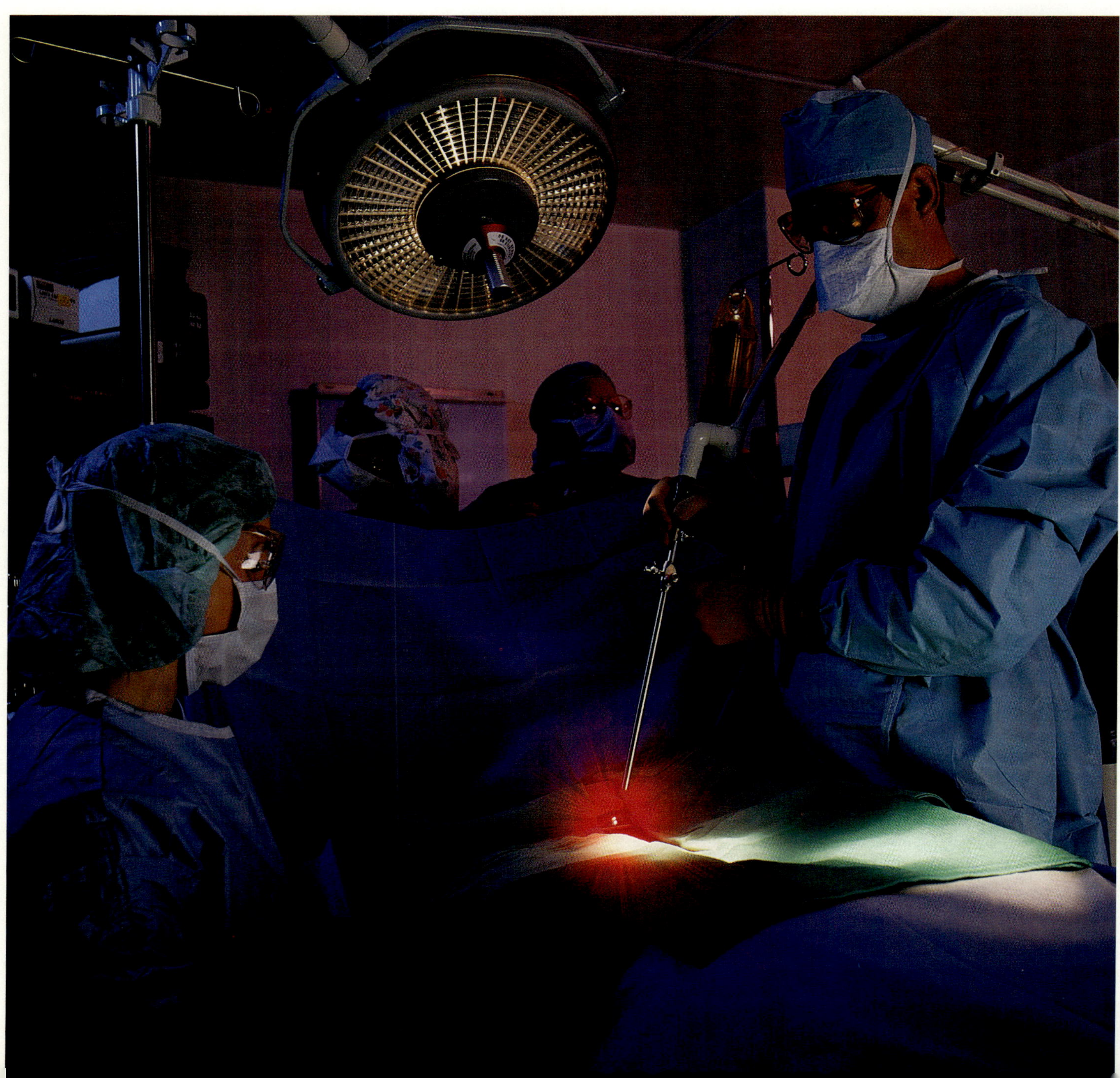

President and CEO of the DCH Healthcare Authority, James J. Ford, Jr., has provided visionary leadership in the expansion of health care for the region.

unique opportunities to practice in diverse capacities," she says. "And opportunities for research abound with the academic and health care systems."

The DCH Regional Medical Center is the cornerstone of Tuscaloosa's exceptional medical and health care community. Originally established in 1923 as Druid City Hospital, today locally owned DCH has grown into a major regional, comprehensive center of quality care and Tuscaloosa's largest employer.

DCH introduced open-heart surgery to the region in 1978. Since then, skilled physicians and nurses here have performed this delicate, life-saving procedure thousands of times. And as researchers developed procedures to dissolve blood clots without major surgery, cardiologists at DCH were among the first in Alabama to offer the advances to their patients.

The DCH Regional Medical Center has also been in the forefront of cancer treatments and advances. From chemotherapy to radiation therapy to advancements in surgery, DCH's cancer treatment center has become one of Alabama's most successful.

Specialists in hematology, medical and radiation oncology lead a dedicated team of nurses, technicians, and other specialists in meeting the emotional and physical needs of cancer patients. For example, Camp

Bluebird, a retreat dedicated to the emotional well-being of adults who have been diagnosed with cancer, is sponsored by DCH.

The birth of a child is an emotionally charged time for a family. At DCH, new parents enjoy peace of mind knowing that one of Alabama's top-rated neonatal intensive care units is available along with an impressive array of special services. Even before the baby arrives, expectant parents are involved in developing parenting skills.

DCH's Trauma Center is yet another example of the role of a regional medical center. Ambulances throughout Tuscaloosa and West Alabama are networked directly to the Trauma Center, linking physicians and specialists directly when a life-threatening emergency occurs. DCH's emergency room, staffed by an exceptional, high-quality staff, is one of the most widely used in Alabama.

DCH's Outpatient Center, one of the most modern in the South, offers a complete menu of health care services in a private, personalized setting designed for convenience and comfort. DCH Sports Medicine offers individual training, physical therapy, and rehabilitation at the Outpatient Center and additionally at Northport Hospital-DCH.

The DCH Healthcare Authority serves the people of Tuscaloosa and West Alabama with a variety of medical services in addition to the comprehensive offerings at the Medical Center.

The Regional Dialysis Center, the first in West Alabama, offers a full range of life-saving treatment, inpatient, outpatient, and home dialysis services. The DCH Speech and Hearing Clinic provides certified and licensed audiologists who offer complete speech and hearing therapy, along with other related testing and support services.

"The citizens of Tuscaloosa have gained much in return for their support over the years," James H. Ford, Jr., the president and CEO of the DCH Healthcare Authority explains. "Because the DCH Healthcare Authority is owned by the citizens of Tuscaloosa County, it offers consumers a choice of facilities while at the same time limiting costly, counter-productive duplication of health care services."

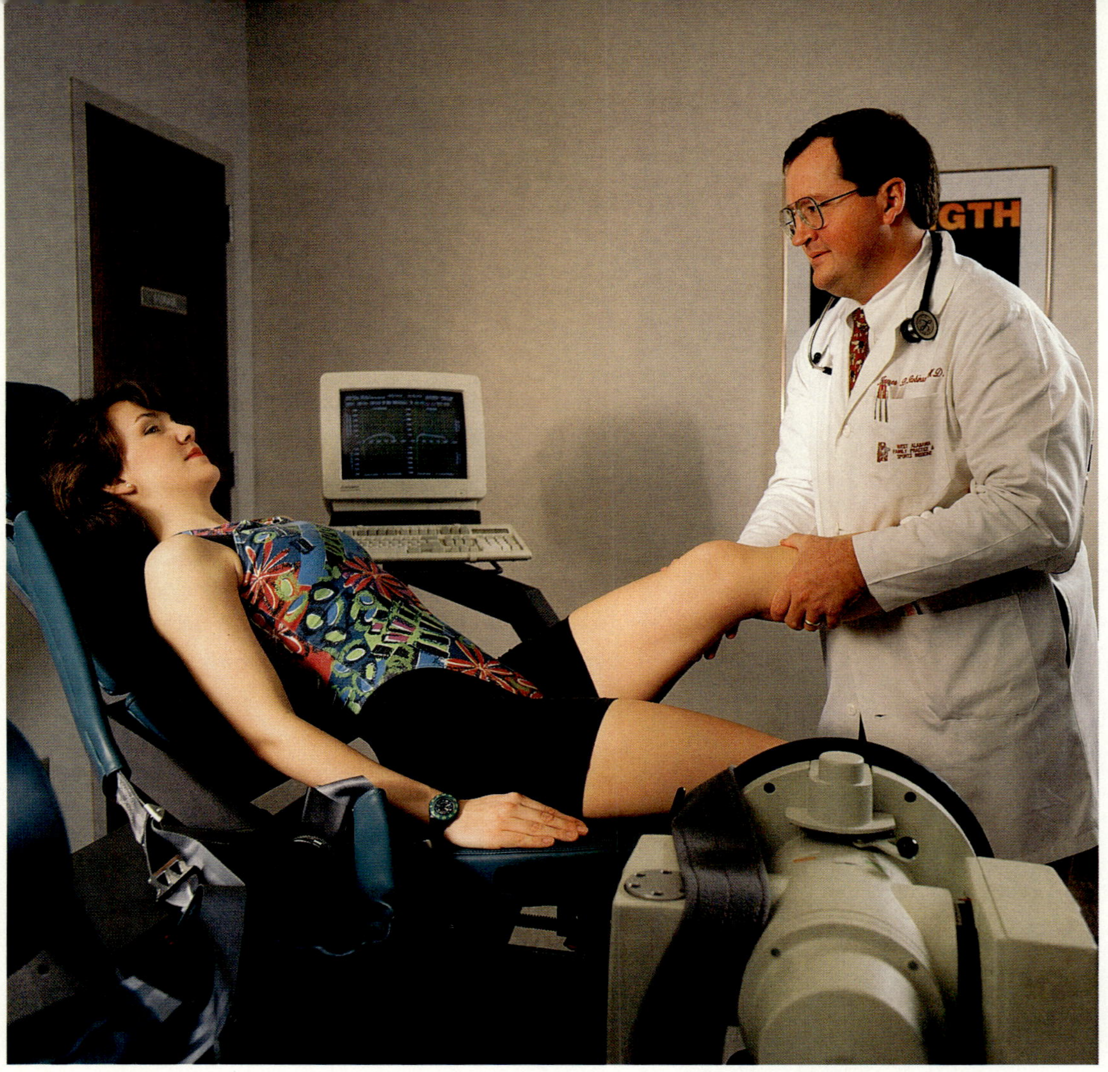

DCH Sports Medicine Program helps every type of athlete from high school and college level players to recreational enthusiasts.

A unique aspect of community support for DCH has manifested itself for well over 20 years through the DCH Foundation, which provides a means to promote and administer gifts to the DCH Medical Center.

Every year, friends and community leaders contribute thousands of dollars through the foundation to support, enhance, and expand programs of the Medical Center. Through projects, such as the highly successful DCH Charity Ball, money has been received over the years to fund a variety of projects.

Another growing aspect of the DCH Healthcare Authority family of services is the DCH Rehabilitation Pavilion. Experiencing phenomenal growth, the rehabilitation center provides an extensive array of services designed to return patients to the community as productive individuals. A team of experienced professionals rehabilitate patients disabled by spinal cord injuries, strokes, amputations, or other neurological and orthopedic problems.

The successful rehabilitation of a patient is always realized through a blending of the professional skills available and the medical center's resources. One of the unique resources is a treatment area known as "Easy Street." This therapeutic system, which was the second of its type in the nation, creates 10 life-size community settings, including a

grocery store, a car, a street scene, and others to provide patients with an opportunity to practice managing the everyday situations they will encounter in the community, once their rehab is completed. Hospitals throughout the United States now use this model program.

In addition, the Acute Long Term Care Unit of the Rehabilitation Center offers a combination of medical care and rehab to help ventilator-dependent patients regain their strength and once again breathe on their own.

Across town in the community of Northport is another of the area's important health care facilities, Northport Hospital-DCH. Formerly privately owned, the DCH Healthcare Authority purchased the facility in 1992, and the hospital continues to grow and expand its offerings of quality health care services.

Northport Hospital-DCH is a full-service community hospital offering a wide range of services, from laser surgery and microsurgery to sophisticated diagnostic techniques. A state-of-the-art Women's Pavilion meets the special health care needs of women with comprehensive services.

The DCH Sports Medicine Program at Northport Hospital-DCH helps every kind of athlete from high school to college to recreational sports enthusiasts. Specially trained physicians, registered physical therapists, and certified athletic trainers provide complete care for sports-related injuries.

Training never ceases at DCH. The Medical Center is a teaching and training site for residents and students from The University of Alabama's College of Community Health Sciences Family Practice Program, for nursing students from the University's Capstone School of Nursing and Shelton State Community College, and for many other specialists including physical therapists, pharmacists, and dietitians.

Over 70 years ago, the people of Tuscaloosa made a commitment to care for the area's health care needs with a comprehensive hospital owned by the citizens.

"Easy Street" therapeutic system provides patients with an opportunity to practice everyday situations during rehabilitation.

STO

The Veterans Affairs Medical Center is affiliated with both The University of Alabama's Medical and Dental School in Birmingham as well as the College of Community Health Sciences in Tuscaloosa.

Today, the DCH Healthcare Authority is meeting that commitment and continuing a tradition of excellence and advanced caring.

A third major hospital located in Tuscaloosa is the Veterans Affairs Medical Center. Situated on a beautifully landscaped 140-acre site, the 582-bed facility along with a 190-bed nursing home, provides primary and secondary medical care and all levels of psychiatric care.

With an annual budget of more than $60 million, and more than 1,000 skilled clinical and administrative professionals on staff, the VA Medical Center provides quality, personal care. In addition, a new $27 million, 270-bed, state-of-the-art psychiatric facility came on line in mid-1994 to upgrade services and resources available through the center.

The VA Medical Center is affiliated with both The University of Alabama's Medical and Dental Schools in Birmingham as well as the College of Community Health Sciences and other related health care fields from The University of Alabama in Tuscaloosa. Support for ongoing research is actively pursued and facilitated by the Medical Center's Research Committee and the Tuscaloosa Research and Education Advancement Corporation.

Contributing to the large, diversified health care industry in the Tuscaloosa area are the Alabama Mental Health Department's major hospitals and health care centers, Bryce Hospital and the William D. Partlow Development Center.

For over 130 years, Bryce Hospital has served the needs of the mentally ill, gaining a world reputation for providing patients with the care and dignity they deserve. Alabama's oldest and largest psychiatric facility, Bryce Hospital serves over 1,200 patients annually with a mission to provide individualized treatment so that disrupted social relationships can be repaired and patients can successfully return to their home communities.

Located on a beautiful 326-acre campus, Bryce Hospital is one of Tuscaloosa's largest employers with over 1,950 employees. While major expansions of the hospital's physical facilities have occurred over the last several years, the original hospital facility is still maintained and is listed on the National Register of Historic Places.

The comprehensive, inpatient services provided are linked with community-based programs that are among the best available nationwide. Through community support groups, such as the "Friends of Bryce," Tuscaloosa has a deep commitment to and understanding of the needs of the mentally ill. The caring attitude of Tuscaloosa reflects the traditions of the hospital's early founders, Dorothea Dix and Dr. Peter Bryce.

In 1847, Dorothea Dix visited Alabama on behalf of those afflicted with mental illness and through her compassion and advocacy, the hospital was established by the Alabama legislature. Six years later, the construction of the hospital began, and in 1860, Dr. Peter Bryce, an internationally renowned leader in the field of mental health arrived in Tuscaloosa as the hospital's first director.

Located only a few minutes across town is another center of caring and treatment, the William D. Partlow Developmental Center.

One of Alabama's largest and primary mental retardation programs and facilities, Partlow Developmental Center is situated on a lovely, tree-shaded campus in the heart of Tuscaloosa and served by over 650 compassionate professionals and staff members.

Another example of the caring thread that runs throughout Tuscaloosa's rich health care fabric is the pioneering, effective initiatives of Tuscaloosa's RISE Program.

Established over 20 years ago, RISE—the Rural Infant Stimulation Environment Program—is now a national model for early intervention and work with children that have multiple disabilities. Both the body and the mind are treated in this unique program, which works with children from six weeks to five years of age.

RISE offers comprehensive services and education for students, who benefit from occupational, physical, and speech therapy. Headquartered on the campus of The University of Alabama, the new Stallings Center, named in honor of The University of Alabama Head Football Coach Gene Stallings and family, provides a "dream come true" facility to meet the needs of children and help them overcome their limitations.

The commitment of caring extends throughout the Tuscaloosa community at every level and every age. Whether through comprehensive adult vocational rehabilitation services, family practice and outpatient centers, or an excellent public health department, Tuscaloosa meets the health care needs of its citizens.

According to Mary Jo Looser of the Department of Public Health, the availability of and access to health services speaks highly of the quality of the community.

"Tuscaloosa is served by a large and very active health department that provides both personal and environmental health services.

Bryce Hospital has served the needs of the mentally ill for over 130 years.

Partlow Developmental Center is one of Alabama's largest mental retardation facilities.

At the health center clinics, new life and those who nurture and care for it continues to be a major focus. If an indicator of a community's health is the availability of public health services and easy access to those services, then Tuscaloosa ranks very high."

The Public Health Department provides an active, diverse menu of services that includes maternity and child health care, nutrition services, family planning, dental services, and social work. In addition, hypertension and diabetes programs are offered along with effective home health services. The department's environmental activities focus on assuring a healthy community through a variety of initiatives such as on-site sewage system inspection, water quality, food and lodging protection, and other services.

The Maude L. Whatley Health Center is another example of outreach to the community and fulfilling of a mission to provide quality care with dignity. Located in West Tuscaloosa, the center's highly trained staff provide a variety of services to patients in an environment that is representative of the highest standards of community health.

Providing quality living and well-being for our senior citizens is also a priority concern in Tuscaloosa. Exceptional nursing homes and retirement centers that provide cheerful environments and home-like atmospheres exist throughout the Tuscaloosa metropolitan area. From high-rise apartments overlooking the Black Warrior River to personalized residential care facilities to garden homes and a complete senior leisure-living community, Tuscaloosa takes care of our senior citizens.

Backing up Tuscaloosa's extensive health care and medical community is exceptional educational, training, and research opportunities for the health care professional. The University of Alabama's School of Medicine enjoys an international reputation for its quality of teaching and research. One highly productive component of the medical school is The University of Alabama's College of Community Health Sciences in Tuscaloosa.

With a unique focus on community health, especially in rural areas, the college plays an

integral role in the education of family physicians and has made a significant contribution to supplying primary-care physicians.

"The presence of the College of Community Health Sciences has been a major factor in the intellectual life of area physicians and in promoting the high level of medical care in Tuscaloosa and West Alabama," says Dr. John Burnum, a longtime, respected Tuscaloosa physician. "It has provided an excellent opportunity for the training of medical students in the clinical years. The special advantage that they have here is working in small groups, often one on one, with their teachers, which has proven to be particularly effective in preparing them for the real world of practice."

Connected directly to the college is one of the most successful and productive residency programs in the Southeast, the Tuscaloosa Family Practice Residency Program. The program works in partnership with the DCH Regional Medical Center, which is the primary inpatient clinical training site, and the on-campus family-care facility, the Capstone Medical Center. In addition, the Tuscaloosa-based program maintains an extensive Health Service Library as well as service and research programs with Bryce Hospital and the Partlow Development Center along with a growing sports medicine program in association with The University of Alabama's Athletic Department.

From sophisticated cancer treatment to a surgeon bypassing a clogged artery of a patient—from extensive sports medicine procedures to meet the needs of an athlete to the birth of a new baby in a home-like environment with high-tech equipment and treatment only steps away—from wellness programs to the compassionate care of our Hospice program—Tuscaloosa cares about the health and well-being of all its citizens.

Dedicated, talented professionals. Public and private sector involvement and investment. A commitment to excellence. In Tuscaloosa, all of these ingredients combine to ensure a high quality of life in a caring environment. ❖

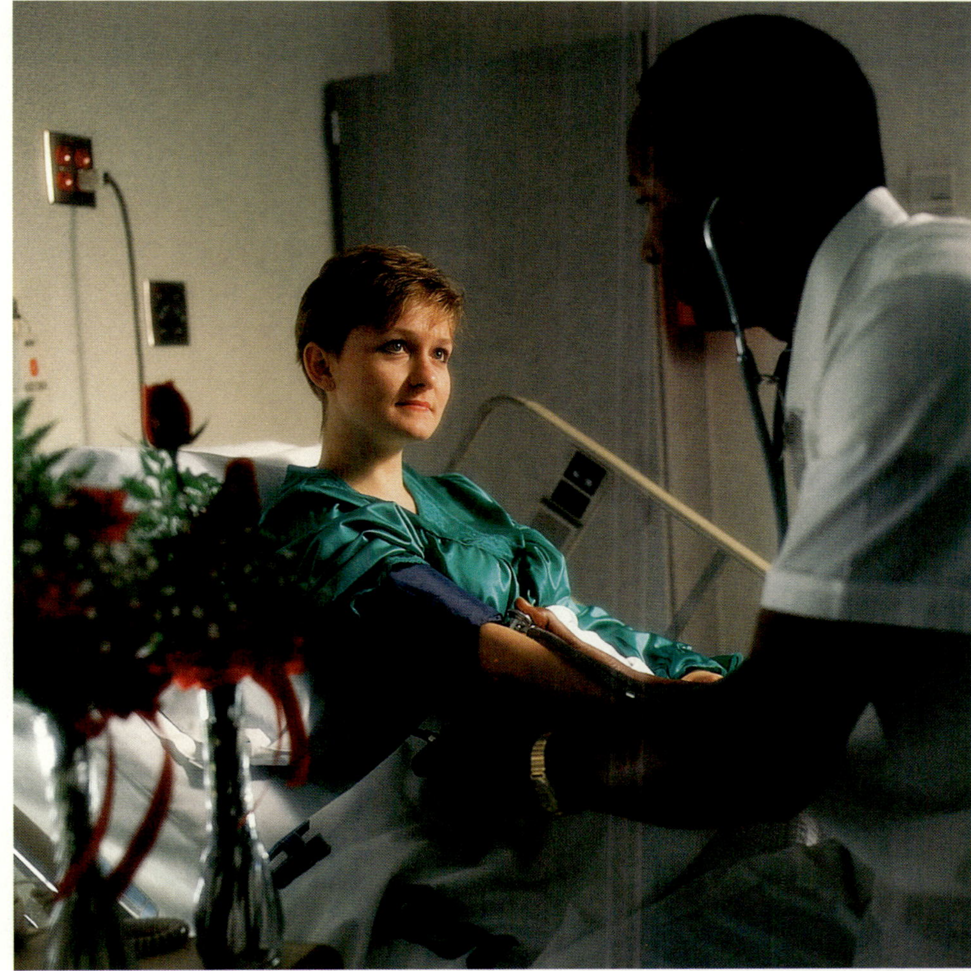

Chapter

Education

From Kindergarten to Ph.D. ... A Capstone of Excellence

There are distinctive threads of caring, challenge, and commitment that run through Tuscaloosa's nurturing environment of educational quality. From preschool to postgraduate work, Tuscaloosa is a community where education is taken seriously, where thinking is nurtured, and where creativity is championed. It is also a metropolitan area where partnerships are productive.

A place of extraordinary opportunity for students from kindergarten

Shelton State Community College is one of Alabama's largest and oldest two-year institutions of post-secondary education.

through Ph.D., Tuscaloosa is proud to be known as the "Capstone of Education" in Alabama.

The area boasts a nationally renowned teaching and research university; a private liberal arts college built on traditions of quality and educational excellence; a community college that meets the area's needs for lifelong learning and training requirements of business and industry; and progressive, quality public and private schools that are enhanced by effective business-education partnerships. Tuscaloosa is truly a leader in academic excellence.

This level of excellence is evidenced in achievement scores that exceed national averages, and in the fact that students and teachers from our public school systems consistently earn national and academic awards, scholarships, and honors for excellence. Indeed, Tuscaloosa has created an environment for learning.

Perhaps that should not really be a surprise in a community that is home to one of the nation's premiere institutions of higher learning—The University of Alabama.

The University of Alabama, the state's first university established in 1831, is a coeducational institution with an enrollment of more than 20,000 undergraduate and graduate students. Offering more than 320 areas of study, The University of Alabama is nationally ranked for its academic excellence, research prowess, and intercollegiate athletic success.

Located on a gorgeous, 850-acre campus along the Black Warrior River in the heart of Tuscaloosa, the university has, since about 1988, been enjoying one of the largest growth periods in its history.

Though certainly well known for its athletic programs, the university has achieved national prominence in a variety of fields over the years outside of the football field. For example, the College of Commerce and Business Administration has been ranked, through a survey of the nation's business college deans, among the top three schools in

The President's Mansion is located on the beautiful 850-acre University of Alabama Campus.

the South providing the most worthwhile business education. The MBA program within the college has been cited by *Business Week* magazine as one of "20 quality MBA programs in the nation that offer consumers the most bang for the buck," while the School of Accounting is consistently ranked as one of the best in the nation.

Because of the university's national prominence and its economic development leadership role, in partnership with other Tuscaloosa institutions and organizations, unique and valuable connections with the "real world" of business, engineering, and industry abound. Practical business and engineering experiences and applied-research linkages are plentiful and productive. Communication school students and graduates often connect with major media outlets such as CNN, *Southern Living*, and a host of other leading print and broadcast media.

There is a special, electric atmosphere about a university community that's difficult to describe. It's a lot like Louis Armstrong's definition of jazz, "If you can't feel it, I can't hardly explain it." But you can feel the excitement in the air at The University of Alabama and throughout the Tuscaloosa community.

There is the excitement of Honor's Day, Graduation Weekend, and Get on Board Day, during which hundreds of students sign up to be involved in more than 250 service, professional, social, recreational, religious, and political organizations. There's the joy and nostalgia of homecoming, when alumni from throughout the nation gather to remember the old days; and then there's just the fun of college life reflected in the unique, annual "concrete canoe" race by engineering students and other fun-loving antics of youth.

And who in America doesn't know the competitive spirit displayed in a loud "Roll Tide?" Crimson Tide athletic teams are consistently nationally ranked. From the football gridiron at Bryant-Denny Stadium, where the legend of Bear Bryant lives, to the parquet floor of Memorial Coliseum, where men and women basketball players excel, to the amazing versatility of the national-powerhouse women's gymnastics team—the university and Tuscaloosa have a championship spirit that you can literally feel.

There is such a vast and diverse array of resources and opportunities available through The University of Alabama. For instance, the university's library system, available for community use, consists of more than two million cataloged items, housed in the historic Gorgas Library along with other key facilities throughout campus, including the state-of-the-art Bruno Business Library and the Eric and Sara Rogers Library for Science and Engineering.

To help foster economic development, The University of Alabama established the Alabama Productivity Center in 1986, in partnership with Alabama Power Company and as an outgrowth of the phenomenal success of the university's involvement with General Motors. Through this partnership, the productivity center is directly enhancing Tuscaloosa and Alabama's economic climate and has become a major draw to new business and industry. The center has been recognized nationally as one of America's more innovative economic development programs by the National Council for Urban and Economic Development.

The opportunity that can be gained through the university is far-reaching and has lasting impact—from the International Trade Center, which provides an effective catalyst for business and industry in a global marketplace, to the extensive opportunities through the College of Continuing Studies for lifelong learning and enhancement of professional and management skills. Whether through a federal tax clinic, Safe State—a unit of the College's Division of Environmental and Industrial programs; the Law Enforcement Academy; or any one of a multitude of continuing education opportunities—the school is enhancing the personal and professional development of people everyday.

The seminary of learning envisioned by the founders of The University of Alabama now flourishes as a nationally prominent, major research and teaching university in partnership with its community. Building on a

tradition of excellence, a cooperative spirit, and an exciting vision for the future, the university's 27th president, Dr. Roger Sayers, shares his views about what makes Tuscaloosa so special: "This is a community blessed with all the components necessary for a comprehensive 'model program' of education. It is one thing to have an array of institutions offering programs at all levels, but it is quite another thing for all these institutions to work together in such a way as to provide an integrated system of education. We achieve that in Tuscaloosa."

One of the truly unique and growing emphases at the university is in the area of children. Through the Child Development Resources and Services Division of the College of Human Environmental Sciences, innovative initiatives are being implemented to meet the growing needs and concerns of children.

In addition to serving as an important resource center for the community on child care services, the university's initiatives connect together other vital community agencies to provide a myriad of enrichment and service programs for children. Among these are the Children's Hands On Museum, YMCA, the Alabama Museum of Natural History, public schools, and the RISE program (an early intervention program for children who are physically and mentally challenged).

Helping people sharpen the skills they bring to the marketplace has been a recurring theme of the university's College of Continuing Studies for nearly 90 years. Whether a neurosurgeon or a small business owner, the notion of continuing education is one of the foremost ingredients of success in today's society.

Located on a serene, tree-shaded, 10-acre campus near Tuscaloosa's central business district on the west side of the community is Stillman College. As you walk across the very personable campus, that caring—along with the institution's history—is deeply felt. Stillman is a four-year, historically black, coeducational liberal arts college of the Presbyterian church.

At one time or another over its illustrious history, Stillman College has operated a seminary, high school, farming college, junior college, trade school, and school of nursing. Founded in 1876 by the General Assembly of the Presbyterian Church of the United States, Dr. Charles Stillman opened the school originally to train black ministers. In 1894, the school's name was officially changed to Stillman Institute, one year prior to Dr. Stillman's death.

Stillman became a four-year college in 1949, graduated its first baccalaureate class in 1951, and was accredited in 1953. Since becoming a senior college, Stillman has flourished and grown in national stature for its quality academic programming, community service, and leadership among America's historically black colleges.

Dr. Cordell Wynn, president of Stillman College since 1982, exemplifies the school's national leadership role and image. In 1993-1994, Dr. Wynn served as chairman of the presidents of the United Negro College Fund's member institutions and co-chairman of the UNCF's Board of Directors, becoming the first Alabamian ever to hold both positions.

With academic excellence as a watchword, Dr. Wynn's continuing vision for his beloved school reflects the deeply caring personality of Stillman College: "The vision I have for Stillman is that, during the decade of the

President of Stillman College since 1982, Dr. Cordell Wynn has held national leadership positions with the United Negro College Fund.

Stillman College is proud to be the home of the world-renowned Stillman College Choir.

1990s and into the 21st century, we are dedicated to the belief that education is a powerful instrument for change . . . the kind of education that prepares students to understand themselves and their world . . . the kind of education that inspires students to help change the world for the better."

Perhaps one of the most meaningful experiences for Tuscaloosa citizens is Unity Day, a joint effort of Stillman College and The University of Alabama in partnership with Tuscaloosa. Each January, the community comes together to remember, commemorate, and recommit to Dr. Martin Luther King, Jr.'s dream of freedom. A time of celebration and inspiration, Unity Day has become an important beacon of hope and guidance in the quest for human dignity for all people.

Stillman College provides that type of caring leadership for Tuscaloosa and West Alabama. Take, for example, the Upward Bound program, a model of community concern and outreach.

A program to help meet the educational needs of disadvantaged high school students, Upward Bound serves young people from low-income areas where secondary school preparation is inadequate, providing strong encouragement and support for the pursuit of post-secondary education.

Vernon Freeman, director of the Upward Bound program explains, "we have a vision

of teaching teenagers not to let their economic background or situation or their family background be a barrier to success. Income doesn't determine your intellect."

Upward Bound targets disadvantaged ninth to twelfth graders in a three-county area of West Alabama. To date, more than 86 percent of the students who have participated have gone on to college, with 62 percent of them attaining college degrees.

To be touched by Stillman College is to have a lasting and marvelous experience. Through the world-renowned, joyous, and moving music of the Stillman College Choir, through the unique educational opportunities afforded adults seeking college degrees in the Stillman Management Institute, or through the inspiration of community-involved and caring teachers, Stillman College is making Tuscaloosa a very special place to live and learn together.

Just a short distance across town, another innovative and unique educational institution serves the needs of students, business, and industry and the Tuscaloosa/West Alabama community as a whole.

Shelton State Community College, one of Alabama's largest and oldest two-year institutions of post-secondary education with over 7,000 students, has a unique mission, role, and tradition in Tuscaloosa and West Alabama.

In 1953, the J.P. Shelton Trade School

opened its doors in Tuscaloosa with 16 faculty members and about 300 students. Today, Shelton State Community College is a comprehensive two-year college offering associate of arts, associate of science, and associate of applied science degrees, in addition to a vast array of certificate courses, lifelong learning opportunities, and highly effective training support for business and industry.

There have been numerous turning points over the years for Shelton, including the building of the new campus for the 21st century, expanded and innovative training programs for industry, and overall expansion of the curriculum. Perhaps one of the most far-reaching, visionary steps taken in recent years, however, was the successful merger and effective transition achieved between C.A. Fredd State Technical College and Shelton State.

The unique merger was an important milestone for both institutions and the Tuscaloosa community, for it was the first time in Alabama history that a historically black technical college had joined with a predominantly white community college. Today, following a successful transition, a new, exciting, cooperative spirit has been achieved in a cost-effective pooling of human, physical, financial, and emotional resources to meet the needs of a broader, more diverse population.

One of the important thrusts of the consolidation was the creation at the C.A. Fredd campus of a regional center for the advancement of minorities in the fields of science and technology. Nontraditional programs are being offered at the center with increased access; and, through the expansion of distance-learning technologies, the center is capable of providing critical allied health and community outreach programs to remote, isolated, and underserved rural areas.

Offering a diverse and extensive menu of academic and technical programs, Shelton also surprises people with its uniqueness. From their Kids Kollege, an enrichment program for children and teens; to courses in travel and tourism management, landscape and turf management, historical presentation, and paralegal studies; from the Vestavia Comes to College program, a program for

fifth and sixth graders from Vestavia Elementary School (Shelton's Adopt-a-School partner); to its Phi Beta Kappa Leadership Development Program—Shelton State delivers a quality product that makes a positive difference.

New Options, a Shelton program, and Career Alternatives, originally a C.A. Fredd State offering, have been merged into a program called "Women Work." This innovative initiative, which has its roots in a displaced homemakers' program from the early 1980s, is designed to empower women from diverse backgrounds and assist them in achieving economic self-sufficiency through job readiness, education, and development.

In addition, Shelton State also houses the Alabama Fire College, which provides training for volunteer and professional firefighters throughout Alabama. The school also offers technical training for water and sewage treatment personnel from across the state through the Alabama Water Resources Training Center.

There is also a strong, working partnership between Shelton State, the county's public schools, Stillman College, and The University of Alabama.

For example, more students transfer to The University of Alabama from Shelton State than any other college or university. While the geographic location is an advantage, Shelton State offers a vast majority of the university's core curriculum, simplifying the transfer of credits. Furthermore, Shelton is a central component of and partner in the West Alabama Tech Prep Consortium of city and county public schools in a seven-county region working to implement an integrated academic/technical curriculum in secondary schools.

The wide range of area businesses and industries that have benefited from Shelton State's efforts form a veritable who's who of the Tuscaloosa business community, including Phifer Wire Products, Uniroyal-Goodrich, Harrison Division of General Motors, JVC

Students and teachers from the Tuscaloosa public school systems consistently earn national and academic awards for excellence.

America, Johnson Controls, Hunt Refining, and a host of smaller businesses. Effective training is provided in electrical studies, electronics, mechanics, maintenance, computer-driven manufacturing, supervisory skills, technology, and other varied technical subjects.

The Tuscaloosa area is indeed entering a new era of technology laced with exciting economic development opportunities, and the key ingredient for our children is educational excellence. Overall, it is their future we are working and planning for.

Innovative programming throughout the public schools of the Tuscaloosa area, coupled with visionary leadership and genuine community support, has created a very special environment for learning and for preparing our children for the future. Both the Tuscaloosa city and county school systems offer a rich academic and technical educational opportunity.

Quality schools are an important issue and asset for business people who relocate to the Tuscaloosa area, particularly those with families. Numerous world-class educational opportunities exist and are growing to meet the needs of a rapidly expanding global society. For example, the Tuscaloosa city schools' budding international baccalaureate program will be awarding a high school degree that can be accepted for admission to universities worldwide; while at the elementary level, growing offerings of a variety of languages are providing our children with early exposure to German, French, Spanish, and Japanese.

International business people who have moved into the Tuscaloosa area attest to the quality of our schools. With a growing, diverse population, area schools have a successful track record of meeting the needs of international families involved with The University of Alabama, JVC America, Michelin Tire, Tuscaloosa Steel (owned by British Steel), Mercedes-Benz, and a host of others.

Edith Merritt, a fifth-grade teacher in the Tuscaloosa city schools and 1993 Presidential Award for Excellence in Math and Science recipient, finds academic strength in diversity: "I think Tuscaloosa is very special in the area of education because of our diversity, commitment, and community support. By diversity, I mean we not only have a broad range of different cultures among our students, but also with reference to the talents and special abilities of our teachers. Tuscaloosa is very committed to the education of all of our children."

Dr. Joyce Sellers, Tuscaloosa County's superintendent of education, explains further: "The opportunities provided through the relationship with and proximity to The University of Alabama give Tuscaloosa-area elementary and secondary schools an advantage through cooperative learning experiences, knowledge-based information, and access to a myriad of services and resources provided by a major research university and other exceptional postsecondary institutions."

There are twelve neighborhood elementary schools in the Tuscaloosa city

Tuscaloosa-area elementary and secondary schools benefit from their relationship and proximity to the Tuscaloosa area resources and educational institutions.

The entire community benefits from the beautiful architecture and environment of The University of Alabama campus.

preparation for an academically challenging high school career.

Central High School is a comprehensive high school for grades nine through twelve. With a student population in 1994 of over 2,500, Central has two campuses, with the west campus serving students in grades nine and ten and the east campus serving grades eleven and twelve.

Having achieved a reputation for excellence in both academics and athletics, Central's victories range from state, regional, and national championships in math, languages, sciences, and other academic competitions to numerous championships in football, basketball, soccer, track, tennis, and golf, for both boys and girls.

An academically centered school, Central High School has achieved more presidential awards for teaching excellence than any other high school in the nation. With a student-teacher ratio of a low 25 to 1 in 1994, this high level of commitment to teaching has directly contributed to a high level of student achievement, resulting in no less than $1 million in academic scholarships being awarded to graduating seniors annually and as high as $3 million in one year.

Never content, however, the Tuscaloosa city schools, through the exciting New Visions program, are moving toward new levels of excellence, innovation, and excitement. Based on the results of the community's Education Summit in 1991, the New Visions program is being implemented to achieve expanded preschool education, parenting education and involvement, use of technology in the classroom, and the Tech Prep program. New Visions also includes the formation of a New Century School, a professional development school and teacher training institute, and expanded business-education partnerships.

From the classroom, elementary school teacher Mary Webster, agrees: "Tuscaloosa has an edge over many communities in that we are willing to work together to address problems and find solutions. We want what is best for our children and are willing to work hard to implement innovative strategies that will help better prepare and educate our children."

system with at least four new elementary facilities in the planning stages. Academic content is strong and consistent throughout the elementary schools with an overall teacher/pupil ratio at a low 1 to 16 as of 1994.

In addition, the Tuscaloosa city schools provide three, community-based middle schools for grades six, seven, and eight, which prepare our children during these critical years of growth, transition, and

The Tuscaloosa County school system has a rich heritage of educational excellence since it was established in 1871. Twenty-five schools, located throughout the county, provide comprehensive, community-based learning centers for students enrolled in kindergarten through grade twelve.

The Tuscaloosa County system also operates a regional education center to provide classes for exceptional students and a student adjustment center, an alternative school for "at risk" students. The Regional Education Center is designed to meet the special class needs of the handicapped, and the TARGET program provides a challenging curriculum for the gifted students.

With low student-teacher ratio, Tuscaloosa county schools enjoy a reputation for results and effectiveness, even with limited resources. Teachers throughout the system have been recognized at every level for their "cutting-edge," innovative teaching methods and excellence.

An example of creativity and leadership exists at Vance Elementary, in the northern part of Tuscaloosa County near the site of the Mercedes-Benz automotive plant. Students are focusing on art, music, and theater, in addition to their academic subjects, in a new approach to fine arts education. Ann Bryan and Beth Pate, two elementary school teachers, aggressively pursued a grant program through the Southern Regional Arts Institute to train teachers and involve students in an innovative visual art, music, and theater program. "Not only is the program providing arts education," according to Pate, it is also "enhancing communication skills and the development of high-order, critical thinking skills."

Through high-level, challenging academic offerings or effective school-to-work transition initiatives and applied technical training, or through an extensive, championship athletic program, Tuscaloosa County schools continue to grow, develop, and meet the needs of our children and young people.

The Tech Prep program is offered and being expanded regularly to meet the needs of students entering the workplace and to create a more effective school-to-work transition. Tech Prep forms a solid foundation of applied academics and technology, upgrades critical thinking skills, promotes technical occupational preparation, and encourages student creativity in a broad range of subject areas.

A unique, meaningful aspect of education in the Tuscaloosa area and an example of the productive partnership between the community and our schools is the year-round calendar of arts education programming.

The Summer Arts Workshop teaches students how to think and act creatively through the arts. Established in 1984, the Bama Fanfare program, an outgrowth of earlier programs of the Tuscaloosa Arts Council, provides opportunities for students in kindergarten through grade ten in a wide range of arts experiences, from symphonic music to theater to classical dance.

For many of our schools, SPECTRA is the bridge to the arts. Involving over 40 participatory artists, the Special Teaching Resources for the Arts (SPECTRA) provides self-contained learning packages, featuring everything from dances around the world to historical happenings, from poetry to art.

Founded in 1985 by The Chamber of Commerce of West Alabama, in partnership with both the Tuscaloosa city and county school systems, the Adopt-A-School program has been recognized on a state and national basis for its results. With 45 individual schools in both school systems matched with over 60 businesses and industries as "adopters," the program is one of the few in the nation managed by a local private-sector-based chamber of commerce that involves multiple school systems.

One of the really interesting initiatives that has been developed through the

Practical engineering experiences and applied-research linkages give Tuscaloosa-area students a great advantage.

The Alabama Fire College, housed at Shelton State, trains volunteer and professional firefighters throughout Alabama.

Adopt-A-School program is Problem Solving Partners. Originated in Tuscaloosa, the program has become a national model that brings adults from adopting businesses together with students at all grade levels to solve real community problems.

From recycling to cultural diversity to economic development issues, teams of students and adults devise solutions through creative problem-solving techniques, brainstorming, research, personal interviews, and other methods. While team competition is used for presenting and stimulating participation, many of the students' ideas gain attention and follow-up from the community at large. Karen Thompson, who organized the Problem Solving Partners program, points out, "Children can actually see their ideas used in the community on real issues, and this is what it's all about. And not only are they working on real problems, but the problem-solving skills learned can be used the rest of their lives."

In addition, the business community, through The Chamber of Commerce of West Alabama, has received state and national recognition and a reputation for leadership in education reform and progress. The Chamber, long committed to building an environment for excellence in education, has achieved results in technical education reform and workplace preparation, was the catalyst for the county's highly successful Education Summit in 1991; and brought 2,000 citizens together in 1993 for Alabama's first and largest "town meeting" on education reform that provided impetus for a statewide, grass-roots movement to improve the schools of Alabama.

Tuscaloosa does enjoy a strong sense of private sector support and involvement, which also manifests itself in exceptional and innovative private schools.

Founded in 1966, Tuscaloosa Academy is a coeducational, independent, college-preparatory school for students preschool through the twelfth grade. Tuscaloosa Academy provides a program built on small classes, individual guidance and instruction, and high academic standards, which incorporate both a solid foundation of college-preparatory classes and electives. In past years, the academy has won the Excellence in Education Award, which is the most prestigious honor given by the Alabama Independent School Association.

A full range of championship athletic programs combine with academic achievements to create a unique educational experience at Tuscaloosa Academy. In addition to sports, the school's trophy case also includes an impressive array of academic competition awards. In 1993, for example, the school's National Geography Olympiad team was second internationally against teams from throughout the world, including Japan, Germany, and Korea.

Catholic education has actually been provided in Tuscaloosa since 1863, although Holy Spirit School was opened in 1963. With over 350 students, Holy Spirit School offers quality Christian education for preschool through the eighth grade. A complete educational program and facilities are provided to carry out the educational mission of the Catholic church.

American Christian Academy is an independent school founded in 1979, with a primary focus on college preparatory curriculum coupled with a strong emphasis on moral instruction for the students. Serving grades kindergarten through twelve, including a preschool and child care program, American Christian offers a challenging curriculum. The school provides a wide range of athletic opportunities as well as award-winning academic competitions in fine arts, math, science, and the scholar bowl.

The Tuscaloosa Christian School accepts students from kindergarten through high school and offers a broad range of academic subjects and experiences. The school continues to adhere to its founding group, the 100-year-old Cottondale Baptist Church, in providing a Christian-based education for its students.

The Tuscaloosa area's newest, and perhaps most unique, school is The Capitol School. Founded in 1993, The Capitol School offers an innovative, flexible approach to education.

Dr. Barbara Roundtree, the school's founder and director, explains that this is "tomorrow's school for today's child."

Located in the historic McGuire-Strickland House at Capitol Park, near the ruins of the old capitol building, The Capitol School offers a diverse program for its students. From weekly lessons in piano, violin, and chorus to an array of sports instruction to personally designed academic curriculum, The Capitol School is an innovative, private school utilizing world-class techniques of instruction.

Tuscaloosa is indeed a unique community blessed with an abundance of world-class educational opportunities, a community where innovation, partnerships, and visionary educational experiences are praised and encouraged.

Looking to the future, the leadership of Tuscaloosa's public and private sector has demonstrated time and time again a deep commitment to our children and their education. Working together and taking action, Tuscaloosa is leading the way to ensure excellence in education for our young people, and a highly skilled educated workplace for today and the 21st century beyond. ❖

The entire Tuscaloosa Community has a championship spirit that you can literally feel.

Chapter

5

The Arts

"The Sounds, The Sights, The Essence of Quality"

An evening with Itzhak Perlman and the Tuscaloosa Symphony Orchestra in the magnificent Moody Music Concert Hall. A rousing concert performance by the internationally acclaimed Stillman College Choir. A perfect October weekend of music and art at the Kentuck Festival. A holiday celebration of *The Nutcracker,* presented by the Tuscaloosa Community Dancers and Theatre Tuscaloosa.

Newcomers are surprised to discover the diversity and richness of Tuscaloosa's cultural life.

Whatever the season or the specialty, Tuscaloosa offers an extraordinary year-round calendar of arts events that rank among the best in the South, surpassing even what can be found in some larger cities. Newcomers are surprised to discover and residents are justifiably proud of the diversity and richness in Tuscaloosa's cultural life.

"The arts have been an integral part of life in Tuscaloosa and West Alabama for many generations. The growth of the area's cultural resources has always been driven by a relentless commitment to quality . . . whatever the art form," emphasizes Kellee Rheinhart, one of the community's active volunteer leaders in the cultural arts. She points out, "by mingling local talent with the faculty and student resources from The University of Alabama, Stillman College, and Shelton State Community College, arts organizations are producing performances, exhibitions, and special events that never fail to dazzle."

The arts shape and inspire both individual lives and Tuscaloosa's character as a whole. "Through the arts," says Gail Skidmore, executive director of the Arts Council of Tuscaloosa County, "Tuscaloosans remember and take pride in their heritage, celebrate the present, and plan for the future."

At the heart of the area's cultural activities is the Arts Council of Tuscaloosa. Through its over two dozen affiliate organizations, the council supports participation in and enjoyment of the arts for people of every age and interest group. Theater, dance, opera, visual arts, music, crafts, festivals, film and educational programs—these amenities and more lend vitality to the community through the council.

For children, the Arts Council provides year-round educational programs. During the school year, children experience theater, dance, music, and art through the highly successful Bama Fanfare and the award-winning SPECTRA program, which provides guest artists for in-school cultural enrichment. Children receive hands-on experiences in the Summer Arts Workshop.

Add to these opportunities, the Children's Hands-On Museum; the nationally renowned Alabama Boychoir, founded and headquartered in Tuscaloosa; Alabama Children's Choir; the superb Tuscaloosa Children's Theatre; a recently formed Tuscaloosa Youth Chamber Orchestra and Junior Strings; and an exciting array of university-based art and music programs—and it is easy to understand why Tuscaloosa has become a thriving cultural resource center for children and families.

Founded in 1985 by Karen Nicholosi, the Alabama Boychoir was formed in response to many parents in Tuscaloosa who wanted their children to have an opportunity to sing. Since its inception, the choir has grown to over 90 boys from a wide diversity of backgrounds. It has delighted music lovers from Tuscaloosa's Moody Music Hall to the National Cathedral in Washington, D.C.—and even to Westminster Abbey and Canterbury Cathedral in England. The choir has become Tuscaloosa's and Alabama's "cultural ambassadors"—and one of our community's richest treasures.

Tuscaloosa Children's Theatre provides ongoing performance and technical experiences each year for hundreds of Tuscaloosa children, producing shows each year with performances for the general public as well as special events at schools. In addition, the performing arts workshop provides concentrated instruction and hands-on experiences in music, dance, and theater for children at all levels of ability.

Even the majestic Tuscaloosa Symphony Orchestra gets in the act through their youth symphony concerts. Aimed at fifth graders, the symphony enriches these young lives with music from Verdi to Mozart to Alabama's own composer, Joseph Landers. It's little wonder Tuscaloosa has earned a reputation for being at the forefront of programming and cultural enrichment for children.

Perhaps at the soul of Tuscaloosa's cultural entertainment is the Bama Theatre. In 1938, the Bama Theatre was the mecca for Tuscaloosa's entertainment, serving as the community's grand movie house.

Following extensive renovation in the 1980s, today the Bama Theatre is again at the center of cultural activities and is still the place people visit for the best in the performing and visual arts. Highly popular and booked for more than 240 days annually, the Bama Theatre, is home to Theatre Tuscaloosa, the Tuscaloosa Children's Theatre, and the Tuscaloosa Community Theatre.

Visiting the Bama Theatre and passing under its brightly lit marquee is an exciting experience. The performing arts center offers a full calendar of music, dance, theater, and stage productions, and provides a home to the Junior League of Tuscaloosa's popular art gallery, which hosts exhibits of local artists, area students, and nationally known visiting artists. An unusual and intriguing mixture of the art deco and lavish renaissance styles, the Bama Theatre's marquee once advertised "iced air" as the first air-conditioned building in Tuscaloosa. Today, inside the renovated interior, designed as the courtyard of a Spanish or Italian Renaissance palace complete with blue sky, clouds and twinkling stars, this comfortable center for the performing arts provides the community with exceptional entertainment.

Across town on the campus of The University of Alabama sits Tuscaloosa's

Tuscaloosa is fortunate to have several talented dance troups that perform throughout the year.

The renovated Bama Theatre is still the place people visit for the best in the performing and visual arts.

other primary cultural, performing arts crown jewel—the Moody Music Building. Opened in 1988 and named for its benefactor, the late Frank Moody, the Moody Music Center is a comprehensive performing and teaching facility that features the centerpiece 1,000 seat Concert Hall, considered to be one of the

The Alabama Boychoir has delighted audiences from the Moody Music Hall and the National Cathedral to Westminster Abbey and Canterbury Cathedral in England.

most acoustically perfect facilities of its kind in the nation. In addition, the building is home to the famous and magnificent Holtkamp Organ. With four manual divisions of more than 5,000 pipes, the Holtkamp is one of the largest mechanical action organs in the nation.

The state's largest comprehensive music complex, the Moody Music Building opened in spectacular fashion with a concert by opera star Marilyn Horne. Since that opening performance, the stage of the Concert Hall has been graced with many of the world's great artists including Cellist Yo-Yo Ma; Metropolitan star Benita Valente; Trumpeter Doc Severinsen; Violinist Itzhak Perlman; Pianist Eugene Istomin; as well as Cicely Tyson, James Earl Jones, and William Warfield.

From The University of Alabama's internationally acclaimed Cadek Trio and the magnificent Tuscaloosa Symphony Orchestra to nationally known ensembles such as the Kronos Quartet and the Guarneri String Quartet to international touring ensembles such as the Ondekoza Japanese drummers and the Dumi Maraire's African musicians— the Moody Music Building has provided the citizens of Tuscaloosa with extraordinary cultural arts experiences in an exquisite setting second-to-none in the nation.

The magical Tuscaloosa Symphony Orchestra calls the Moody Music Building home. Formed in 1979, this exceptional symphony has grown to become a vital part of the Tuscaloosa community and one of the region's only professional symphony orchestras.

"The Tuscaloosa Symphony's goal," according to the orchestra's marketing director, Bobbie Rafferty, "is to expose the widest possible and the most culturally diverse audiences to musical programs of the highest quality, which, in turn, will enhance the cultural reputation and quality of life in the community." That goal is being met by a symphony that has never run on operational deficit.

Dr. Michael Gattozzi and Margaret McCain formed the Tuscaloosa Area Community Orchestra in 1979, which officially became the Tuscaloosa Symphony Orchestra during the 1981-1982 season. Since that time, the symphony's musical directors have included Terry Gates; Tuscaloosa's native and internationally acclaimed Flutist Ransom Wilson; and Adrian Gnam, who was appointed director beginning with the 1993-1994 season.

Offering five subscription concerts annually, the Tuscaloosa Symphony Orchestra draws its personnel from The University of Alabama's School of Music faculty, advanced university music students, former members of the Alabama Symphony, and other additional community members. Each year, the symphony draws capacity audiences to its concerts, which feature some of the nation's best artists as guests.

The Symphony's Guild, which is a volunteer support group, also has a full slate of outreach activities. These performances and activities reach approximately 4,000 school children and nearly 20,000 residents of the region annually.

"Standing Ovation," a pops concert and fund-raising event, also provides the community with exciting entertainment annually, as well as revenue for the Tuscaloosa Symphony. Each year, popular artists such as

The Tuscaloosa Symphony draws capacity audiences to their concerts and features some of the nation's best artists as guests.

Founded as a tiny street festival in 1971, Kentuck Festival is filled with invited artists from all over the country.

and technical professionals have been drawn into the community, each bringing ideas and innovations from other regions of the country.

Technical, administrative, and artistic support continues to flow from The University of Alabama and from Tuscaloosa's newest addition to the academic and cultural community, Shelton State Community College. With the support of Theatre Tuscaloosa as an established part of Shelton State's long-range mission, community theater has blossomed into a dynamic force in Tuscaloosa.

Theatre Tuscaloosa has grown from humble beginnings in the 1920s to an organization with a permanent home in Downtown Tuscaloosa, the T. Earle Johnson StageCentre, with offices, a scene shop, and three rehearsal halls.

There is hardly a night of the year that some type of theatrical entertainment is not available. Dramas, comedies, musicals and operas—there is something for everybody. *Oliver, Little Shop of Horrors, Amadeus, The Grapes of Wrath, Fiddler on the Roof*, and a host of other plays and musicals at the Bama Theatre; and Theatre Tuscaloosa's more adult-theme SecondStage at StageCentre— theater indeed can boast a reputation as an artistic, cultural, and economic force in Tuscaloosa.

"Tuscaloosa provides a unique atmosphere for theater in that all the ingredients for outstanding productions are at work in the area," comments Paul Looney, Theatre Tuscaloosa's artistic director. "Talent is abundant; skilled, motivated theater professionals are available to lead, teach, and work with interested participants; and a caring, contributing group of corporate citizens has become a motivating force."

Diverse theatrical experiences are part of the fabric of the arts in Tuscaloosa. For example, the exquisite Tuscaloosa Community Dancers, bringing together the area's premier jazz, tap, and ballet students, performs *Giselle* or *The Nutcracker* and numerous other offerings throughout the year.

The University of Alabama's Department of Theatre and Dance also provides the community with exceptional, quality productions. Each season, University of Alabama Theatre

Pete Fountain, Roger Williams, Toni Tenille, Peter Nero, and others perform at those pop concerts. The symphony offers exceptional, high-quality entertainment for the people of Tuscaloosa and West Alabama, which sets the community apart in a very special way.

The warmth, emotion, and joy of Tuscaloosa's cultural arts is often best experienced in the community's own little Broadway—Theatre Tuscaloosa, Alabama's top community theater group.

From its earliest days in the 1920s, community theater has positioned itself as an integral member of Tuscaloosa's robust arts family. With "Little Theatres" blossoming throughout the nation, talented theater artists from all segments of Tuscaloosa's social fabric joined together—in what would eventually grow into Theatre Tuscaloosa—to entertain their friends and neighbors with thought-provoking and exciting plays.

Theatre Tuscaloosa's name has changed three times in the past 70 years—from Tuscaloosa Little Theatre to Tuscaloosa Community Players to Theatre Tuscaloosa— each name reflecting the tastes and ideals of the community.

As the economic and cultural hub of West Alabama, Tuscaloosa has always been rich in talent. But perhaps the single-largest factor in the establishment and growth of interest in the theater stems from the presence of The University of Alabama. Through the university's influence, talented theater artists presents faculty-directed productions are presented in the Gallaway Theatre as well as plays performed in the Allen Bales Studio Theatre.

The Alabama Repertory Dance Theatre, founded to prepare students for a professional dance career, often performs in the 700-seat Morgan Hall Theatre as does the student company, Dance Alabama! Both groups participated in the Fifth International Dance Biennial in Lyon, France, in 1993.

The University Dance Company and Dance Alabama! maintain active outreach programs, lecture demonstrations and performances for schools and community organizations. Often, theater, music, and dance students collaborate to provide exciting mainstage productions in the Gallaway Theatre and Morgan Hall.

University programs cross many disciplines in bringing to Tuscaloosa outstanding speakers through their lecture series—while the Horizon's Performing Arts Series provides a diverse menu that ranges from *Steel Magnolias* and the *Flying Karamazov Brothers* at the Bama Theatre to Windham Hill's *Winter Solstice* at the Moody Music Concert Hall. Across campus, at the Riverside Amphitheatre, jazz concerts and "Radio Free Tuscaloosa" programs are popular spring and fall offerings.

The sounds and essence of quality are embodied in the diversity and joy of our music. The internationally acclaimed, inspiring Stillman Choir touches the hearts of people every time they perform on the Stillman College campus, at the Moody Music Concert Hall, or any number of other venues throughout Tuscaloosa.

The Tuscaloosa Music Club, organized in 1926 and comprised of music enthusiasts from throughout the community, holds regular musical programs as well as the musical productions of the club-sponsored Tuscaloosa Civic Chorus. The Tuscaloosa Community Singers, specializing in classical choral repertoire, regularly delight local audiences at the Moody Concert Hall.

While Tuscaloosa's performing arts are diverse and exceptional, our visual arts are just as marvelous and extensive. Local artist Richard Brough points out that "beneath the quiet surface, Tuscaloosa is a unique

creative arts community. There is extraordinary talent in our community, and the sincerity and quality of working, creative people is overwhelming."

Louise Pinion Wilson, for whom the Tuscaloosa City Hall Art Gallery is named, emphasizes that "Tuscaloosa has achieved a reputation as a vibrant visual arts community that provides quality experiences for all our citizens. There is growing awareness and appreciation of artists, past and present, who have and are contributing to a world of beauty all around us."

No review of the visual arts in Tuscaloosa would be complete without mention of the Warner Collection, one of the most extensive collections of American art in the nation. Housed at Gulf States Paper Corporation's

Local artist Richard Brough is just one of the talented and creative people active in the Tuscaloosa arts community.

dramatic, Oriental-style national headquarters, the collection features primitive artifacts, oriental art and artifacts, and sculpture and paintings by American artists.

Over 150 pieces are on display, ranging from classical to modern including the works of well-known artists such as Remington, Russell, Eastman, Wyeth, Bierstadt, and Basil Ede, considered history's foremost painter of birds. Throughout the complex, a variety of other items are displayed ranging from bronze and porcelain sculptures to primitive artifacts from around the world.

As an extension of the collection, antique furniture, antique dolls, and paintings by such artists as O'Keefe, Sargent, and Hassam are on display at the Mildred Warner House, a restored antebellum home in Downtown Tuscaloosa.

Founded in 1958, the West Alabama Art Association plays an important role in encouraging interest in and support of the visual arts. The group books juried shows and has been successful in establishing gallery space, arranging exhibits, and promoting interest in the arts among all age groups. Meanwhile, the Tuscaloosa and University Women Painters actively support opportunities that meet the needs of serious female artists, providing interaction and encouragement as well as exhibitions of members' works during the year.

It's virtually impossible, however, to discuss the arts in the Tuscaloosa area without moving across the Black Warrior River to Northport, an arts community with an exceptional, regional reputation for high-quality, traditional and contemporary craft and visionary folk art.

Georgine Clark, former director of Kentuck, sums it up well. "To please the senses while meeting a practical need is the aim of all fine handicrafts." She goes on to explain, in discussing the Kentuck Arts Center located in Downtown Northport, that "the most exciting element about the center is that it is a community of artists and that makes for a stimulating environment. They are constantly being artists."

The Moody Music Building has provided the citizens of Tuscaloosa with extraordinary musical experiences such as the internationally acclaimed Cadek Trio.

Craig Nutt blends humor and artistry into unique wood pieces that have been displayed in the Smithsonian.

Kentuck is an extensive, growing network that includes the Kentuck Art Center; the Kentuck Museum; and the Kentuck Festival of the Arts, which has grown into one of the most important regional arts and crafts festivals in the Southeast attracting more than 200 invited artists and over 30,000 festival goers from throughout the United States annually.

Founded as a tiny street festival in 1971, Kentuck Festival booths are filled each October with invited artists from throughout the country, nationally acclaimed visionary folk artists, and expert traditional craftsmen demonstrating their skills. This visual arts presentation is complemented with performances by legendary musicians, children's arts activities, and southern and ethnic food specialties.

At the Festival's Art Market, visitors can see and shop for superb art, from small pleasures to one-of-a-kind quilts and paintings, created by award-winning artists from over 14 states. Contemporary jewelers, potters, fine woodworkers, glass artists, sculptors, photographers, metal artists, and painters—the quality of the art available is accented by continuous performances of blues, jazz, bluegrass, folk, gospel, and classical music. Prestigious artists, whose work has literally been shown around the world, long have practiced their crafts in studios in this historic, downtown community.

Craig Nutt, an exceptional artist and fine-furniture maker, blends humor and artistry into unique, imaginative wood pieces that have made their way to the Smithsonian in Washington, D.C. Steve Davis pounds out copper and brass into masks, pictures, and weather vanes as a metal sculptor and renaissance craftsman. Matt Henderson and Tim Webber and Valerie Wall have all created graceful, flowing art through their passion for pottery. Musical instrument maker Anden Houben specializes in harpsichords. Together, over the years, these artists and more have created the magic that is Kentuck.

Back at the Kentuck Museum, located at Northport's Civic Center, traveling and invitational exhibits of arts and crafts delight residents and visitors alike. The museum has become a southern mecca for quality exhibits of pottery, sculpture, woodworks. glass, and paintings by artists from all across the country. The focal point for the Alabama Crafts Council, Kentuck maintains a year-round, superb collection and exhibits of Alabama arts and crafts.

Whatever the season or the specialty, the Tuscaloosa area offers an extraordinary year-round calendar of arts events and experiences that rank among the South's best.

In a community where championships are a way of life, the arts have become another standard bearer of excellence—the heart and soul of a people with a commitment to excellence and quality living. As a result, Tuscaloosa's cultural assets are interwoven with economic progress and vitality, as they enrich the lives of our people. ❖

Chapter

6

Quality Living

Meeting Human Needs Through Gracious Living

People everywhere want to live fully, to have needs met, to see their talents developed, to watch children grow up in a nurturing environment, to have dreams realized.

The surroundings and environment in which an individual strives to be fulfilled and enjoy life are of critical importance in truly being able to claim that a community is a great place to live, work, and raise a family. Tuscaloosa, according to natives

The Gorgas Home is an architectural landmark dating back to 1829.

Rural Infant Stimulation Environment Program (RISE) is a national model for early intervention for children with multiple disabilities.

and new residents, passes the test. This is an ideal place to raise a family, to call home.

The Tuscaloosa area is a community built around family values and diverse, caring neighborhoods with inspiring places of worship. This is a vibrant, special community where people make the difference, where neighbors genuinely care about each other.

From Northport, one of Alabama's fastest growing communities, to North River, from West Tuscaloosa to Brookwood and Vance and on to Moundville in the south, the Tuscaloosa area is a rich, diverse quilt of tradition and wonderful people. The grace of

friendliness, an easy acceptance of people, and a special pride in the community cause doors to swing open with a heartfelt welcome.

Whatever the lifestyle, there's a place for anyone; whatever makes a person feel at home, one of the area's neighborhoods is likely to have it.

Revitalized, tree-lined, historic areas, where young and old alike have restored the ambience of earlier times, are popular near the downtown area, as well as in tucked-away, quaint neighborhoods throughout the metropolitan area. Then, only minutes away,

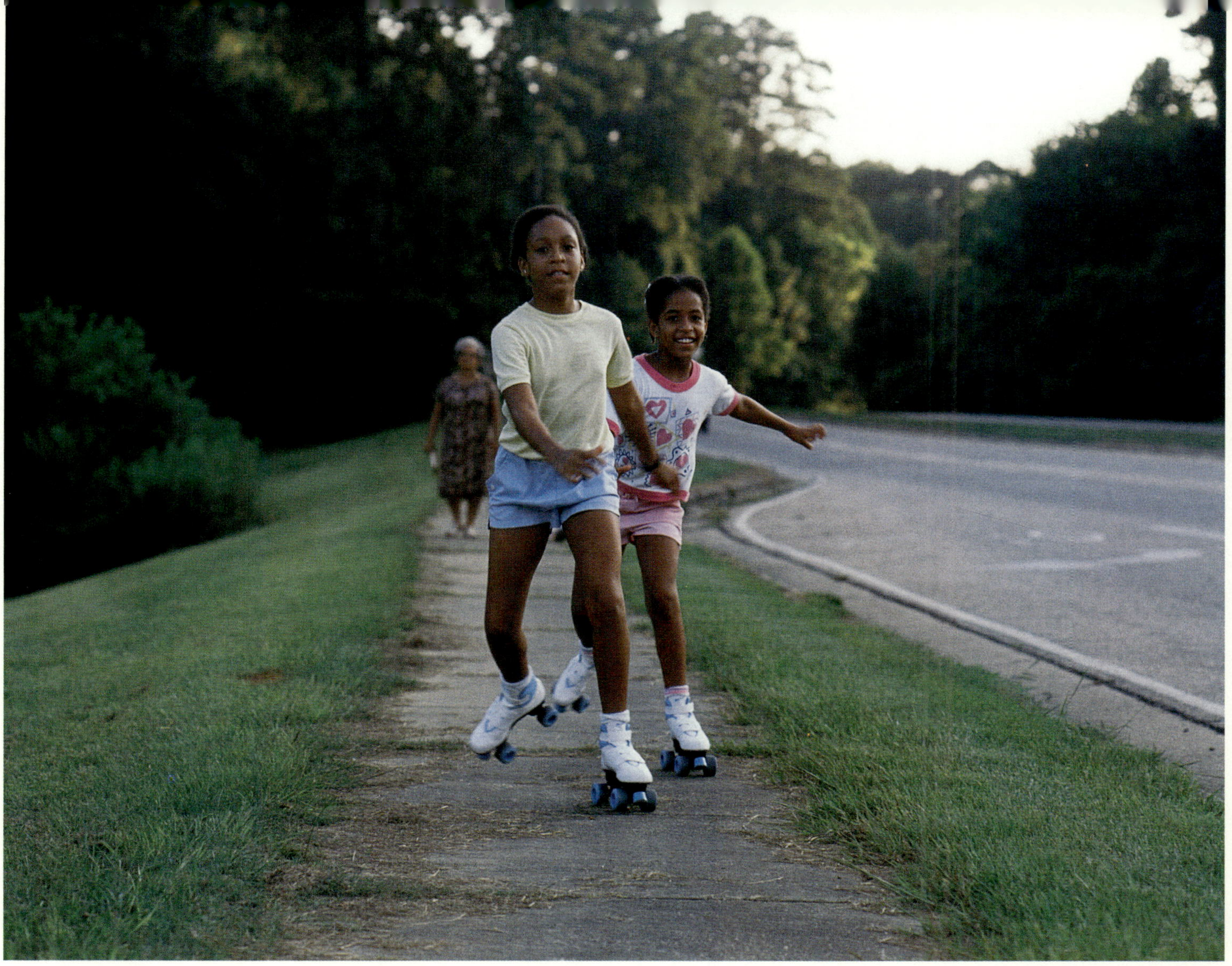

there are neighborhoods and homes where you can awaken with the morning sun breaking over a hilltop or at a lake's shore with the gentle sounds of nature all around.

You can find a home in prestigious, planned developments with the elegance of the English countryside—quiet, secluded, wooded settings—or in small neighborhoods with tree-lined sidewalks, where neighbors chat across the backyard fence and children play along peaceful cul-de-sacs.

Throughout the metropolitan area, virtually in every neighborhood, our citizens can escape from the pressures of work and enjoy their families and friends, yet only be minutes away from shopping, restaurants, theaters, schools, health care, and recreation. In Tuscaloosa, you can enjoy a small town environment with all the advantages of a larger metropolitan area.

Whether running home for a quiet lunch with the family, in the course of a busy day at the office, or taking time away from work to visit our children during school or just enjoying a leisurely break with good friends at one of our many and varied restaurants, Tuscaloosa is a delightful, inviting place to live that has retained traditions of neighborhoods and community.

Over the past several years, there has been consistent expansion in the area's housing market with new residential construction at all levels and of all descriptions—from riverfront and lakefront developments to elegant estates to new, affordable housing for low- and moderate-income buyers.

Our neighborhoods all have distinctive, delightful personalities. Some have been carved out of rolling hills, some out of woodlands, some along the lakefront—and virtually all have been enhanced by the beauty of well-kept, manicured lawns or azaleas, Bradford pear trees, crepe myrtles, or flowering plants. But it takes more than streets, houses, and lawns to make a neighborhood; it takes people caring for each other.

In Tuscaloosa, you can sense the spirit of neighborhoods and see, firsthand, people working for the benefit of all.

One example—a national model, in fact—is Community Service Programs of West Alabama. Organized in 1967 and expanded in 1987, this nonprofit, community action agency has

Tuscaloosa is built around family values and diverse, caring neighborhoods where people make the difference.

Marvin Harper, former director of the Tuscaloosa County Preservation Society, stands in front of his historic home in old Downtown Northport, which is undergoing revitalization.

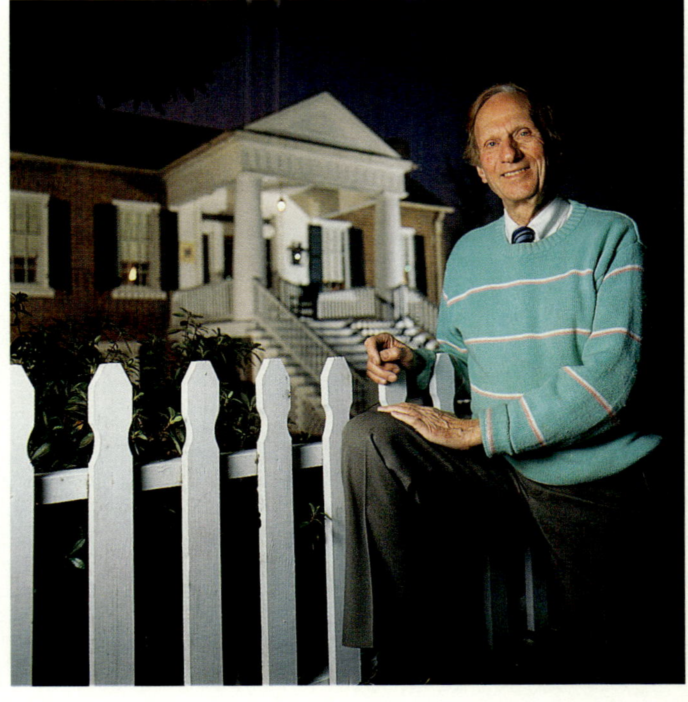

become a leader in providing opportunities for home ownership among low-income citizens. Working in partnership with government, the private sector, banks, and churches, CSP constructed or rehabilitated 329 homes valued at over $9.75 million between 1987 and 1994.

Whether through helping people obtain decent, affordable housing, developing small businesses, weatherization of homes, Meals on Wheels, or helping to alleviate problems associated with poverty, Community Service Programs of West Alabama attempts to improve the quality of life for people with special needs by involving the total community in innovative partnerships.

As one of CSP's bank partners pointed out, "CSP doesn't wait for a problem to come to them; they seek out ways to create a better community."

In Tuscaloosa, people are willing to give of themselves, and that's the essence of community life. An Alabama Outdoor advertising billboard reads, "Commit a Random Act of Kindness," and there are wonderful examples of that every day throughout the community.

United Way, YMCA, Boys and Girls Clubs, Boy Scouts, Girl Scouts, Habitat for Humanity, FOCUS on Senior Citizens, and many, many more provide meaningful vehicles for volunteer service in meeting the needs of our people. Volunteerism is a way of life in the Tuscaloosa area. Our citizens are willing to give not only their financial resources, but their time, talent, and leadership too. People have a strong sense of responsibility towards their neighbors.

United Way of Tuscaloosa County has been serving needs through volunteer action since 1946. With hundreds of volunteers active annually, United Way has consistently met its annual financial goal, reaching $2 million annually, in order to provide support for 23 local charitable organizations, educational, health, service, and youth agencies—from Hospice to Big Brothers/Big Sisters to Family Counseling Services. United Way uses 90 percent of every dollar raised to provide services for children, families, the handicapped, and the needy in the community.

Innovative programming to meet the needs of our young people has been an exciting ingredient in Tuscaloosa's success. The Boys and Girls

James Horton and many other volunteers are supporting Tuscaloosa's young people by helping them develop leadership and citizenship qualities.

A diverse selection of churches and synagogues fill the city with the ringing of bells each weekend.

The Tuscaloosa-Northport area has retained the traditions of neighborhood and community life.

Clubs are developing leadership and citizenship qualities through the Better Foundation program while working through their nationally recognized drug and alcohol prevention initiative, "Smart Moves." The Black Warrior Council of the Boy Scouts serves 12 counties in West Alabama, involving more than 7,000 young people and 2,000 adult volunteers. And hundreds of young people are active year-round in the YMCA's extensive sports programs. Through The Chamber of Commerce of West Alabama's Adopt-A-School program, hundreds of business and industry volunteers from over 60 local firms and organizations are involved in enriching the education of our children in 45 city and county schools.

Caring for each other and our citizens is not the exclusive preserve of our volunteer agencies or our schools or our health care professionals. For hand in hand with the many traditions that make Tuscaloosa such a caring community comes a deep sense of worship and faith.

More than 250 churches and synagogues, representing approximately 35 denominations and faiths, fill the metro area each weekend with the sounds of praise. During the week, their members reach out into the community, offering a hand and heart to those in physical and spiritual need. Building houses through the acclaimed Habitat for Humanity; feeding hungry people through the Community Soup Bowl; helping the homeless and needy through the Salvation Army; providing prison ministry; or any number of other outreach efforts, our people's faith extends well beyond the church door.

Dr. Rick Lance, pastor of the area's largest church, First Baptist Church of Tuscaloosa, sums it up: "Tuscaloosa is a good place to live. The outstanding virtues of the South still remain in our people . . . good, neighborly attitudes, a cooperative spirit, a positive work ethic, a respect for human life, and a desire to worship God."

The Tuscaloosa community's sense of caring, graciousness, and family extends beyond our boundaries to people from throughout the world. Tuscaloosa citizens are actively involved in meaningful educational and cultural exchanges with our sister city in Narashino, Japan. The partnership, formed in 1985, has provided regular student and teacher exchanges between each city, and a full-scale Japan House model is being built at our Children's Hands-On Museum.

There is even a Host Family program through the Women's Division of The Chamber of Commerce of West Alabama. The program, originally established to assist with the transition of Japanese families into the Tuscaloosa area following the establishment of JVC America, has been extended and expanded to provide for German families moving to Tuscaloosa with the new Mercedes-Benz automotive plant. Through the Host Family program, families from around the world have learned firsthand why Tuscaloosa is the ideal place to call home.

To accomplish and sustain these volunteer community activities, there is an ongoing community leadership training program in place and available to all citizens. Leadership Tuscaloosa, founded by The Chamber of Commerce of West Alabama in 1983, has trained over 300 emerging leaders through 1994. From all walks of life, these people provide a network of leadership and a foundation for the community's future.

Most neighborhoods have distinctive personalities enhanced by the beauty of well-kept lawns, azaleas, and lovely flower gardens.

Over the years, Tuscaloosa's name has appeared regularly in the top rankings of the "best places to live" in the country, including surveys conducted by *Money* magazine and *USA Today*.

A mid-sized community of 78,000 permanent residents, Tuscaloosa connects and blends with Northport, Brookwood, Vance, and other smaller unincorporated communities to make up the 150,000-plus citizens of one of Alabama's strongest and most progressive areas, Tuscaloosa County.

Northport, one of Alabama's fastest growing cities, is a popular place to live with a rapidly expanding commercial and small-business base. Construction and growth is a regular sight in and around the Northport area. Northwood Lake, Vestavia, Huntington Place, along with many new subdivisions, are popular addresses in the Northport area.

A self-sufficient city of over 19,000 residents, Northport, on the north side of the Black Warrior River, was settled in about 1813. First known as "Canetuck" or "Kentuck," Northport's popular and nationally known arts and crafts festival bears the community's original name, the Kentuck Festival.

Today, Northport is in the midst of significant expansion and a renaissance. The City of Northport has been working on a Renaissance Development Plan for the revitalization of the downtown area and the development of the riverfront along the Black Warrior.

Spearheaded by the late Dick Platt, who served as Northport's planning director until his untimely death in 1994, the Northport Renaissance Plan has captured the attention

Volunteerism is a way of life in the Tuscaloosa area.

of the entire metropolitan area with its exciting commercial, recreation, historic, and tourism potential.

Construction of a flood-control levee, which will also double as a scenic promenade, will contribute to preservation initiatives designed to protect the tradition and character of the area. The Renaissance Plan also includes plans for the Black Warrior River Heritage Museum, an improved Kentuck Festival site, an amphitheater, and major physical renovations in the downtown Northport area.

About 20 miles northeast of the Tuscaloosa-Northport metropolitan area, in the northern portion of the county, is the small community of Vance. The small town of 248 people captured the international spotlight in September, 1993, when Mercedes-Benz selected a site nearby for its first all-activity vehicle assembly plant in America.

Actually, the Mercedes project was not the first time Vance has captured this type of attention. Back in 1984, following some tough decisions by the Vance City Council and citizens to tighten their financial belts instead of facing bankruptcy as a town, national and international media proclaimed the "all-American spirit of Vance." Vance tightened its belt rather than go into debt or tax their residents.

For over 170 years, the "spirit of Vance" has lived in this tiny rural community. Settled sometime prior to 1830, Vance was originally known as Trion and was supposedly a campsite for Davy Crockett. The community was later renamed to honor Dr. William Vance, a physician and founder of the town's first school.

A clear brook running through stands of pine, oak, and dogwood are the elements of nature that inspired the name of Brookwood. Located about 13 miles north of the Tuscaloosa metropolitan area, Brookwood was incorporated in 1977. Extensive coal deposits make Brookwood a center of coal mining and a major location for coalbed methane gas development. Brookwood is home to Jim Walter Resources, one of Tuscaloosa County's largest employers.

Brookwood—a friendly town, where neighbors are always helping each other—prides itself on the quality of its public services and its schools, which are centerpieces of community involvement. With a growing population of over 660 and easy access to the new Mercedes site, Brookwood's residential and commercial development prospects are bright.

From Hinton Place and Wood Bank in the south to Wellington, North River, and Rivermont; from Woodland Forrest, Skyland Park, and Woodland Hills to Northwood Lake and Huntington Place, quality living opportunities abound throughout the Tuscaloosa area, with a location right for any and every taste.

Tuscaloosa enjoys a moderate climate with an average temperature of about 64 degrees. The summer gets very warm, but winter months are normally fairly mild, even though, every once in a while, we may get lucky and experience a little snow. But even when summer sizzles, a dip in the pool, an afternoon on the lake, or a glass of iced tea under a shade tree will cool things off.

Fall and spring bring glorious seasons of color and perfect days and nights for outdoor recreation and family outings. The reds, pinks, and whites of dogwoods, azaleas, redbuds, and flowering fruit trees in the spring and the golden, rich colors of orange, rust, and yellow in the fall all work together to provide a gorgeous backdrop.

If you want to leave the beauty, serenity, and enjoyment of home to experience a weekend getaway, Tuscaloosa's location is strategic. Within only a few hours, you can enjoy the fast pace of Atlanta, the music of Nashville, or the jazz, food, and cuisine of New Orleans. Or you can enjoy the Great Smokey Mountains to the north and the world's most beautiful beaches on the Gulf of Mexico less than five hours to the south.

Grace Adams, a physical therapy coordinator at DCH Regional Medical Center, is a native of Jamaica who moved from California to Tuscaloosa in 1979 with her husband, who had accepted a job with The University of Alabama. "Having lived in California and New York, I was apprehensive at first about moving to Tuscaloosa and the South. But after moving to the community and through my work, there was the opportunity to meet so many different people, and people were so accepting of all different cultures. Tuscaloosa is really a nice place to live, and there's so much to do to help a child grow. The longer I live here, the deeper I fall in love with the community," she says.

But, as the old saying goes, there really is no place like home, and home in Tuscaloosa is synonymous with quality living and a positive family environment. So, we've ended up right where we began—at home with family. ❖

In Tuscaloosa, you can enjoy a small town environment with all the advantages of a larger metropolitan area.

Chapter

7

Connecting Points

Connecting People to Each Other

The day begins in Tuscaloosa with a multitude of separate events taking place, seemingly unconnected with each other.

A child waits for the school bus while hundreds of people move down miles of streets and roadways heading for work. Stores begin to open downtown and in the many shopping centers spread throughout the area. In the myriad of offices, factories, and commercial centers, computers begin to hum and phones begin to ring.

Literally tons of commodities are transported daily along the Black Warrior River.

Many, many small events that weave the ever-changing pattern of a typical day in Tuscaloosa.

These are not, however, separate or unconnected events, for each moment is linked in a layered pattern that binds together the community. There are many connecting points—geography, history, and tradition—in the lives of the people of Tuscaloosa.

Flying over Tuscaloosa in an airplane, you see other connecting points: The concrete curves of highways and bridges, the steel of railroad lines, the pattern of phone and power lines and lights, and one of the most timeless, powerful connectors of all, the Black Warrior River.

The Tuscaloosa area's transportation, communications, and energy resources keep our people, information, and commerce networked and circulating inside and outside the metropolitan area.

Transportation always plays a vital role in the development of any community, and Tuscaloosa is no exception. Between the banks of the Black Warrior River, right where Tuscaloosa is now located, early settlers and businessmen from the South encountered the river's first significant shoals and rapids. To ship their products further to the north, early traders had to unload their boats and transport the goods over land to the Tennessee River, where river transport could again be used.

The need to ship north gave rise to the formation of the first toll road in Alabama, the Byler Road, which generally followed the

Harriet Mattox takes samples for comprehensive testing at the Ed Love Water Filtration Plant in Tuscaloosa.

The rail system has become a vital transportation link for the area and leaders are exploring the possibility of a high-speed rail line through Tuscaloosa.

alignment of the present-day U.S. 43 from Tuscaloosa to the Tennessee Valley.

Just as in its earliest days, Tuscaloosa is still a connecting link between the Gulf of Mexico and Mobile and the Tennessee Valley and points north. Even more important today is Tuscaloosa's strategic location and transportation network to the major metropolitan markets of the Southeast.

Automobiles and trucks from Tuscaloosa travel I-59/20 to Atlanta via Birmingham in less than four hours or southwest to New Orleans in about five hours. Via U.S. 43, Mobile and the Gulf of Mexico are also only about four hours to the south. Nashville and Memphis; Jackson, Mississippi; and Pensacola, Florida; are all within 200 miles, while Jacksonville, Florida; Charlotte, North Carolina; Lexington, Kentucky; and Charleston, South Carolina; are within a 400-mile radius of Tuscaloosa.

The central business district of Tuscaloosa is connected to I-59/20 by I-359, a controlled access six-lane highway; while U.S. 82, designated McFarland Boulevard within the metro area, provides the city with an east-west connector.

Tuscaloosa has planned well for the location of new industrial and distribution centers, the growth of which is directly linked to the availability of developable land and the proximity of transportation arteries. The Tuscaloosa County Industrial Park, at the Tuscaloosa Municipal Airport off of U.S. 82, and the Interstate Industrial Park, on

I-59 near the JVC plant, are ideally suited for these requirements. And with the location of Mercedes-Benz fronting I-59 at Interchange 86, an exciting, new economic development corridor is fast becoming a reality.

A metropolitan urban beltway around the Tuscaloosa-Northport area is on the drawing board—a vision and partnership initiative of the public and private sector. The first phase, a third bridge across the Black Warrior River, is expected to be constructed in the mid-1990s. This important, developmental corridor and four-lane divided roadway with controlled access points will extend from I-59 east to U.S. 82 west of Northport and eventually will encircle the metropolitan area, opening up opportunities for new residential, commercial, and industrial projects.

Through the year 2000, more than a quarter of a billion dollars is scheduled to be spent on the highway system in the Tuscaloosa metropolitan area. Local government and businesses constantly are working together to aggressively plan for future development and achieve long-range transportation goals.

State-of-the-art technology, computerized traffic signal systems, professional transportation and planning expertise, all coupled with farsighted initiatives, puts Tuscaloosa in the enviable position of being well prepared for the community's future development.

Tuscaloosa law enforcement agencies provide a high level of public safety and security.

Van de Graff Municipal Airport provides commercial, corporate, and private air transportation with a full range of services.

Coalbed methane gas producers are dedicated to meeting residential, commercial, and industrial needs of the nation.

The Tuscaloosa Metro Transit System helps to reduce the volume of traffic on Tuscaloosa-area streets and meets the transportation needs of citizens. Serving most of the city 6 days a week, 12 hours a day with modern buses, the metro also operates specially equipped vans for the physically disabled and provides "on demand, door-to-door" service.

A growing distribution center, Tuscaloosa's trucking industry has assumed an increasingly greater role over the years in commodity transportation. With a growing emphasis on flexibility, just-in-time inventories, and delivery requirements within the manufacturing sector, Tuscaloosa's 34 trucking firms provide a critical connector between transportation efficiencies and productivity. From contract carriers that maintain large terminals for the transfer and storage of commodities, to the private fleets serving manufacturer's and retailer's warehousing and distribution needs, Tuscaloosa's transportation system is growing and vital.

Rail has also become a vital transportation link for the area. Tuscaloosa is situated at a juncture of and served by KCS Transportation and Norfolk Southern. Amtrak's "Crescent" passenger line provides daily service between New York and New Orleans. Always with an eye on the future, governmental and business leaders are exploring the possibility of a high-speed rail line through Tuscaloosa, connecting Atlanta and New Orleans by the first part of the 21st century.

Located strategically 4.5 miles northwest of Downtown Tuscaloosa and contiguous to the Tuscaloosa County Industrial Park, Tuscaloosa's Airport, known as Van de Graff Municipal Airport, provides commercial, corporate, and private air transportation with a full range of services. Regional passenger airline service is provided to Nashville daily by American Eagle. In the past, service to Atlanta has been provided via ASA and most recently, GP Express.

With its excellent proximity to the Industrial Park, coupled with its quality charter services and corporate and private air service capabilities, Van de Graff Airport's potential has yet to be realized. For that reason, a Municipal Airport Master Plan was completed in the early 1990s that could result in major expansions and improvements to this important transportation asset.

A reflection of Tuscaloosa's history, our people, industry, leisure, beauty, and personality, the Black Warrior River connects us in a powerful way and symbolizes parts of our lives that will always be unique to the area. The river is an image that lies deep in the minds and hearts of Tuscaloosans; and, without its presence, Tuscaloosa just wouldn't be the same.

From its headwaters at the southern end of the Appalachians, the Black Warrior River flows through the coal-rich Warrior Basin, through the Tuscaloosa-Northport Metropolitan area, to Demopolis where it joins the Tombigbee River and flows on to Mobile and the Gulf of Mexico. The entire river system is also connected to the Tennessee River and the nation's 16,000-mile inland waterways via the Tennessee-Tombigbee Waterway.

On any given day, the Black Warrior means different things to different people. Picnickers relax at River Road Park, and boaters move up and down the river. People enjoy old-fashioned Christmas fun as lighted, glittering floats dazzle the eyes during Tuscaloosa's Christmas Afloat. And thousands of our citizens move back and forth across the Hugh Thomas and Woolsey Finnell bridges that span the great, scenic river.

Tuscaloosa's economic vitality is directly tied to the river. The Alabama State Docks at Northport. New residential and commercial development along the riverfront, from Rivermont to River Walk to Northport's exciting Renaissance Plan. The huge mounds of coal and tons of other commodities that are transported daily along the Black Warrior River. These barges and the men who work, sleep, and eat on the tows seem to say something about the people of our area, about the independent spirit in all of us.

All along the scenic Black Warrior, you can sense the river's influence, its connecting points to the life of Tuscaloosa. River Road Park, the Jack Warner riverfront park system, Riverside Amphitheatre, walking and bicycle trails, a youth sports complex—these and other riverside attractions all contribute to the special spirit of Tuscaloosa. Even The University of Alabama's nationally regarded literary magazine is proudly entitled *The Black Warrior Review*.

Tuscaloosa's energy resources also play a critical role in connecting the community's economic vitality to present and future needs, job creation, and the very essence of quality living. Suppliers of energy and utilities, such as Alabama Power Company, Alabama Gas Corporation, South Central Bell, and various coalbed methane gas producers, are dedicated to not only meeting residential, commercial, and industrial user needs, but you will often find their employees in key leadership roles throughout the community. From United Way to The Chamber of Commerce, from the Industrial Development Authority to churches, social service agencies, and charitable organizations, Tuscaloosa's utilities and their employees connect to the heart of our people and the spirit of community.

Alabama Power Company, an affiliate of the Southern Company, is linked to other systems in adjacent states, creating a grid of high-voltage transmission lines that ensures reliable service. Alabama Power's industrial rates are among the lowest in the Southeast, and it has a deep commitment to economic and community development and a wide range of assistance programs to industry.

Tuscaloosa is blessed with an abundance of conventional natural gas as well as coalbed methane gas. These clean-burning, environmentally correct fuels are delivered through 1,000-plus miles of pipelines to homes and industrial consumers.

Alabama Gas Corporation serves as the distributor for residential, commercial, and industrial customers with the majority of industrial sites being served by high-pressure distribution lines. Offering firm, noninterruptible service for any natural gas requirements, as well as service for users with interruptible requirements, Alagasco is one of the few local gas distribution companies in the nation that has on file a Firm and Interruptible Transportation Tariff, a competitive fuel clause, and an industrial development rate.

Welborn Transport is one of Tuscaloosa's 34 trucking firms that provide a critical connector between transportation efficiencies and productivity.

Charles Land is the current publisher of _The Tuscaloosa News_ which has made a significant impact on the progress, direction, and civic climate of the area.

In the late 1980s and early 1990s, Tuscaloosa and West Alabama was a beehive of activity for the development of the coalbed methane industry. Thousands of people were employed and hundreds of millions of dollars spent developing our region's substantial methane resources. The industry, which began in the coal mines as a way to improve mine safety and capture methane that would otherwise escape into the atmosphere, has come into its own.

Today, the industry is larger than ever before. In 1993, coalbed methane production passed the 100-billion-cubic-foot mark, enough to meet the needs of all residential gas customers in Alabama for a year. Production of coalbed methane in Tuscaloosa and West Alabama has propelled Alabama into the top 10 natural gas producing states in the nation and contributed significantly to Alabama's status as a net exporter of natural gas.

With over $2 billion invested in West Alabama for the development of coalbed methane resources, the industry is contributing in aggressive, innovative ways to environmental protection. The coalbed methane industry was the first in Alabama to develop and implement a statewide plan to control erosion from well sites. And a majority of the operators formed a voluntary cooperative to install a first-of-its-kind monitoring system along the Black Warrior River, using computer technology to continuously monitor water quality.

Prospects for continued coalbed methane development are exciting. The industry uses high-tech methods and constantly develops

This allows flexibility in meeting a customer's energy needs.

An interconnected web of people and technology, South Central Bell has built an infrastructure to meet Tuscaloosa's present and future communications needs. A technologically advanced telecommunications system, South Central Bell provides a full range of services through an integrated digital network. Tied together by fiber-optic cable, South Central Bell is providing customers, especially business and industry, with virtually limitless capacity for transmitting data, voice, and video. Served by 11 long distance companies and 2 cellular telephone systems, Tuscaloosa citizens are connected to each other and the world through state-of-the-art telecommunications.

new technical information, research, and production techniques. Tuscaloosa has become a center of coalbed methane technology transfer to the rest of the nation and around the world.

Connecting our people to each other and to the day-to-day world is the area's community and service-oriented media. Beyond delivering the current events and news happenings of the day, members of the Tuscaloosa media are often found in leadership roles and in partnership with the community—enhancing the area's quality of life and creating innovative opportunities for citizen involvement.

The Tuscaloosa News, West Alabama's award-winning daily newspaper, has served the community almost continuously since 1818. Published under different names over its distinguished life, *The Tuscaloosa News* is today an affiliate of *The New York Times*. The paper is deeply interconnected with the history and progress of Tuscaloosa.

Throughout its history, *The Tuscaloosa News* has provided important community and statewide leadership and insight on many fronts. From James Boone, Sr.'s Pulitzer Prize-winning editorials in 1957 on the breakdown of law and order, to Charles Land's vital role in economic development and community harmony as today's publisher, to the newspaper's advocacy role in education reform, cultural development, and social unity, *The Tuscaloosa News* has made a significant impact on the progress, direction, and civic climate of the area.

But then you'll find the media throughout the Tuscaloosa area in partnership with our people in a myriad of ways. WCFT-TV, Tuscaloosa's honored and highly rated CBS television affiliate, and WDBB-TV, an independent television operation, are often in the forefront of community issues, providing visible leadership for our schools and a multitude of cultural and entertainment events.

An active and competitive media market, Tuscaloosa has 13 commercial FM and AM radio stations of every description; community-oriented Comcast Cable; and outdoor billboard companies that often share their space for community causes and events. While in competition, Tuscaloosa's media often come together in partnership to make

good things happen such as Market Place, promoting a "Shop Smart, Shop Tuscaloosa" campaign, or supporting a multitude of diverse charitable, cultural, and entertainment programs. Tuscaloosa's media truly connects us to each other.

People are interdependent and all of those thousands of seemingly unconnected daily events do indeed link our people together in a larger context known as community. Whether it's moving commerce, goods and people, energy or information, Tuscaloosa is blessed with extensive networks of people that care about one another—and it is that collaboration and partnership with each other that connects Tuscaloosa to its high quality of life and bright future. ❖

Tuscaloosa's strategic location and transportation network are important to the major metropolitan markets of the Southeast.

TOURNAMENT OF ROSES
Alabama 29 ★ Stanford 13
★ National ★ Champions ★
1935
COACH HANK CRISP DEDICATED HIS LIFE TO ALABAMA FOOTBALL AND PARTICULARLY TO THE PLAYERS. IN 1970 HE WAS INDUCTED INTO THE ALABAMA SPORTS HALL OF FAME.
NOTRE DAME ATHLETICS AWARD GIVEN TO FRANK W. THOMAS IN 1922—SIGNED BY KNUTE ROCKNE.
AWARD GIVEN TO DON HUTSON BY THE FOOTBALL WRITERS OF AMERICA FOR HIS SELECTION TO THE ALL-TIME ALL-AMERICAN TEAM, 1969
1942 COTTON BOWL TROPHY. ALABAMA BEAT TEXAS A&M 29-21.
THE JACK RISSMAN AWARD GIVEN TO ALABAMA FOR THEIR WIN IN THE 1935 ROSE BOWL
SWEATER WORN BY JIM DILDY, 1931
BALL USED IN 1926 ROSE BOWL. ALABAMA CLAIMED THE NATIONAL CHAMPIONSHIP IN THE 1926 ROSE BOWL WITH A VICTORY OVER WASHINGTON, DESTROYING THE MYTH OF EASTERN/WESTERN FOOTBALL. IT WAS THE BEGINNING OF THE BOWL TRADITION IN WHICH ALABAMA HAS APPEARED IN MORE BOWL GAMES THAN ANY OTHER SCHOOL.
THE EVERTS COTTON BOWL TROPHY

Chapter

8

Recreation & Attractions

Just for the Fun of It

Experience the excitement of a crimson-filled Saturday on a gorgeous autumn afternoon as one of college's traditional football power-houses takes the field at Bryant-Denny Stadium. Take a candlelight stroll down streets filled with history. Enjoy a diverse, appealing collection of festivals that delight both visitors and residents alike. Relax in the serenity of a sunset sail on Lake Tuscaloosa or a cruise on the Black

The Paul W. Bryant Museum captures the tradition and spirit of 100 years of the Alabama Crimson Tide.

The Alabama Museum of Natural History has one of the South's most important archaeological research programs. Photo by Barry Fikes. Courtesy of the Alabama Museum of Natural History.

forests—and moderate climate, outdoor sports and activities are plentiful and popular. Tuscaloosa is full of surprises.

You can explore scenic streams. Search for fossils. Be part of an archaeological dig and explore the past. At the Alabama Museum of Natural History, experienced naturalists guide visitors who investigate plants, collect rocks and fossils, discover great swimming holes, or get involved in serious archaeological digs.

You can get in touch with nature in Tuscaloosa. Enjoy an idyllic river cruise on the Black Warrior River as you lounge on a 70-foot houseboat. You may even spot a rare bald eagle. Or simply relax as you sail on Lake Tuscaloosa, surrounded by forests and inviting lake homes. Once a person experiences a sunset on the lake, they're hooked on Tuscaloosa for life.

From sailing regattas to championship bass tournament fishing to the excitement of The University of Alabama's water ski team, Tuscaloosa satisfies the water enthusiast's desire for fun and relaxation.

Lake Tuscaloosa, a man-made 5,885-acre body of water created in 1969, is a popular location for boating, skiing, sailing, lakefront homes and retreats, and fishing. The lake yields fine catches of bass, bream, crappie, and catfish, and has been the site of several regional and national fishing tournaments.

Holt Lake is a 3,200-acre, 18-mile-long lake that cuts a deep gorge through the high bluffs. A fully developed lake area with tent and trailer camping areas, hiking trails, and swimming beaches, Holt Lake's 42 miles of shoreline are filled with wildlife including white-tailed deer, eastern wild turkey, and a diversity of bird species such as American bald eagles.

Lake Lurleen State Park, named for Alabama's only woman governor, the late Lurleen B. Wallace, is a 1,625-acre park and scenic lakeshore retreat set on the banks of a 250-acre lake. Built in 1956, Lake Lurleen is a popular area for swimming, boating,

Warrior River or a quiet canoe trip down an unspoiled, scenic stream.

And there's so much more. You can play tennis or golf. You can hunt or fish. You can swim, ski, birdwatch, hike, pick camellias or winners at the dogtrack. Or you can enjoy one of the most extensive park systems and public recreational programs of any community, anywhere.

For over 175 years, Tuscaloosa has been maintaining a genuine sense of fun in an easy-paced atmosphere of family and friendliness. There is simply so much to enjoy and do—museums, music, world-renowned barbecue, prehistoric Indian mounds, art galleries, elegant historic homes, folk festivals, college sports, a lazy river, softball, annual spring pilgrimages—and so much more.

Because of Tuscaloosa's geographic setting—our abundant lakes, rivers, and camping, or family activities 12 miles northeast of the metropolitan area. When you include all of the area lakes, including Lake Nichols and Oliver Lake, you can see why it's often said that delightful water recreation is only minutes from any Tuscaloosa resident's front door.

You can see them up early on Saturday morning, the anglers. They've driven only a short distance to that favorite fishing hole. They'll spend the day on the boat or the bank relaxing—sitting in the shade of the trees, casting out line and reeling it back.

Then there are the tournament fishermen. Tuscaloosa is home to the nation's largest bass club, the West Alabama Bass Fishing Association. The enthusiasm of local anglers draws people from throughout the nation to some of the best fishing anywhere.

Our lakes and rivers are also bordered by miles and miles of hardwood and pine forests, a hunter's paradise. An unusually large deer population attracts hunters from throughout the Southeast and hunting clubs dot the West Alabama landscape. Doves, quail, and wild turkey are plentiful, as are waterfowl, especially mallards and wood ducks.

Beyond the plentiful outdoor sports opportunities, Tuscaloosa provides all of our citizens with perhaps one of the most extensive communitywide recreational programs to be found anywhere.

Known as PARA, the Tuscaloosa County Parks and Recreation Authority has enjoyed enormous success as the only countywide program of its type in Alabama. Created in 1969, today PARA operates and maintains over 31 parks throughout Tuscaloosa County totaling approximately 1,700 acres of public park land. In 1993, it was estimated that almost seven million visits were made to area parks annually, and almost 500,000 visitors and users enjoyed PARA's extensive network of recreational facilities.

Swimming pools, 3 athletic complexes with 17 ball and soccer fields, 16 lighted tennis courts, numerous picnic and family pavilions, public

boat landings on Lake Tuscaloosa and the Warrior River, walking trails—and a new 104,000-square-foot multipurpose outdoor area with drawing power for events from national-level horse shows to garden shows, from rodeos to concerts—PARA creates opportunities for fun and family recreation.

PARA's programs and services are diverse and accommodate almost any recreational interest, including outstanding therapeutic activities for youth and adults who are physically and mentally challenged.

Tuscaloosa takes care of our children's sports and recreational appetites regardless of the level of expertise, skill, or experience. The McDonald Hughes Center, Boys and Girls Club, Big Brothers/Big Sisters, the YMCA, the Police Athletic League—these and other programs provide exciting and enriching recreational opportunities for all our young people, from soccer to basketball, from baseball to track.

The YMCA's Compute and Shoot program centers on developing communication, grammar, and computer skills by allowing children to produce a newspaper using a desktop publishing program, while playing

The nationally ranked women's gymnastics program at The University of Alabama keeps the fans coming back for more, year after year.

The Moundville Archaeological Park is one of the premier Native American cultural centers in the U.S. Photo courtesy of Dr. Jim Knight, University of Alabama Anthropology Department.

From greyhound racing to archaeological digs, there is entertainment for all tastes in Tuscaloosa.

today on The University of Alabama campus in Smith Hall, named in honor of Professor Eugene Allen Smith, a former state geologist and member of the university faculty for 54 years.

Today, Smith Hall and the Alabama Museum of Natural History display growing and extensive geological, mineralogical, botanical, zoological, and archaeological collections. One of the South's most important archaeological research programs, the museum continues to add diverse Alabama geological, geographical, and historical collections.

About 13 miles south of Tuscaloosa, in the small community of Moundville, the Alabama Museum of Natural History operates the Moundville Archaeological Park, one of the premier Native American cultural centers in the United States. It is internationally recognized as one of the best-preserved sites in North America.

Travelers literally come from around the world to visit the park, sometimes referred to as Mound State Monument. People visit to learn more about a fascinating Indian culture that existed over 800 years ago, as well as

on basketball teams. Grades, learning, teamwork, and sports—it's a winning combination!

Tuscaloosa also offers children a place where they can explore and discover science, history, and arts. At the Children's Hands-On Museum, they can enter a Choctaw Indian village or navigate the Black Warrior River on the *Captain Tim Parker*, a replica tugboat wheelhouse, or discover Tuscaloosa's past by strolling through the T-Town Gallery that includes the Maxwell General Store and Grandmother's Attic.

Another excellent area museum is the Alabama Museum of Natural History, housed to enjoy the year-round natural beauty of the area.

Moundville is also a popular recreational center. The 317-acre park, which sits among 20 intact Indian mounds, is also home to the Annual Moundville Native American Festival, the premier educational event of its kind in the region.

The festival, a six-day event each October, features Choctaw, Creek, Cherokee, Seminole, and Shawnee Indians from Alabama, Georgia, Tennessee, and Florida, demonstrating such traditional skills as the making of pottery, silver jewelry, and musical instruments, along with beadworking, dressmaking, woodworking, and a variety of other crafts.

Tuscaloosa's newest museum emphasizes a totally different subject—insurance and natural disasters. Opened in March, 1992, the Insurance Hall of Fame Museum is housed in Alston Hall on the campus of The University of Alabama.

Developed and funded by major insurance companies and individuals from more than 50 countries, the museum highlights major natural disasters that have occurred all over the world. Memorabilia, photographs, history, and other data of insurance industry leaders is displayed.

From the historic costume collection at Doster Hall to Ma'Cille's Museum of Miscellaneous, an eclectic collection of Americana tucked away near Gordo—from numerous public and private art galleries to the Alabama Room at the university's main library, which contains rare books, maps, and historical documents—from the Will J. Murphy Museum, with its exceptional collection of African-American and Civil Rights history to the replica of Supreme Court Justice Hugo Black's study at The University of Alabama Law School—Tuscaloosa is filled with the repositories of very special treasures.

Perhaps no other museum in Tuscaloosa, however, captures the tradition and essence of our community like the Bryant Museum. Located on the campus of The University of Alabama near Coleman Coliseum and next door to the state-of-the-art Bryant Conference Center, the Paul W. Bryant Museum offers 100 years of the Alabama Crimson Tide.

Considered a "must see" by casual visitors and sports aficionados alike, the museum is named in honor of the legendary Paul "Bear" Bryant. Opened in 1988, an average of 30,000 visitors annually experience the great tradition of Alabama football through exhibits of memorabilia, video presentations, old films dating to the 1920s, photographs, and a sports research library.

The Battle Friedman Home is one of the beautiful landmarks of Tuscaloosa tradition.

In the fall, The University of Alabama alumni and Crimson Tide fans descend on Tuscaloosa for home football games at Bryant-Denny Stadium.

The "Crimson Spirit" permeates the very fabric of Tuscaloosa, and our community is filled with traditions and opportunities that one only finds in a college town—a winning edge that sets us apart.

The essence of that spirit and tradition is felt on autumn weekends, as thousands of University of Alabama alumni and Crimson Tide fans descend on Tuscaloosa for home football games at Bryant-Denny Stadium. With 12 national championships and more bowl appearances than any college team in history, Alabama football is synonymous with gridiron glory.

Thousands of crimson-clad fans and local citizens gather at pre-game festivities, "tailgate parties," and around hundreds of recreational vehicles to reminisce with old friends and simply enjoy the essence of a glorious,

fall football weekend. They experience the aura of a place where the greats have demonstrated their skills and competitive spirits. Names like Joe Namath, Ozzie Newsome, Bart Starr, LeRoy Jordan, Harry Gilmer, Cornelius Bennett, Jon Hannah, Derrick Thomas, Kenny Stabler, Dixie Howell, and Don Hutson—and coaches dedicated to excellence such as Gene Stallings and, of course, "Bear" Bryant.

Still, the spirit of college sports in Tuscaloosa means more than just football. Over at the 15,000-seat Coleman Coliseum, men's and women's championship-caliber basketball and one of the nation's most successful women's gymnastics programs keep the fans coming back for more year after year.

With over 1,200 victories and a consistent Southeastern Conference championship contender, Alabama has played more than 320 men's basketball games in Coleman Coliseum, drawing 3.1 million fans since the facility opened. The men's team is ranked fourth in NCAA appearances among SEC schools. Meanwhile, the women's basketball team has grown into one of the nation's best. Consistently ranked in the top 10, and an NCAA Final Four participant in 1994, a first in Alabama's history, the women's basketball team is a joy to watch. Coleman Coliseum has hosted a number of NCAA and NIT basketball events, providing local fans with the opportunity to see the best of college basketball in Tuscaloosa.

In women's gymnastics, two national championships, numerous regional and Southeast Conference titles, and a host of All-American performers have taken the Alabama's women's gymnastics program to the highest level of collegiate competition and excellence, under the outstanding coaching of Sarah and David Patterson.

Coleman Coliseum is one of the most versatile indoor facilities in the nation. The King, The Dipper, The Shack, Bosephus— they've all played here! Coleman Coliseum regularly hosts athletic events, community and alumni gatherings, student convocations, commencement exercises, musicals, and concerts—a broad array of programs, from Ray Charles to Bob Dylan, from Lionel Richie to

Reba McEntire and Hank Williams, Jr., and even a speech from President Ronald Reagan.

On beautiful spring afternoons, many residents head for Sewell-Thomas Stadium, on the campus of The University of Alabama, to watch Crimson Tide baseball. A modern, 2,700-seat stadium, Sewell-Thomas Field is home to the Alabama baseball team and the many great players who have enjoyed "America's pastime" since Alabama baseball began in 1892.

Nearby, at the Alabama Aquatic Center, one of the nation's "fastest" pools has played host to over 150 major swimming and diving competitions, including some of the most prestigious in the sport.

While University of Alabama sports provide an extra dimension to local athletics, Tuscaloosa has even more to offer. From a broad array of sporting events at Shelton State Community College and Stillman College to traditional Friday night high school football games to weekend youth soccer and baseball leagues, Tuscaloosa energizes its citizens, whether they are participants or spectators.

Sports aside, you can step back into history in Tuscaloosa very easily and experience a legacy of stately mansions, churches, and public buildings. More than 100 pre-Civil War structures stand in Tuscaloosa, Northport, and the surrounding area today. A resident or a visitor can literally take a stroll down streets of history past some of the most magnificent and architecturally important homes of any community in the South.

These architectural landmarks include the Gorgas Home, a raised birch cottage and home of General Josiah Gorgas, a University of Alabama president and Confederate General, dating back to 1829, and once used as a student dining hall; the 1820 Mildred Warner House, restored beautifully in 1977,

today it houses one of the area's first collections of 18th- and 19th-century antiques and original works of famous artists; and the Murphy-Collins House, built in 1923 by Will Murphy, Tuscaloosa's first black mortician and home to an outstanding collection of black-heritage memorabilia. The University Club, a University of Alabama private facility built in 1829, is an exceptional example of Greek Revival architecture and houses an outstanding art collection. The gracious, beautiful President's Mansion, on the campus, was built in 1841.

Built in the late 1850s and 1860s by one of Tuscaloosa's early legislators and business leaders, the Jemison-Van de Graff mansion is the beautiful headquarters today of the Tuscaloosa Convention & Visitors Bureau and serves as the community's Visitor Information Center. The home, which has housed the Tuscaloosa County Library, is of significant historical value as well as being one of only four remaining Italianate-Style houses in Alabama.

Over at historic Capitol Park, you can see the renovated foundation and site of Alabama's State Capitol from 1826 to 1846. Within the park area, you can visit The Old Tavern, built in 1827, which was the home of Alabama Governor John Gayle and also served as an inn and stagecoach stop in earlier years. The McGuire Strickland House, a two-story, raised cottage built in 1820, is the oldest structure in Tuscaloosa and presently houses The Capitol School. The Old Jail is a two-story, 1850's structure that today is home to UA's American Studies program.

Original buildings at The University of Alabama and Stillman College, as well as beautiful churches, contribute to Tuscaloosa's

history. Christ Episcopal Church (1829) and St. John's Catholic Church (1845) are two of the oldest structures; while the First African Church, organized in 1866, has historic significance as a major civil rights headquarters; and the First Baptist Church, organized in 1818, has the distinction of being the oldest church in Tuscaloosa.

Throughout Tuscaloosa, there are numerous historic collections and landmarks that delight visitors. The Gulf States Paper Corporation has one of the most unique collections of Alabama landmarks restored and relocated to a site near North River. Included in this collection are: the Old Center Church (1870), the Umbria Schoolhouse (1820), the Gainesville Bank (1835), and the Dogtrot Cabin (1837).

History and tradition is alive and well in Tuscaloosa and threads throughout the rich fabric of the community in not only structures, but in our events. Heritage Week, an annual April event that includes an exceptional Pilgrimage of Homes, has gained regional attention for its graceful, exquisite activities amid the beauty and glory of blooming azaleas and dogwoods.

The Tuscaloosa area has become known as a "community of festivals," providing a vast array of events year-round that appeal to people of all ages and all interests.

The largest and perhaps best known is the Kentuck Festival in Northport, held each October. There is no other event quite like Kentuck, where families, residents, and visitors from throughout the nation gather to see and hear traditional craftsmen share their talents and secrets. The festival stages are filled with blues artists and storytelling, and everywhere there is the tempting aroma of barbecue, sweet potato pie, and funnel cakes filling the air.

Kentuck has become one of the South's major arts and crafts festivals, hosting over 30,000 visitors and more than 200 artists and craftsmen from across America each year.

Cityfest is yet another Tuscaloosa happening that has gained much popularity and a dedicated following. Originally developed by Downtown Tuscaloosa Unlimited, Cityfest combines children's activities, crafts, and a regional barbecue cookoff competition with an extensive, diverse musical menu. Stages throughout Downtown Tuscaloosa come alive on the fourth weekend in October, and

Residents and visitors from throughout the nation gather to see and hear traditional craftsmen share their talents at the Kentuck Festival in Northport.

Christmas with roving minstrels, hot cider and roasted chestnuts, caroling, and an appearance by Father Christmas.

Major events and attractions such as the historic trails, pioneer homes, and rustic environment of the pre-Civil War Tannehill Iron Works in the wooded hills north of Tuscaloosa; the sleek, fast greyhound racing at Greenetrack south of Tuscaloosa in Greene County; the traditional carnival rides, exhibits, nationally known entertainment, and just plain family fun at the annual West Alabama State Fair are all just minutes away.

The Bama Theatre's performing arts center; the Bryant Conference Center, a state-of-the-art facility that provides the ideal environment for major events, lectures, community happenings, and trade shows, such as West Alabama's largest small-business event, "MarketPlace;" the Moody Music Center, a focal point for exceptional entertainment and culture featuring some of the world's greatest artists; and Denny Chimes, perhaps Tuscaloosa's most identified and photographed landmark on the campus of The University of Alabama, rings its chimes and plays lovely late afternoon concerts to the delight of passersby—Tuscaloosa has it all!

And after the fun and entertainment, the tours and sports, many Tuscaloosans simply enjoy being together over a delicious meal, a cup of specialty coffee in one of our growing number of coffee houses, or a sumptuous dessert. Tuscaloosa's restaurants are growing and made to order. Good eating and lots of it is a Southern and Tuscaloosa tradition.

You can take yourself on a real gastronomic adventure and explore a wide variety of spots to indulge. Casual, cozy places mixed with charming local color and tradition— riverfront sites where you can enjoy the late afternoon sunsets, exciting music and entertainment mixed with specialty foods along "The Strip"—the world's best barbecue— these and a growing variety of restaurants provide the perfect settings for fun, relaxation, and just good fellowship.

Whatever whets your appetite for entertainment, exercises your creativity, inspires, excites, or just relaxes you; the recreational and attraction menu in Tuscaloosa is full, week after week. ❖

the crisp autumn air is filled with music for all tastes.

One of Tuscaloosa's most unique events and celebrations is the month-long Sakura Festival, beginning in March of each year. Sponsored by The University of Alabama and in cooperation with Tuscaloosa's Sister City Commission, the Sakura Festival highlights a wide range of Japanese cultural exhibits, demonstrations, and activities.

Two of the area's newest events are held in December. Christmas Afloat is a parade of brightly colored, decorated boats and barges down the Black Warrior River; while in Downtown Northport, the Dickens Christmas celebrates an old-fashioned, English-style

The City of Tuscaloosa operates out of a beautiful and functional city hall complex in downtown Tuscaloosa.

Chapter

The Public Sector

Building Bridges of Progress and Service

From progressive local governments to vital public institutions serving the needs of people, the Tuscaloosa area is built on public and private partnerships that work to sustain and enhance the community's quality of life.

Downtown Tuscaloosa remains the major center of government with city, county, state, and federal offices. And government is the major local employer with almost one-third of the work force employed in the public sector.

However, the vast majority of the work force classified as the public/governmental sector are employed at The University of Alabama, Bryce Hospital, Partlow Development Center, the Veterans Administration Medical Center, Shelton State Community College, our two public school systems, and DCH Regional Medical Center.

So Tuscaloosa is by no means a government town. Rather, it is a center of education, health care, business, and industry—where local governments work in partnership to provide an enabling framework to foster economic growth; to provide quality infrastructure and a network of roads and highways to efficiently move goods, services, and people; to provide parks, recreational opportunities, and other essential services for residents and businesses.

The City of Tuscaloosa operates with a mayor-council form of government out of a beautiful and functional city hall complex in

Tuscaloosa County residents have the most modern, efficient service for emergency communications and assistance.

downtown Tuscaloosa, originally built in 1909 as a federal courthouse and post office. The City of Tuscaloosa purchased the building in 1968, and with extensive renovations, coupled with the construction of a new annex in 1989, Tuscaloosa's City Hall has become a state-of-the-art municipal center while still maintaining the charm and tradition of the original structure.

The City of Tuscaloosa made a smooth and efficient transition to the present mayor-council form of government in 1985. The seven-person council, elected by districts, along with the mayor, elected at-large, has provided a forum for broader citizen participation and resulted in the election of Tuscaloosa's first African-American council members in 1985—Charles Steele, Jr. and John England, Jr., and Tuscaloosa's first woman council member in 1989, Sarah McBroom. Today, Tuscaloosa's municipal government continues to be inclusive and respectful of the diversity of a growing city.

The City of Tuscaloosa has traditionally been one of the better fiscal-managed communities anywhere, with a per capita debt of only $115 as of 1993. But the city hasn't been budget conscious at the expense of moving forward with visionary projects to meet the expected needs of the future.

Through the year 2000, more than a quarter of a billion dollars is scheduled to be invested in expanded highways in the metropolitan area, including the development of a metropolitan loop around the Tuscaloosa-Northport area. On the major state and local thoroughfares of the community, loop detectors and computers electronically talk to each other, constantly monitoring the flow and density of traffic to enhance the safe movement of goods, services, and citizens.

Tuscaloosa's water and sewer system has always been on the cutting edge of technology and poised to meet the needs of future development. It takes a great deal of water and sewer capacity to supply a growing metropolitan area with an annual consumption of more than 8 billion gallons and counting. Tuscaloosa is blessed with the vision and foresight to have water for today's use and tomorrow's growth.

Tuscaloosa's virtually inexhaustible water supply comes from the man-made lakes that have a total capacity of more than 44 billion gallons of water. The largest, Lake Tuscaloosa, is an engineering marvel of 5,885 acres built in 1970. Two smaller lakes, Harris and Nichol, are located in the same general vicinity north of the Black Warrior River. Meanwhile, the city's water and sewer systems have been sufficiently expanded to meet the growing needs of residential customers as well as industrial and commercial users.

Originally built in 1976, the Ed Love Water Treatment plant doubled its size in 1994 and can, today, produce over 45 million gallons of water daily. Tuscaloosa's wastewater treatment facilities, also upgraded and expanded in 1994, can handle up to 24 million gallons a day. It treats more than 15 million gallons daily. A state-of-the-art facility, the plant has been recognized as a model system cited by the Alabama Water and Pollution Control Association as the state's "Best Operated Plant."

Tuscaloosa's abundant water resources and planning have become vital ingredients in the community's successful industrial recruitment efforts over the years. Extension of water and sewer lines and other infrastructure into areas outside Tuscaloosa's corporate limits has played a key role in stimulating and enhancing economic development initiatives in recent years. Investment in infrastructure reaps big dividends for the whole area.

Only a few blocks away from City Hall, the Tuscaloosa County Commission oversees and directs the daily business of Alabama's

Local government and private business work together to provide a high-quality infrastructure to meet the growing need for new roads and facilities.

Local law enforcement works to create a better understanding and positive relationship with the community.

second-largest geographic county with over 1,340 square miles. The Tuscaloosa County Courthouse, a modern, 280,000-square-foot facility in Downtown Tuscaloosa, is the center of all county governmental operations and functions.

The Tuscaloosa County Commission is made up of four commissioners, elected by districts, and is chaired by the commission chairman, who is elected at-large and also serves as probate judge. Similar to the City of Tuscaloosa, the mid-1980s saw an expansion of broader representation with the election of Joe Mallisham as the first African-American member of the county commission.

To meet the growing demands of a vibrant economy and expanding population, the county government often turns to the private sector for leadership and support.

Through the county commission's Blue Ribbon Task Force, a private-sector group organized to help county government be more efficient and cost-effective, Tuscaloosa County has implemented major cost-saving recommendations in massive road, highway, and bridge operations and has received recognition for the application of Total Quality Management within the county courthouse. Guided by The University of Alabama's Productivity Center, Tuscaloosa County is a customer-oriented governmental operation. TQM within the Tuscaloosa County Courthouse is reinforcing the belief that public employees are indeed there to serve the public.

Throughout the area, from Northport to Brookwood and Vance, you will find local government maintaining close, responsive ties to citizens while working to meet the demands of growth and development. In Northport, Tuscaloosa's neighbor across the Black Warrior River, the people are served efficiently by a mayor elected at-large, five council members elected by districts, and a dedicated, professional city administrator. Brookwood and Vance are also served by mayor-council forms of government.

Even though the various local governmental units may provide some form of water, sewer, police and fire protection, sanitation services, parks, or any number of varied governmental services, there has been a long tradition of working together when an opportunity to benefit the whole area presents itself. Local governments have come together in partnership with highly productive results and in some areas have consolidated their efforts.

The Tuscaloosa Parks and Recreation Authority, one of Alabama's largest and diverse countywide recreation initiatives; the Tuscaloosa County Public Library; local law enforcement's combined West Alabama Narcotics Squad, Juvenile Division, and Homicide Division; Tuscaloosa County Clean Community Commission, Tuscaloosa County Solid Waste Authority; the Tuscaloosa County Industrial Development Authority— these and others are effective, consolidated efforts of local governments in the Tuscaloosa area.

The Tuscaloosa County Public Library is a countywide system serving 150,000 citizens from its main library near Downtown Tuscaloosa and its Weaver-Bolden branch on Tuscaloosa's west side, the Northport branch, and the Vance library. Founded in 1921, the library collection contains over 170,000 cataloged entries in addition to its growing, diversified community service programs.

Used by citizens from every socioeconomic group, from preschoolers to senior citizens, the library's resource center, community meeting facilities, and outreach programs touch the lives of local citizens. Through its Ready, Set, Read program, Children's Center, the rapidly expanding services to retirement homes, Boys and Girls Clubs, mental health centers, metro jail, or any number of other growing outlets, the Tuscaloosa Public Library is a unique source of ideas, information, education, and enrichment.

Another example of collaborative initiative among local governing bodies and the private sector is the Tuscaloosa County Clean Commission. Founded in 1988 through a cooperative effort of the citizens of Tuscaloosa and Northport, Tuscaloosa County, and The Chamber of Commerce of West Alabama, the commission today is the lead agency in serving the environmental needs of Tuscaloosa County.

An independent agency funded by the three local governments, the Clean Community Commission develops and implements programs to achieve a litter-free community. Educational and school initiatives, anti-litter awareness, and law enforcement are the three primary program areas that have gained some impressive results recognized statewide. Adopt-A-Mile, a 24-hour litter hotline, recycling initiatives, door-to-door, countywide garbage pick up, and other efforts by the Clean Community Commission are making a significant impact on the area's environment, safety, health, and quality of life.

A small child knows how to dial 911 in an emergency. But the caller in trouble may be a mute person who cannot give the police information, or an elderly person who passes out just as the fire department asks for the home address. With a coordinated, countywide emergency service system, E-911, Tuscaloosa County residents have the most modern, efficient service for emergency communications and assistance. The service saves critical minutes in response time to emergencies.

Tuscaloosa law enforcement agencies work in cooperative efforts with each other as well as in partnership with the area's citizens to provide a high level of public

Jim Fitts consults the plans for one of the many public and private buildings he has designed in the area.

safety and security that directly impacts quality living. Working together, our law enforcement network is able to focus on a host of community safety concerns that are outside their traditional role.

"When I talk with law enforcement officials from other areas of the state and nation, they are impressed with how effective our metro law enforcement concept works. The close working relationships between law enforcement agencies in our community denies the wrongdoer any advantage of crossing a jurisdictional boundary. This is another edge Tuscaloosa has over many other cities," says Tuscaloosa's Chief of Police Ken Swindle.

Operating out of model, high-tech law enforcement headquarters built in 1992, the Tuscaloosa Police Department's programs are structured so that officers work as change agents within our community and in nontraditional roles to create better understanding between the police and the public.

An effective Crime Stoppers program, involving a partnership between business, the media, and the law enforcement community,

is making an impact. The Police Athletic League is building bridges with the community and our young people. The DARE program, Drug Abuse Resistance Education, involves the Tuscaloosa Police Department and the County Sheriff's Department with elementary schools throughout the area. The Sheriff's Citizens Academy, the Lake Tuscaloosa Patrol, the "Eye in the Sky" Helicopter Unit, Bike Patrol—these and various other innovative techniques are reaching out to meet a growing community's needs.

"Morals, ethics, values, and education are why Tuscaloosa's people are our most valuable resource. I've had the opportunity to travel throughout the United States as well as around the world. Tuscaloosa is one of the best-kept secrets—a growing, thriving community where our people are quick to face a challenge by working together," Tuscaloosa County Sheriff Ted Sexton says.

Communication between public agencies is one of the strong points of the community, but it's not limited to just law enforcement. Exceptional fire departments, the Department of Transportation, ambulance services, a

The many construction sites in and around the city are a sure sign of growth.

The City of Tuscaloosa moves forward with visionary projects and careful fiscal management.

highly effective West Alabama EMS, area hospitals, and law enforcement, are always prepared and constantly striving to enhance their response and capabilities to ensure a safe, secure environment for our people.

Traditionally, business and industry have enjoyed a close working relationship with local government. In partnership with the private sector, local government has been a catalyst and stimulus for important economic expansion and industrial development successes.

The Tuscaloosa County Industrial Development Authority, founded in 1973, is the focal point by which our community sells itself to potential industrial investors. Funded by the cities of Tuscaloosa, Northport, Brookwood, and Vance and by Tuscaloosa County, the IDA has evolved into an effective partnership between business, community, and governmental leaders, The Chamber of Commerce of West Alabama, and major institutions of higher education in the expansion and support of new and existing industries.

The public sector provides a critical framework that enables public-private partnership efforts to work: Tuscaloosa County's industrial development parks. Investment in expanded water and sewer to meet long-term needs. Northport's exciting Renaissance Plan and riverfront development. Tuscaloosa's Convention and Visitor's Bureau. Downtown Tuscaloosa's streetscaping project. These and a host of other vital initiatives have contributed to an atmosphere and foundation for Tuscaloosa's reputation as an ideal home for business.

Communities exist to meet human needs, and local governmental entities in Tuscaloosa provide a framework to accomplish that basic objective. But there also must be opportunities for citizens who live in a community to participate in the decision-making process and to respond to the challenges faced by a city. There must be mutual concern and mutual support. In Tuscaloosa, that opportunity and concern exists.

And out of this stimulating interdependence and interchange of energies and partnership comes an exciting dynamism. You can feel it in the air in Tuscaloosa. You can sense it in a positive climate for business and economic expansion. It is an energy that creates vision, guides problem solvers, and nourishes leadership.

Over its 175-year history, much has changed with government in Tuscaloosa. Local government has grown into a vital planning component that provides an infrastructure to enhance livability in an expanding, diversified economy. ❖

Northport is served by a mayor-council form of government which is housed in a beautiful City Hall complex.

Epilogue

10

The Vision

The Future, The Promise, The Hope

It's the year 2005 in Tuscaloosa. The 21st century is well underway as Tuscaloosa celebrates its 186th Anniversary. The community has grown steadily over the past decade to a population of over 125,000 in the Tuscaloosa-Northport metropolitan area, with over 165,000 residents countywide.

More than 25 years have passed since Tuscaloosa has experienced any major economic downturns and significant job losses because of a highly productive partnership between business and industry, education and government, established in the early 1980s and continuing to produce positive economic results today.

Through all the fast-paced changes, advancements and global challenges, Tuscaloosa has established and sustained itself as a nationally and internationally recognized community of world-class technology, manufacturing, health care, and education. Meanwhile, the quality of life and natural beauty that have always characterized the community have been carefully preserved, directly enhancing the cherished traditions and spirit of the area's residents and impressing newcomers from throughout the world.

Tuscaloosa has not become an uncontrolled "boom city" of the 21st century but, instead, a community of moderation and solid, quality growth confident in its shared vision. The metropolitan development plan envisioned in the mid-1990s has served the entire area well, bringing managed growth that has not put undue stress on the community's support systems and infrastructure.

All of Tuscaloosa County's neighboring communities have grown together over the past 10 years, not just in terms of geography, but in spirit, cooperation, and even in the elimination of some costly duplication of services and consolidation of major governmental units. Yet, communities within the region have still maintained their own unique personalities and identities.

Throughout the Tuscaloosa-Northport metropolitan area, new, exciting centers of commerce operate profitably within one of the nation's best business and entrepreneurial environments. Centers of technology, engineering, and innovation consistently take new ideas from the labs and classrooms straight to product development and the global marketplace, as Tuscaloosa has retained its leadership in industrial development and the effective transfer of technology to the market.

In the year 2005, Tuscaloosa has secured its leadership position as the ideal home for business, proving the predictions of the mid-1990s. Back in 1994, Cognetics, a Massachusetts-based consulting firm that tracks business activity, selected the Tuscaloosa-Birmingham market as one of the top 10 markets in the nation to start and grow a business.

Tuscaloosa's regional marketplace has continued to expand and develop. Revitalized central business districts in downtown Tuscaloosa, Alberta City, and West Tuscaloosa have become models of commercial innovation while one of the region's most popular entertainment and cultural arts centers thrives in downtown Northport's Renaissance District. Meanwhile, many national and recognized regional retailers and restaurants anchor the area's retail market, which has almost doubled over the past 10 years to $2.5 billion in annual retail sales.

The riverfront along the Black Warrior River is now bustling with sophisticated, quaint retail shops, exciting restaurants, commercial and office centers, and residential developments; yet a balance has been carefully maintained to include relaxing riverfront promenades and leisurely parks where families and tourists alike enjoy the scenic splendor of the Black Warrior.

Meanwhile, I-59 between Tuscaloosa and Jefferson County, has grown into one of the nation's premier high-technology corridors. Anchored by JVC and Mercedes-Benz, the corridor is lined with high-tech manufacturers, strategic distribution centers, and research and development centers connecting Tuscaloosa to the world marketplace.

In addition to research and development parks that now dot the landscape, Tuscaloosa County's Industrial Park has grown into an efficient intermodal center of industry, transportation, and exports. Anchored by the Tuscaloosa Municipal Airport, which has been carefully developed into a strategic center of corporate, private, and freight distribution services, Tuscaloosa is linked to the world in all directions by rail, four-lane highways, and an industrial canal to the Black Warrior River.

Moving goods, services, commerce, and people in the year 2005 is an efficient, cost-effective blend of public transportation and a high-quality road and highway network. Initiated almost 20 years ago, the Warrior Urban belt-way is in place along with efficient four-lane arteries east and west and north and south.

With the growth and economic expansion experienced over the past 10 years, the public and private sectors have increased investment in new and expanded opportunities for recreation and the arts. Not only do riverfront activities draw residents and visitors, but so do the area's new championship public golf courses; nationally known festivals such as Kentuck, RiverFest, and Heritage Week; and an enlarged 84,000-seat Bryant-Denny Stadium where all the Crimson Tide's home games are now played.

While the technology renaissance has continued to transform virtually all facets of our lives, the year 2005 still sees the Tuscaloosa-area community anchored by strong, well-defined neighborhoods where people genuinely care about each other.

Tuscaloosa is still the ideal place to create a home. Strong family values thread through the community. There are safe, secure streets for all. The advantaged reach out to nurture, support, and encourage the disadvantaged. Because of protective public-private partnerships in the community, all of the Tuscaloosa area's citizens have access to adequate and affordable housing, health care, and human services.

People are working together in the year 2005. The community's vision process and goal-setting are inclusive, involving our citizen's everywhere, from neighborhoods to city hall. Tuscaloosa has become one of the nation's model communities for valuing and managing multi-culturalism, which has contributed to the area's harmony and strength through diversity.

The significant underpinning to the area's exceptional quality of life and standard of living in the year 2005 has been our world-class schools and educational institutions. All of our schools, from prekindergarten to postdoctoral, are producing globally competitive, academically and technically competent people with the skills to engage in lifelong learning and to achieve their full potential.

In the year 2005, our schools are adequately and equitably funded because of increased local support for world-class education. Challenging curriculum with high standards; international baccalaureate programs; magnet schools for math and science, technology and the arts; effective school-to-work transition initiatives—these and other 21st-century technologies have created a state-of-the-art learning environment for all of our children.

In addition, parents are involved with their children's education at every level.

The work ethic and economic education are core components of every student's learning. There is respect and discipline in the classrooms, which have become cornerstones for our children's growth and education.

This crystal ball picture of Tuscaloosa in the year 2005, or at least part of it, may prove to be somewhat out of focus when the 21st century actually dawns. But even given the unreliability of crystal balls, it's still a vison that is very attainable.

Attainment of this vision is possible in Tuscaloosa because there is a spirit that recognizes our interdependence with one another as well as new levels of relationships and opportunities that require us to think globally and locally at the same time. A community, in the long run, differentiates itself from all others because of human resources and the winning spirit of its people. And that's Tuscaloosa's edge.

The people of Tuscaloosa have long cherished a tradition of solving problems and meeting challenges together, focusing our energies and interests on what is best for the total community. This tradition becomes more exciting and challenging as regional growth brings diversity of interests, backgrounds, and lifestyles.

Entering the 21st century, Tuscaloosa is an exciting, dynamic center of commerce, education, and quality living with timeless traditions, values, and charm. Its promise is as bright and inspiring as the dawning of a new day. ❖

With strong family values threading through the community, Tuscaloosa is the ideal place to create a home. Photo by Dale South.

Part Two
Tuscaloosa's Enterprises

Chapter

Networks

Tuscaloosa County Industrial Development Authority

The industrial recruitment successes enjoyed by the Tuscaloosa County Industrial Development Authority in the past two decades have changed in a most positive way the face of economic development, the business climate, and the quality of life in the Tuscaloosa area.

In fact, the Authority, in concert with government entities, development agencies, financial institutions, and existing industries, has hit some of the longest home runs in the history of industrial recruitment, effectively putting Tuscaloosa on the economic development map in the United States and around the globe.

Founded in the 1970s by an Act of the Alabama Legislature, the Tuscaloosa County Industrial Development Authority was created to assist area governments with economic development and industrial recruitment—specifically in soliciting manufacturing investment and convincing industrial companies to locate plants in Tuscaloosa County.

The recruitment of manufacturers takes into account the economic advantages of attracting industrial concerns to a geographic region. Manufacturing enterprises are a time-honored way of creating wealth because such businesses utilize moderate-to-large amounts of skilled labor and bring new dollars into a community by selling finished products in other markets. As a result, recruiting manufacturing jobs is one of the most efficient ways of improving the living standards in a community.

The Tuscaloosa County Industrial Development Authority, or IDA, has played a major role in developing the Tuscaloosa area

as we know it today. Companies such as Mercedes-Benz, JVC, Tuscaloosa Steel, Harrison Radiator (to name but a few) were recruited by the IDA. Now they have become an integral part of the fabric of the area's business community. The recruitment of JVC America in the 1980s was the most significant industrial development success in Alabama history—at least until 1993 when Tuscaloosa County landed the American manufacturing plant for the German automaker Mercedes-Benz. While that success took the cooperative effort of dozens of entities—from state development officials and the governor's office to area governments to the economic development initiatives of major corporations such as Alabama Power Company—the Tuscaloosa County Industrial Development Authority was naturally the "point man" on the huge project.

The major governmental bodies in Tuscaloosa County—the cities of Tuscaloosa, Northport, Brookwood, and Vance, as well as the Tuscaloosa County government—operate the authority by pooling their resources and acting together in the interest of economic development. The government entities appoint 22 people to serve as the board of directors for the authority, which employs just four people on a full-time basis.

To facilitate its industrial recruitment efforts, the Tuscaloosa County Industrial Development Authority issues industrial revenue bonds to assist in the financing of projects and owns the Airport Industrial Park and a speculative building for potential industrial recruits, as well as other parcels of real estate appropriate for development.

The marketing effort employed by the IDA is sophisticated and multifaceted. Seeking prospective companies from a wide variety of sources, the authority identifies prospects that are likely to expand and then systematically

and periodically places the merits of Tuscaloosa County before the company's decision makers. For corporations actively involved in the early stages of an expansion, the authority works hard to convince the company to add Tuscaloosa County to its list of potential industrial sites.

Once a company is interested in Tuscaloosa, the IDA gathers and places at the company's disposal the data that addresses the prospect's needs, concerns, and requirements. The authority builds relationships with other development entities and utilizes their resources in recruiting a prospect. Similarly, the IDA has relationships with financial institutions and educational/training facilities whose resources may play a pivotal role in the decision-making process. The University of Alabama—with its first-class facilities and

At the announcment ceremony, Mercedes-Benz Chief Executive Officer and Chairman of the Board, Helmut Werner, discloses that Tuscaloosa County is the chosen site for manufacturing the Mercedes-Benz Sport Utility Vehicle. Photo by Neil Blake.

Johnson Controls, an internally recognized company, located in the Airport Industrial Park and began production of plastic automotive components in 1989.

talent—is often a vitally important community component put to work to recruit a new company to the area.

Often the best marketing agent the authority can employ is a recently recruited company that is now operating in the area. The IDA often calls on existing industrial companies to help in the recruitment effort. That's part of the reason why a major emphasis of the Tuscaloosa County Industrial Development Authority is what might best be described as service after the sale. The authority follows through carefully with companies that move into Tuscaloosa County—fulfilling their needs and making certain that promises made have been promises kept—to assure that these companies become the best sales tool Tuscaloosa County ever had.

Tuscaloosa County competes in the big leagues of industrial recruitment. For example, if JVC had not moved here, the company was headed to the vaunted Research Triangle area of North Carolina. The area also competes in an international arena. Many of Tuscaloosa's greatest recruitment successes have come with European or Asian companies.

Still, success has not come naturally or easily for Tuscaloosa. In 1978, the county had a work force of 55,000 with about 15,000 people employed in manufacturing—most often in moribund industries such as textiles. The late 1970s and early part of the 1980s were not kind to Tuscaloosa's manufacturing base. In the late 1970s, unemployment in Tuscaloosa County had sunk well into double digits bottoming out at about 17 or 18 percent—the highest in Alabama.

That was the environment that surrounded the birth of the Tuscaloosa County Industrial Development Authority. Something had to be done and something was. By the late 1980s, Tuscaloosa County had become the second fastest growing metropolitan area in Alabama in one of the most remarkable stories of economic development on record.

The Tuscaloosa County Industrial Development Authority has been so successful in its recruitment because the employees who lead the effort are talented economic development professionals and because they have a good product to sell.

Tuscaloosa County has many of the assets and positive attributes that companies are looking for in communities. For one thing, local governments have been progressive in their efforts at improving the infrastructure of their communities—from roads to schools. Teamwork has also come into play with many governmental and business entities coming together beneath the IDA banner to attract new investment. The recruitment of Mercedes Benz, for one example, was an unprecedented example of cooperative effort. The University of Alabama has been an excellent community asset, as has progressive leadership in state and national political offices in Montgomery and Washington, D.C. But perhaps the clearest advantage employed by all of those interested in economic development in Tuscaloosa County has been an ability to think and act in the most progressive and broadest possible manner, beyond the boundaries of corporate or city limits.

The challenge ahead for the Tuscaloosa County Industrial Development Authority lies in keeping the economic development team moving in the right direction, with an eye towards continuing improvement in the quality of community resources and the diversification of the area economy. ❖

JVC America, which began operations in 1986, was the first major international company successfully recruited by the Tuscaloosa County Industrial Development Authority.

Alabama Power Company

Tuscaloosa is a thriving community of good neighbors and hard working citizens who share a vision of making Alabama a better place to live. Alabama Power is a partner in that vision. From producing electricity which keeps the wheels of business and commerce spinning, to serving in key leadership positions throughout the state, Alabama Power plays a vital role in the life of the community.

Alabama Power provides reliable, low-cost electric power to 1.2 million homes, businesses, and industries in the lower two- thirds of the state. It is one of the five operating utilities of The Southern Company—one of the nation's largest investor-owned electric utility groups.

Tuscaloosa, the hub of Alabama Power's operations in west Alabama, became part of the company's service area in November 1923. The city is headquarters for the company's Western Division which serves over 181,000 customers. Five-hundred-seventy-six division employees live and work in communities throughout fifteen counties in west Alabama. In addition, 605 Alabama Power employees work at five company generating facilities located within the division's boundaries—Greene County Electric Generating Plant near Demopolis, Gorgas Electric Generating Plant and Smith Dam near Jasper, and Holt and Bankhead Dams near Tuscaloosa.

Competitive pricing, reliable electricity, and world class service are cornerstones of Alabama Power's commitment to its customers. During the last decade, inflation rose over 40 percent, while the price of electricity in Alabama rose less than 1.5 percent. Alabama Power consistently has prices in the lowest quarter of utilities in the United States.

Ensuring that electricity gets to customers with minimal interruptions is a core value at Alabama Power. The company knows a reliable energy source is critical, especially in energy-sensitive industrial and commercial processes. New technologies, intensive maintenance programs, and automated equipment help the company restore service quickly should an interruption occur.

To ensure very satisfied customers, Alabama Power continuously adds valuable services. For example, residential customers now have price options which help them use energy more economically. One option sets prices according to the time of day electricity is used. The other option reflects electricity costs on a seasonal basis. Both pricing methods benefit customers who incorporate energy-saving measures in their homes.

Commercial and industrial customers also have a variety of price options from which to choose, and Alabama Power employees work to provide individualized service to all customers, often developing specialized solutions to meet individual user energy requirements.

Advanced technology is used to improve customer service. For example, customers with rotary telephone dial service can now report outages using new voice-activated technology. New products, such as power surge suppressors for residential customers and "PowerCall," a device that automatically notifies the company if power is interrupted, are being test marketed.

Alabama Power takes action to add convenience for customers. The company has expanded office hours, added drive-through payment windows, and installed night

More than 14,000 miles of distribution lines and 2,000 miles of transmission lines deliver electricity across Alabama Power's Western Division.

World-class customer service is the foundation of positive customer relationships.

payment facilities throughout the division. A full-service Customer Convenience Center has been opened at Northbrook Plaza Shopping Center in Northport to complement service provided at the company's Queen City Avenue office. In addition, the company has established convenient neighborhood bill payment locations.

Helping customers succeed in a competitive marketplace by keeping electricity prices low demands that the company pursue innovative ways to control costs. For example, improved generating plant efficiency has saved customers more than $400 million in fuel costs over the past 11 years. And, the company continues to take advantage of improving financial markets to refinance long-term debt, significantly lowering financing costs.

Maintaining a well-trained, empowered workforce at appropriate staffing levels is a

Alabama Power Service Organization volunteer gives the gift of time to help special-needs children at the RISE Program in Tuscaloosa.

key component of an effective competitive strategy. The company provides cross-training and job rotation opportunities to help employees become multi-skilled. Training courses and mini-seminars, some adapted to a new teleconferencing format through the Alabama Power Television Network, help keep employees up-to-date on company operations, strategies, and goals.

Since its inception, Alabama Power has remained true to its vision of helping create a state of opportunity and economic vitality. New and expanding industries improve the quality of life for Alabamians by providing jobs, enlarging the tax base, and improving training and educational opportunities. Alabama Power is a leader in Alabama's economic development efforts.

The company's Alabama Resource Center provides site selection information to companies looking to expand or to locate in Alabama. The Alabama Resource Center database highlights the state's abundant industrial and business resources—from transportation systems to the labor force. Alabama Power's ability to provide stable electric prices is an excellent marketing tool for economic development efforts in the state.

Satellite centers were opened in Mobile and Decatur to supplement the efforts of Resource Centers in Birmingham and Montgomery. The original center in

Birmingham now houses the Alabama World Business Center to help state businesses broaden their trade and export activities.

In 1993, Tuscaloosa and Alabama made history by winning the economic development prize of the century. An aggressive public/private partnership that included Alabama Power convinced Mercedes-Benz to build its first U.S. plant in Tuscaloosa County.

As a major employer in the state, Alabama Power is committed to exemplary corporate citizenship. Alabama Power employee volunteers, members of the company's nationally recognized Teacher Corps, make classroom presentations in schools. The company also awards grants to teachers developing innovative programs and provides seed-money and grants for local educational foundations.

In Tuscaloosa, Oak Hill School, a public school for children with special needs, is the company's adopted school. Employee-sponsored fundraisers, including an annual bass tournament, have generated $80,000 for programs and facilities at Oak Hill such as a wheelchair-accessible playgound. These volunteer efforts resulted in a Governor's Point of Light Award recognizing Western Division employees for their work with handicapped children.

Alabama Power encourages employee and family involvement in the community. Employees and spouses volunteer time and energy to work on charitable projects. The Alabama Power Service Organization in the Western Division, one of the nine chapters comprised of employees and spouses, focuses efforts and resources on critical needs such as education and child health and safety.

The company is a leader in sponsoring other charitable projects. Project SHARE, created in 1982 with $50,000 seed money, has

provided $10 million in energy assistance to more than 100,000 Alabama families. The Alabama Power Foundation, created in 1989, has contributed more than $12 million to help charitable, educational, and cultural entities in the state. And, the Alabama Business Charitable Trust Fund, created by Alabama Power in 1992 to provide energy assistance to those not assisted through other programs, contributed $1.7 million to 8,800 families by the end of 1993.

As the latter half of the decade approaches, tremendous opportunities for success lie before Alabama Power and the Tuscaloosa community. As a responsible citizen of the state and as a reliable, low-cost energy provider, Alabama Power plays a critical role in that success. Alabama Power is committed to make the Tuscaloosa community and Alabama the very best it can be. ❖

Thanks to laser-speed technology, economic development prospects can research the entire state without leaving one of four Alabama Resource Center locations.

South Central Bell

The story of South Central Bell is the inspirational tale of the birth and development of a network, an interconnected web of people and technology woven together in a pattern of growth and ever increasing knowledge. South Central Bell is a corporation of people and material resources put to work to find better ways to communicate, melt the distances between people, and smooth the flow of ideas and commerce.

While South Central Bell is a gigantic, multi-state company, it works very much on

South Central Bell employees lay down the infrastructure for the communications of tomorrow.

the local level. The people and technology that make up the Tuscaloosa operations of South Central Bell serve the communication needs of the western half of Alabama.

South Central Bell employees are not only concerned with their work, but they are also active in the community. The Telephone Pioneers of America—an employee and a retired employee group—contribute thousands of hours of community service each year. There are also many Tuscaloosa area South Central Bell employees active in organizations such as scouting, United Way and the Chamber of Commerce of West Alabama.

The community and its school systems have enlisted the help of South Central Bell in a variety of efforts aimed at improving public education. A South Central Bell initiative, the Teacher Mini-Grants Program, awards up to $500 to help teachers implement innovative classroom projects, and the company participates in the Adopt-A-School program. The company makes available training slots in management institutes for school principals to improve performance and hone leadership skills.

In all, about 185 people are employed by South Central Bell in the Tuscaloosa area. Three call-switching centers with state- of-the-art digital electronic equipment are tied together by a digital network and serve some 70,000 customers.

That service comprises some of the most technologically advanced telecommunications available. High-speed, high-quality voice and data communication now move through a growing network of fiber-optic cables. One fiber-optic cable can carry more than a million conversations at once, with the communications traveling several hundred times faster than they

South Central Bell is finding better ways to communicate and smooth the flow of ideas and commerce.

would over traditional copper wires. South Central Bell employees are busy placing fiber-optic cable on main routes throughout the service area with eventual branching off into subdivisions—laying down the infrastructure for the communications of tomorrow. Nowadays, the Integrated Services Digital Network (ISDN) makes possible simultaneous transmission of voice, data, and video on one digital line. In years to come, ISDN will serve customers' homes where monitoring temperature and security systems on the home front—even electronically linking appliances and communication devices—will be possible.

Also available to customers is the full range of TouchStar service options that allow customers to automatically dial back numbers, program distinctive ringing patterns, or block annoying calls. Caller ID lets customers see on a digital readout the number of the person calling. MemoryCall service is a voice messaging service that turns a telephone into an electronic mailbox.

All of the high-tech access put into place by South Central Bell takes the wonders of telecommunications and makes them applicable to the present and future needs of people and businesses. In reality, the telephone now most closely resembles a computer terminal in its ability to impact our lives. And the most exciting advances in telecommunications are yet to come, making the future unlimited and the role of an innovative company such as South Central Bell in that future assured. ❖

Alabama Gas Corporation

Alabama Gas Corporation is one of the most dynamic and progressive natural gas distribution companies in the United States. The largest subsidiary of Energen Corporation, Alagasco excels at serving customers and providing reliable, economical gas service to some 425,000 customers in 180 cities and towns across Alabama.

In 1992, Alagasco was included in the book, *The 100 Best Companies To Work For In America*, a national recognition of the organization's finely tuned sense of customer and employee needs and its caring, progressive corporate culture.

Alagasco has always broken new ground when it comes to seeking out sources of energy. It was the first distribution company to buy natural gas from West Alabama fields in Fayette and Pickens counties and today purchases gas from nontraditional sources such as coalbed methane wells in east Tuscaloosa County.

In the Tuscaloosa District, Alagasco has grown and expanded its business at more than twice the national average for utility companies. Seventy employees serve 35,500 customers in Greene, Pickens, Hale, and Tuscaloosa counties.

Marketing at Alagasco is an all-encompassing effort. All employees are encouraged to become marketers of natural gas for the home, promoting everything from water heaters and clothes dryers to fireplace logs, gas grills, and an appliance that combines heating, water heating, and cooling in one unit. In addition to developing new markets for natural gas in the homes of customers, the company promotes natural gas as a clean-burning fuel that can be used to power vehicles such as the trucks in Alagasco's fleet. Also, natural gas is used to incinerate hazardous waste, and to cool the air without ozone-damaging CFCs.

Alabama Gas Corporation takes seriously its commitment to the communities in which it does business. The Company and its employees are deeply involved with the United Way, FOCUS on Senior Citizens, the American Red Cross, Temporary Emergency Services, and similar social service agencies. Every employee is a member of an educational support organization and many work "hands on" in the Adopt-A-School program. The award winning Operation Assist program hired teenagers to weatherize more than 15,000 low income homes in Tuscaloosa between 1985 and 1991. The program helped needy customers stay warm while providing jobs, training, and hope to at-risk young people.

Of paramount importance to Alabama Gas Corporation is its relationship with its customers. It offers money saving energy systems, free safety inspections and monitoring of potential emergencies for elderly customers, help for customers having trouble paying their bills, and even bills designed for the blind. **Customers come first at Alagasco!** ❖

Tuscaloosa County has proven to be a rich source of natural gas from coal seams, providing clean energy for Alagasco customers in Tuscaloosa and around the state.

The company serves more than 425,000 customers in central Alabama, providing energy for heat, hot water, cooking, clothes drying, grilling and outdoor lighting.

The Tuscaloosa News

The *Tuscaloosa News* serves readers and advertisers in a primary marketing area of nine West Alabama counties, packaging local, state, national, and international news in a strong community newspaper with roots that run deep in the region's history.

The News is part of the New York Times Regional Newspaper Group (and has been since 1985), one of 31 mostly Southeastern and primarily daily newspapers owned by the company whose flagship is arguably the world's best known newspaper.

The News places a strong emphasis on local news, serving readers with information they can't get from any other source—news items that are vitally important to their understanding of their community, neighborhood, local government, schools, and area businesses. The paper also serves as a complete source for news about the state of Alabama, regional concerns, and national and international developments.

Located at the center of a hotbed of collegiate athletics, sports also naturally play a large role in the news package Tuscaloosa

The Tuscaloosa News team takes seriously its responsibilities of presenting clear and carefully considered opinions on its editorial pages.

and West Alabama readers receive. In addition, *The Tuscaloosa News* takes seriously its responsibility of presenting clear and carefully considered opinion on its editorial page, a long and proud tradition at the paper. *The News* won a Pulitzer Prize for its editorial writing in 1957, and has won numerous state honors since.

Full color printing long has been a signature strength at *The News*. The paper has been successfully reproducing attractive color images for more than 20 years.

The Tuscaloosa News' history—through ancestral related newspapers—goes back to the beginning of the 19th century. The first newspaper in Tuscaloosa, *The American Mirror*, began publishing in June, 1818. Its name was changed in 1827 to the *Tuscaloosa Chronicle*. In 1833, the *Chronicle* merged with the *Sentinel*.

When the state capitol moved to Tuscaloosa in 1826, the leading newspaper at the time, *The Alabama State Intelligencer*, moved with it. Unfortunately, all of the files and records of the *Intelligencer* were destroyed in a fire set by Union soldiers who invaded the city in April, 1865. Various newspapers operated in Tuscaloosa in the years immediately following the Civil War, including the *Independent Monitor*, which was banned for about a month in 1868 by Reconstructionist authorities.

The more immediate ancestor of *The News* was the *Times-Gazette*, which began publishing as a merged newspaper in 1903. *The Tuscaloosa News* was launched in August, 1910, and merged five years later with the *Times-Gazette* under the banner *Tuscaloosa News/Times-Gazette*.

The Tuscaloosa News serves readers and advertisers in a primary marketing area of nine West Alabama counties.

By 1929, the newspaper came under the ownership of Tuscaloosa Newspaper Publishing Co. and began publishing under the name of *The Tuscaloosa News*. General Newspapers, Inc. bought the paper in 1947, and James Buford Boone, Sr. of Georgia became publisher. In 1954, stock in the paper was sold to the Public Welfare Foundation, a philanthropic organization that used newspaper profits to fund good works. The Boone family leased the paper from the foundation, giving *The Tuscaloosa News* local control and management.

Under the Boones, the paper had many successes, commercially and editorially. As a crusading newspaper it was able to have a real impact on the safety and conscience of a community during difficult periods of social change.

The News continues to flourish today under the leadership of publisher Charles Land. As an institution, the newspaper has emphasized the need to improve the state's public schools as well as state-supported higher education, and *The News* has helped play a role in setting the climate for local industrial and economic development and expansion.

Quality continues to be a hallmark of *The Tuscaloosa News*, which won recognition in the category of general excellence in statewide newspaper competition in 1993, as well as numerous other distinctions.

That dedication to excellence was reflected in newspaper sales, as circulation at *The News* reached its highest point ever in 1993. ❖

Comcast Cable

A subsidiary of one of the largest and most respected cable television operators in the nation, Comcast Cablevision of Tuscaloosa is the area's leading source of broadcast entertainment and information.

Comcast's corporate headquarters are in Philadelphia, Pennsylvania and the company serves approximately 2.9 million subscribers throughout the country. Locally, more than 34,000 families in the city of Tuscaloosa, the city of Northport, and portions of unincorporated Tuscaloosa County turn to Comcast Cablevision for the best value in round-the-clock news, exciting sports events, and family entertainment.

Comcast purchased the Tuscaloosa cable system from Group W in 1988. Since that time, the company has invested both time and money to give local residents the best in customer service, reliability, and picture quality. Ensuring that telephone calls are answered promptly and completely, scheduling service calls in a fast and convenient manner, and providing flexible office hours for personal visits are all important to the overall goal of providing Tuscaloosa with an outstanding customer-focused operation.

Comcast's programming reflects the interests of the subscribers. Networks like TNT, ESPN, Discovery, Arts & Entertainment, QVC, and the Weather Channel are included in the 35 channel "preferred basic plan." Popular premium channels such as Showtime, HBO, Cinemax, and the Disney Channel are also available. Rounding out the selection are Viewers Choice channels of Pay Per View offering just released movies, special concerts, and unique sporting events.

A new service, Music Choice, is also available to Comcast subscribers. Often referred to as "cable variety for your stereo," Music Choice provides thirty different channels-from jazz to classical to New Age to rock—24 hours a day and all commercial free.

Comcast Cablevision of Tuscaloosa likes to describe itself as the information source for the community. To do that, the cable system devotes a lot of effort into providing specialized local programming. The city of Tuscaloosa's annual Christmas Parade is broadcast, as well as other events of broad interest such as the University of Alabama's football championship parade in 1993. Comcast also produces a weekly business and community affairs show for the Chamber of Commerce of West Alabama.

Recognizing its unique ability to promote worthy causes, Comcast makes its facilities and employees available to produce public service announcements for such worthy local community organizations as the United Way, the Salvation Army, and Toys for Tots.

Comcast Cablevision of Tuscaloosa is the area's leading source of broadcast entertainment and information.

Comcast realizes that its long term success as a business rests with a dedication to quality in every phase of its operation. Comcast is proud to be part of this community. ❖

Comcast Cable provides Tuscaloosa with outstanding customer-focused services.

Chapter

12

Manufacturing & Distribution

Industrial Warehouse Services

Flexibility and service are the key words to remember about Industrial Warehouse Services. Since its founding in 1968, IWS—a holding company that oversees warehousing, packaging, and trucking concerns in three states—has focused its business on providing exemplary, responsive, and flexible service and fulfilling the needs of industrial customers.

Tuscaloosa Warehouse can handle bulk hopper car unloading, blending, and transferring.

The warehousing services that IWS provides cut to the very heart of an efficient industrial operation. Every step of the way in its relationship with customers, IWS operates as a business partner, lending peak efficiency to industry and allowing for such modern techniques as Just In Time delivery. And the service-oriented philosophy of IWS will become even more valuable as business efficiencies such as Just-In-Time—a delivery system that saves companies the expense of the high cost of inventory—grow ever more popular.

In Tuscaloosa, IWS operates the Tuscaloosa Warehouse, a site convenient to both the interstate and other highways as well as rail lines. KCS Railroad services the site with the added efficiency of being open to reciprocal switching. Due to the reciprocal agreement, the warehouse is also served by Norfolk Southern Railroad.

Tuscaloosa Warehouse contains 375,000 square feet of warehouse space with plenty of additional land at the site available for expansion. All of the interior space is equipped with sprinklers and protected by fire and security systems. All temperatures are centrally and carefully controlled. Inventory management at the facility is top shelf and computerized with on-line services and printouts.

Some of the special services offered at Tuscaloosa Warehouse for customers include import/export storage and distribution, dry chemical blending and packaging, break bulk sorting, blending, batching, segregating, and labeling. In addition, Tuscaloosa Warehouse can handle bulk hopper car unloading, blending, and transferring. Such preproduction services allow a customer to avoid investing in equipment and manpower to accomplish these necessary, but capital intensive, tasks. Those sorts of services are examples of the innovations offered by IWS, services that really help the productivity of customers.

Approximately 90 employees work at Tuscaloosa Warehouse and Service Express (overall about 250 people work at IWS facilities in Alabama, Mississippi, and Texas). One of the real strengths of the company is its dedicated work force of experienced personnel.

The company's in-house carrier trucking line, Service Express, is one of the aspects of the exceptional service that IWS and Tuscaloosa Warehouse provides for customers. Service Express operates 50 tractors and 110 trailers moving freight for customers throughout the eastern half of the United States, and meeting their shipping and JIT delivery needs with an exceptional service and safety record.

Aside from the IWS warehouse in Tuscaloosa, the company has additional operating facilities in other parts of Alabama, Mississippi, and in Texas.

Southeastern Packaging Co. (SEAPAC) meets the materials handling and packaging needs of customers with a 210,000-square-foot facility in Mobile, Alabama, and a 300,000-square-foot facility in Baytown, Texas, just outside of Houston. The IWS operating company specializes in dry solids processing and packaging from bulk railcar or truck. Because of the company's locations in port cities, access to international markets is superior.

IWS also operates the company's Marht facility in Cottonton, Alabama, near Eufaula and Phenix City, a 210,000-square-foot complex designed to efficiently receive, sheet, rewind, slit, and ship coated board. Strict standards of quality and accuracy infuse every aspect of operations at Mahrt, saving customers downtime due to poor quality sheets and significantly enhancing their bottom line.

A Jagenberg Synchrovert sheeter is a state-of-the-art piece of machinery that generates a minimal amount of dust and produces a clean-cut, perfectly square sheet of coated board. Computers monitor production at the plant to ensure a maximum level of precision in quality control. A computerized labeling system assures accuracy in shipping to customers or end-users.

In Columbus, Mississippi, Industrial Warehouse Services' Triangle Warehouse Complex offers customers 207,000 square feet of warehouse, light manufacturing, and packaging space and services. The facility is well situated to meet the transportation efficiency needs of customers. The Tenn-Tom Waterway, highways, and rail service are all easily accessible. As with all IWS facilities, the Columbus warehouse is fully bonded, sprinklered, and secured. And with careful quality assurance and J-I-T shipments, customers receive their deliveries on time and in good order.

The secret of Industrial Warehouse Service's success is the strongly held corporate belief that the best way to operate a company is to treat your customer's business as if it were your very own. That kind of commitment naturally leads to satisfied and loyal customers and a growing, energetic business.

IWS responds to the needs of its customer—whether that need lies in the arena of preproduction processing of materials, Just-In-Time delivery, or computerized warehousing.

In-house trucking. Adept materials handling. Cost-efficient warehousing and inventory management. Those are the products that have arisen from the dedicated management of Industrial Warehouse Services. The company's experienced and committed managers are focused on providing solutions to the challenges faced by industrial companies.

Flexibility is an important attribute to display in any business, but in the warehousing, packaging, and trucking business—where so many different customers depend on you every day to deliver your best, so that they in turn can effectively serve their clients—flexibility is especially critical. A company like IWS must be flexible in order to be responsive and earn the trust and business of customers.

The operations of all IWS facilities are geared to reflect the needs and concerns of the company's manufacturing customers. Customized solutions offer the best opportunities for companies to realize their production goals, and customized solutions for inventory management is precisely the specialty of the professionals at Industrial Warehouse Services. ❖

Some of the special services offered are blending, batching, dry chemical blending and packaging.

Tuscaloosa Warehouse contains 375,000 square feet of warehouse space.

Tuscaloosa Steel

Tuscaloosa Steel has carved out a unique niche in the steel industry by manufacturing, in a uniquely wide range of dimensions, the highest quality flat-rolled steel, produced by people who are motivated by a time-honored sense of pride in their own work.

Wholly-owned by British Steel, PLC. which purchased the plant in January, 1991, Tuscaloosa Steel operates a hot strip/plate mill that produces coil-based carbon and stainless steel in a wide range of flat-rolled product dimensions and gauges. The company is the only American domestic steelmaker and one of only a handful in the entire world that can produce plate from coil in such a large variety of dimensions—in gauges from 0.187 of an inch to 1 full inch and up to 101.5 inches wide.

Tuscaloosa Steel utilizes a steady supply of continuously cast steel slabs in a low-cost, technically efficient method of converting the slabs into coiled steel products. About 50 percent of the plant's raw material supply comes from the United Kingdom, with the balance coming from Europe, South America and Asia. The plant's geographic location on the Black Warrior River makes for ease of movement in the transportation of materials by barge.

Tuscaloosa Steel's product line is utilized by the transportation sector in truck bodies, railcars, barges and shipbuilding; the construction industry in fabrication beams; in

East end of TSC's Hot Rolling Mill with processed coils ready for rail, barge or truck transport.

storage tanks for oil, water, LP gas and liquefied natural gas; and as structural steel in bridges, guardrails, and pipe.

While earning a reputation for outstanding customer service and unparalleled quality, Tuscaloosa Steel has developed into one of the most shining success stories in the American steel industry. It is the only flat-rolled mill in the United States to receive JIS (Japanese Industrial Standard) certification, one of the highest standards of production excellence recognized the world over. An application for a world quality standard ISO 9000 designation will be completed in 1994. Tuscaloosa Steel is also the only U.S. mill that can roll titanium more than 40 inches wide and produce the widest coil of stainless steel available.

Tuscaloosa Steel employs a system of Total Quality Performance that assures the company is measuring up to the toughest standards of customer service. Management and workers toil together to make certain that customer requirements are continually satisfied, productivity is consistently improved and a quality workplace for employees is constantly provided. Tuscaloosa Steel operates with the guiding principle that a company committed to quality is one destined for long-term success.

Another superlative at Tuscaloosa Steel is the quality of the work force. A non-union shop, the company workplace is an excellent example of a modern industrial plant that features the latest in automation and computer technology, and employs highly skilled and well-trained workers that can operate the mill

Entrance to Tuscaloosa Steel Corporation's Holt Road Facility.

Slab yard inventory with overhead slab handling crane.

at peak efficiency. The management of the company strives to create a corporate culture where empowerment is the key to successful operations. The employees are really a part of what makes the company a success. As a result, morale among Tuscaloosa Steel's approximately 295 employees is very high.

The company's philosophy of maintaining the highest quality manufacturing processes and customer service is grounded in an approach to business that is uniquely effective and inclusive. Tuscaloosa Steel considers customers, employees and vendors to be stakeholders in the company, and builds relationships among all of these to allow for wide-ranging business success. Customer Value Teams and Customer Partnering Programs are designed to help customers reach their goals, building up the businesses of customers as surely as Tuscaloosa Steel builds its own successful future.

Tuscaloosa Steel began operations in November, 1984, built at the location of an old industrial site on the banks of the Black Warrior River. Since the mill opened, more than four million tons of steel have been produced at Tuscaloosa Steel. The original capacity of the mill was 250,000 tons annually. In only its second year of operation, Tuscaloosa Steel produced about 480,000 tons of steel and has stayed at about that level throughout much of the company's existence. An expansion creating melt facilities at the mill may mean an increase in capacity of up to one million tons annually.

A world-class competitor, Tuscaloosa Steel exports a percentage of its output, although the majority of the mill's production is sold to the domestic market. Real competitive advantages can be found in the company's capabilities for producing coil and strip mill plates, carbon and stainless steel products, which feature heavy gauges, wide widths, close tolerances and unique chemistries. The customer is left with a product that offers a combination of quality, customer service and price, which translates into an unbeatable value for steel users.

Secondary coil storage facility adjacent to plate cut to length facility and newly erected environmentally controlled indoor plate storage building.

Value, worker productivity and pride and quality company performance are the pillars that undergird the success of Tuscaloosa Steel. Yet these abstract concepts and perceptions have real-world applications in the day-to-day operations of the company.

Tuscaloosa Steel operates on a Package Mill concept that employs a highly motivated work force, quality control processes and low-cost technology to bring world-class, flat-rolled steel—coils and plate cut from coils—to market.

The whole operation begins with the unloading of continuously cast steel slabs secured with long-term commitments from suppliers. The slabs are reheated in the walking beam furnace and trimmed to a customer-specified width in the vertical edging stand. A high-pressure water descale system leaves slabs scale-free, top and bottom. In the plant's unique Four High Reversing Hot Steckel Mill, the slabs, either carbon grades or stainless steel, are converted into coils in a highly automated and efficient manner. The reversing mill features two coiling furnaces and two distinct operational modes, roughing and

finishing, for the greatest possible efficiency. The computerized control of temperature and dimensions—and workers who really care that things are done right—yields the best possible products.

And, in the end, that's what Tuscaloosa Steel is all about: a quality product, created by cost-efficient technology and the best work force in the steel business. ❖

JVC America, Inc.

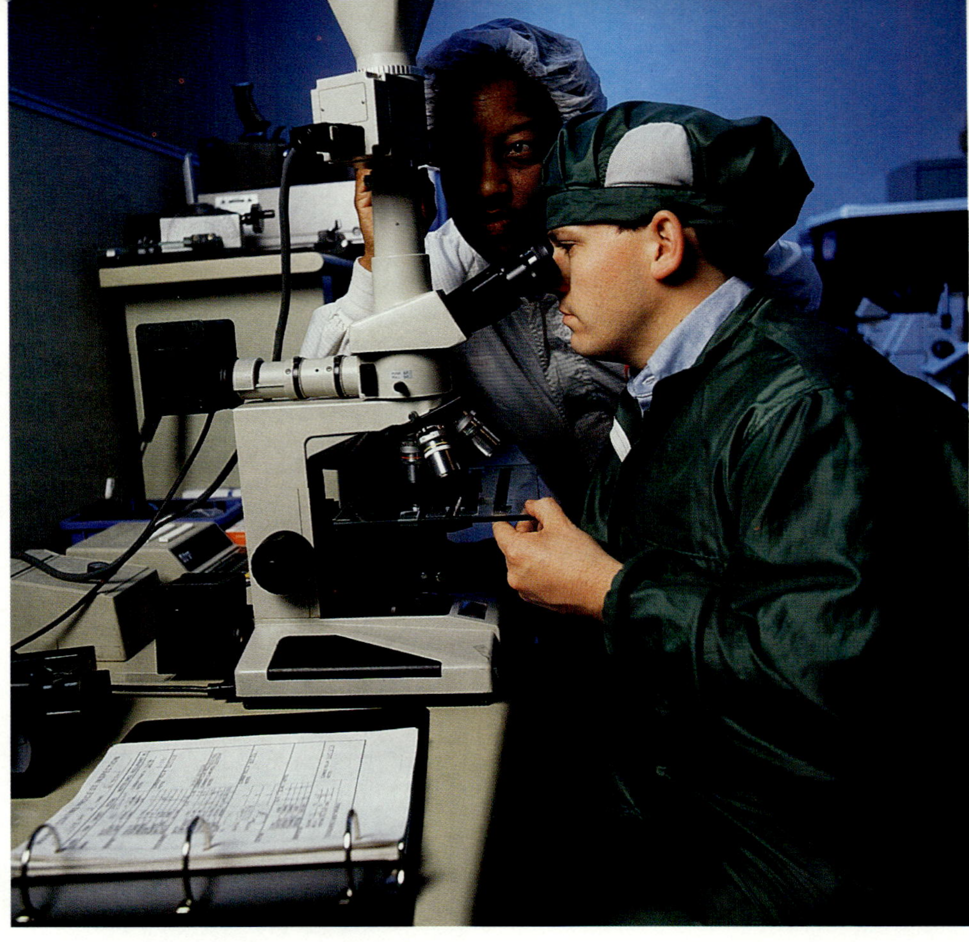

JVC America, Inc., headquartered in Tuscaloosa, manufactures electronic software for the information and entertainment industries worldwide. Established in Tuscaloosa in January 1986, the company operates two manufacturing divisions, JVC Magnetics America Co. and JVC Disc America Co., which began production in Fall 1986 and Spring 1987 respectively.

JVC Magnetics makes VHS videotape, and videocassettes for both consumer and tape duplicator markets. The division produces more than 30 million videocassettes per year for domestic and foreign markets.

JVC Disc produces more than 50 million compact discs a year for entertainment and information publishers who market music, games, and interactive and multimedia CDs. Its product line includes CD Audio, CD Graphics, the emerging CD Movie, and the popular CD ROM.

Six hundred highly-skilled and efficient employees produce and ship high quality media products in a clean and highly technical environment. Clean-room manufacturing environments, proprietary manufacturing processes, and an aggressive quality program are integral to the manufacture of JVC's Tuscaloosa-made products.

JVC houses its advanced manufacturing technology in two facilities—totalling 364,000 square feet—on a 100-acre site in

The technical and cultural resources available at The University of Alabama have made Tuscaloosa an ideal position from which to compete in global markets.

Tuscaloosa's Interstate Industrial Park. The attractive manufacturing campus fronts on JVC Road and Interstate 20/59. The company's Tuscaloosa location is central to the majority of its domestic markets, with convenient access to transportation services for

JVC America's Tuscaloosa location is central to the majority of its domestic markets.

domestic and international customers.

In addition to enhancing Tuscaloosa's reputation as a technology center, JVC has contributed to the community's increasing international presence. With a customer-base spanning 45 countries worldwide, JVC has helped Tuscaloosa develop the infrastructure and services necessary to conduct business on a global scale. Conversely, the ability of local banking, insurance, finance, and transportation services to adapt to the demands of international business has been a key factor in the growth and success of JVC America, Inc.

Those services, along with the technical and cultural resources available at The University of Alabama, have made Tuscaloosa an ideal position from which to compete in global markets geared toward rapidly developing technology.

The Alabama company's corporate parent, Victor Company of Japan, Ltd., was itself born in 1927 as the Asian subsidiary of the U.S. firm, the Victor Talking Machine Co. Alabama's JVC America, Inc., is a significant part of JVC's global strategy—it is the company's only manufacturer of videotape and compact discs outside Japan.

JVC America's customers are the makers of software—various companies that create and market computer programs, popular music, Hollywood movies, computer animation, or reference materials of every description. In the world of information storage and technology, products used in communications, entertainment, and archival fall mainly into two categories: hardware and software. JVC's role lies in manufacturing software media, the materials on or in which the information resides. Examples are the compact disc that contains the music of Mozart, a multimedia encyclopedia or courthouse records, or the tape that carries the latest from Hollywood or cherished family memories.

Media consumers know that demand for both the CD format and magnetic tape products will continue to increase as science finds new ways to compress data into smaller bits. And as data compression technology advances, JVC's two Tuscaloosa operating divisions anticipate constant demand for new and innovative products—along with the new manufacturing technologies to produce them.

Its talented workforce is committed to meeting each new future challenge.

And in the meantime, JVC America, Inc. is making the products of tomorrow in today's Tuscaloosa. ❖

(top) JVC produces and ships high quality media products in a clean and highly technical environment.

(bottom) Alabama's JVC America, Inc. is JVC's only manufacturer of videotape and compact discs outside Japan.

The Uniroyal Goodrich Tire Company

The Tuscaloosa plant of The Uniroyal Goodrich Tire Company is the largest industrial enterprise in the Tuscaloosa area, and one of 14 tire plants operated in North America by Michelin.

The Tuscaloosa plant manufactures radial passenger and light truck tires in a full range of sizes for the original equipment and replacement markets. The products are manufactured under the BFGoodrich brand as well as Uniroyal and private and associate brands. The plant produces high-performance tires in the H, V, and Z speed capabilities—including the Comp T/A, a premium tire for high-performance vehicles both on and off the road.

Products from the Uniroyal Goodrich plant are shipped to both domestic and foreign markets. Sister plants to the Tuscaloosa facility are located in Fort Wayne, Indiana; Ardmore, Oklahoma; Opelika, Alabama; and Kitchener, Ontario. They all operate as part of Michelin North America's Small Tires business unit.

The Uniroyal Goodrich facility in Tuscaloosa is one of the largest tire plants in the United States. More than 1.5 million square feet of factory space is available in the plant. More than 35 acres are under roof at the plant site, which is located on a 212-acre tract of land on the outskirts of Tuscaloosa.

With approximately 2,000 employees, the plant boasts a payroll economic impact in excess of $100 million. The tire plant operates 24 hours a day, 7 days a week. Twenty-one shifts of workers each week come through the plant gates as part of the world-class manufacturing team that produces high-quality tires for American and selected foreign markets.

The huge manufacturing plant is a very impressive sight. From some perspectives, the building stretches seemingly as far as the eye can see. But size is not the only thing that makes this particular manufacturing facility something special. The men and women who work here are absolutely committed to quality—ensuring that the products they manufacture are the very best they can be.

Raw materials utilized by the plant include such items as polyester and nylon cord fabrics, natural rubber, synthetic rubber, steel bead wire, carbon black, sulphur, and other chemicals and pigments. Yet the most important ingredient that goes into their products is the quality consciousness and dedication of the company's well-trained work force.

The Tuscaloosa plant is the only Uniroyal Goodrich manufacturing facility built with bomb-proof walls. That bit of trivia is important in terms of the fascinating history of the plant. Construction on the plant was begun in the waning years of the Second World War. The U.S. government started the plant in order to manufacture tires for military vehicles.

In 1945, when construction on the plant was 65 percent complete, mobilization and industrialization for the war effort began to slacken. B.F. Goodrich purchased the facility from the federal government and completed the unfinished plant in 1946. The first tire came off the assembly line on October 23, 1946.

The plant was originally designed to employ only about 500 people. In the years since its original construction, more than a million square feet of factory space has been added to the facility. The rate of modernization has kept pace with the physical expansion of the facility, so that today the plant is a shining example of the latest in a modern tire manufacturing environment.

In its storied history, the plant has participated in a number of important manufacturing milestones. In 1954, B.F. Goodrich invented the tubeless tire; the tires were first manufactured in Tuscaloosa. In 1965, B.F. Goodrich was the first U.S. company to

| The Tuscaloosa plant.

Employees stroll down "TA Boulevard" in the Tuscaloosa plant.

produce radial ply tires, and they, too, first rolled off the assembly line at the Tuscaloosa plant.

The BFGoodrich Company operated the Tuscaloosa plant from 1946 to 1986. In 1986, BFGoodrich and Uniroyal Inc. merged their respective tire operations to form The Uniroyal Goodrich Tire Company. In 1990, Uniroyal Goodrich was purchased by Michelin. Today, it operates as a part of the parent company's domestic subsidiary, Michelin North America.

Because of its varied and important business history, the Tuscaloosa facility of The Uniroyal Goodrich Tire Company is clearly one of the most interesting success stories among area businesses.

Certainly, the plant's size, economic impact, and status rank it in the top echelon of Tuscaloosa business enterprises.

As the largest industrial operation in the Tuscaloosa area, the plant enjoys a prominent position in the business community. But the company also plays a major role in the community at large. For example, it is the largest annual contributor to the area's United Way effort.

Personnel at the Tuscaloosa plant are active participants in many civic organizations and community initiatives. Improving educational standards in the Tuscaloosa area is a top priority. The plant was one of the four original partners in the local Adopt-A-School program.

From manufacturing tires that meet the world's highest standards to staying active and involved in a community it has called home since 1946, Uniroyal Goodrich's Tuscaloosa facility is a plant that cares about quality. ❖

Gulf States Paper Corporation

From a small family enterprise that had its first great success a century ago making a single, ingeniously simple product, Gulf States Paper Corporation has grown into one of the nation's largest privately-held forest-products companies, producing packaging, paperboard, and a host of other forest-related products and services.

The integrated forest products company has operations in seven states and customers all over the globe. But back in 1884, the company that would become Gulf States operated only a small mill in Marseilles, Illinois; powered by a water wheel, the facility made wrapping paper from wheat straw.

After a few years of operating small mills, the young company's real growth began—appropriately enough—with the opening of a paper sack. Company founder Herbert E.

Westervelt invented the E-Z Opener paper bag machine, patenting the product that opened at the flick of a wrist and became an American standard. All those years ago that invention pointed the way to a business premise that guides the company to this day: design products that make the lives and businesses of customers easier and more efficient.

Herbert Westervelt also invented something else in those early days. He came up with a motto "Quality Counts" that the company and its chairman, Westervelt's grandson, Jack Warner, still live by.

In 1929, Gulf States' operations were consolidated in Tuscaloosa, introducing the modern paper industry to Alabama. Today, the corporation's Tuscaloosa headquarters is a showcase that has charmed visitors from all 50 states and scores of foreign countries. The modern buildings are efficiently and beautifully designed and evoke the glories of Oriental architecture; a lush and inviting Japanese garden offers peace and solitude right in the heart of the bustling business complex. The headquarters of Gulf States house the Warner Collection, one of the finest and most extensive collections of American art to be found anywhere. More than 150 works of art in the collection—along with artifacts and sculpture from many ages and

Gulf State foresters begin with improved seedlings from the company's own nursery, plant them on specially prepared sites and follow their progress through the years until harvest.

cultures—are displayed throughout the headquarters buildings, turning great art into a part of everyday life for employees, customers, and visitors.

Gulf States employs about 1,200 people in Alabama and another 900 or so at plants and offices in other states. The company also has sales offices in major metropolitan areas. Gulf States is an ardent supporter of projects that improve the quality of life in the communities where the company has a presence.

Four operating divisions—Natural Resources, Wood Products, Pulp & Paperboard, and Paperboard Converting—make up the fully integrated Gulf States Paper Corporation. The company is the ninth largest U.S. producer of SBS paperboard and holds fifth place in U.S. market share in the SBS folding carton category.

Timber and land resource management professionals are the stewards of Gulf States' sizable land holdings (400,000 acres of Alabama woodlands) that provide the raw materials for the company's products. The goal is to produce high-quality trees that grow quickly to usable size, and then scientifically replant to ensure the future viability of the land and the timber.

A large part of Gulf States' program of land management is tied into environmental concerns. The company maintains close ties to the scientific and regulatory communities to make certain that policies and procedures

Gulf States Paper Corporation's national headquarters in Tuscaloosa was built with an Oriental design and is one of the showplaces of Alabama, housing the company's corporate art collection.

Gulf States' Moldwood Products Company in York, Alabama, uses a unique process of blending wood shavings with resins and glue additives to form core plugs for rolls of products such as paper, aluminum, film, and textiles.

on company lands and at facilities are followed with the utmost respect for high-quality environmental standards.

As a fully integrated company, the products of the various divisions of Gulf States might be sold on the open market or dedicated to supply another aspect of the company's total operations. For example, the Wood Products Division utilizes some of the timber Gulf States harvests for the green and finished lumber mills it operates.

Log Industries, a Gulf States company located near Tuscaloosa, converts trees to lumber destined to be further processed. It also prepares the straightest and tallest trees to be used as utility poles. Gulf States' Loper Lumber Company is a finishing mill that manufactures specialty lumber products for various markets. Moldwood Products Company, a Gulf States facility in York, Alabama, manufactures molded wood products from wood shavings, resins, and glue additives. The products—such as core plugs for rolls of paper or textiles and more esoteric

component parts that solve specific design problems for manufacturers of everything from furniture to speaker baffles—are strong competitors against parts made from particle board or plywood. Molded wood products are very convenient and versatile.

The Pulp and Paperboard Division at Gulf States manufactures bleached pulp and solid bleached sulphate paperboard at its Demopolis, Alabama, facility. About one-half of the mill's high-quality, bright, and durable paperboard is used in other Gulf States facilities to make packaging for food and consumer goods. The remaining paperboard and excess market-pulp is sold on the open market.

With plants in five states—Alabama, Kentucky, North Carolina, Missouri, and Texas—the Paperboard Converting Division manufactures consumer packaging in a dizzying array of styles, sizes, and categories, but with an overriding concern for quality and customer service. The product mix offers a preponderance of food packaging in such categories as frozen food, bakery, dry goods, and fast food, though packaging for health care products also figures prominently into the mix.

The company is always searching for new opportunities, devising new packaging to meet both the needs of consumers and environmental concerns. An example: Ovenable packaging that allows consumers to cook and eat in the box. The packaging adds greatly to consumer convenience while reducing solid waste.

In addition to the major business areas of Gulf States Paper Corporation, the company is involved in timber management services; minerals and mining operations; and land

development. NorthRiver, a country club and residential development of Gulf States in Tuscaloosa, is the area's premier address for gracious, elegant living.

All of the major divisions and facilities of the company are dedicated to highly ethical salesmanship, quality, and superior customer and technical service. Superior safety standards are emphasized in all manufacturing environments in the company, along with total quality management and adherence to ISO-9000—an international standard for business process quality.

As an international corporation, Gulf States is committed to competing in the global marketplace by understanding customer needs, delivering top-quality products to meet those needs, and holding a strong position in product design, technology, quality/service, and professionalism.

Over more than a century of operation, Gulf States Paper Corporation has earned its reputation as an exemplary company with which to do business. ❖

Gulf States' innovative new line of ovenable frozen-food packaging provides consumer convenience, cost savings and reduces packaging waste.

Welborn Transport

The City of Champions has produced yet another star—this time in the trucking industry. Tuscaloosa is the proud home of Welborn Transport, a motor freight carrier whose reputation for reliability, efficiency, and safety have proven it to be a contender among other southeastern freight haulers.

Already the major truck line in Tuscaloosa County, the company serves its many customers with a fleet of flat-bed trailers and dry freight containers. Most of the operation is dedicated to flat-bed hauling; transporting such materials as steel, pipe, lumber, and roofing products. But it has recently developed a van division; a move that will allow the company to further meet the needs of its growing customer base.

The strength of Welborn Transport lies in the vision of its founders, Miller Welborn and Steven Rumsey. After attending the University of Alabama, both sought to make their mark in Tuscaloosa. "We were both born and raised here," says Rumsey, "so it's only natural that we would start our own families here." Welborn went on to run a local trucking firm, while Rumsey started a waste collection company that has also grown into a successful business. Although they pursued separate interests, their college-born friendship remained, and in time, they recognized a similar vision: a quality trucking company that could provide reliable freight service to the many manufacturers in the Tuscaloosa area.

In the years following, the friends became business partners, buying tractor trailers and leasing them to the company managed by Welborn. Then, In October, 1989, they put their dreams to the test and opened the doors to Welborn Transport.

The company has seen remarkable growth since its beginning. Starting with about 40 trucks, Welborn Transport initially served the local roofing plants, moving their products to points in the southeast. Today, more than four years later, the company operates a fleet of over 200 trucks, transporting freight to cities and towns from the Great Plains to the Atlantic seaboard.

So what's the secret behind their incredible

Welborn Transport services its customers with a fleet of over 200 trucks. Photo by Barry Fikes.

success? Welborn explains, "We're committed to on-time delivery. And we accomplish that by working as a team. Whether you're a driver, dispatcher, or work in safety or maintenance, each person plays a part in moving the freight from point A to B."

"It's the family atmosphere that makes it all work," Rumsey adds. "The company is family owned and operated, everyone's on a first name basis, and if anyone needs to talk to Miller or me, all they have to do is pick up the phone."

Getting the freight to its destination however, is only half the job. Having freight to move is a key ingredient to success in this industry. "It's just as important to get a load coming back into the state as it is to get a load going out," says Welborn. To meet the needs of their inbound customers, Welborn Transport has agents in Atlanta, Tampa, Knoxville, Houston, and New Orleans, with additional offices to be opened soon in the Carolinas. "These offices communicate daily with our home office in Tuscaloosa, as well as our other Alabama offices in Birmingham, Mobile, and Muscle Shoals, to provide our customers the dependable service they expect."

Reliable freight service. That was the goal four years ago, and it's the same goal today. When you consider what they're working with: professional drivers, late-model equipment, complete shop facilities to handle everything from regular maintenance to engine overhauls, an exemplary safety record, and a sales staff that is second to none, you'll see why their motto is right on target— "WELBORN TRANSPORT: dependable." ❖

Miller Welborn, Chairman; Steven Rumsey, President of Tuscaloosa based Welborn Transportation. Photo by Barry Fikes.

TWR, Inc.

TWR, Inc., the only locally owned and operated waste removal company, provides waste containment, collection and disposal services to Tuscaloosa County businesses, multifamily residential facilities, industrial plants, and construction sites. The Company, founded in 1987 by Steven Rumsey, operates on the business philosophy that customer service and satisfaction must remain its foremost objective. TWR operates 365 days a year, utilizing a radio dispatched system, and makes every effort to service the waste collection needs of its customers by scheduling pick-ups at low activity times of the day. Thus, the waste collection and disposal needs of its customers are met in an efficient and environmentally sound manner—again, reflecting the

Company's goal in achieving customer satisfaction.

At its inception, TWR, Inc. owned one truck, employed one driver, and offered 50 dumpsters. At that time, Rumsey served as its sole management employee while completing his undergraduate degree at the University of Alabama. Today, after five years, this young Company operates eight trucks, employs approximately 20 employees, and services hundreds of waste containers in place at customers' facilities, including residential and commercial construction sites. Mr. Jeb Green presently serves in the capacity of Vice President and General Manager for TWR.

TWR is unique in Tuscaloosa County in that it is the only locally owned and operated waste removal company. The company's owners and managers live and work in this community, thereby taking a personal, and business interest in the Company's customers, productivity, and employees. Other owners of TWR include Jackie Cummings, Charlie O. Sealy, and Miller Welborn.

In today's environmentally conscious climate, waste containment, collection, and disposal services have become an increasingly important component of the day-to-day management of a business. TWR, Inc. provides businesses with the opportunity to meet such needs in a prompt, efficient, and cost effective manner, while dealing with a locally owned and operated company. ❖

Providing waste systems to meet all needs, a TWR employee services a large container filled with construction debris.

TWR, Inc. services a large leak proof garbage compactor at area Inn and conference center.

Hunt Refining Company

Dedicated to supplying high-quality petroleum products, Hunt Refining Company has built its stellar reputation as a petroleum refiner by remaining totally committed to supplying and servicing its markets, while striving to always be a good employer and a well-respected member of the business community in the Tuscaloosa area.

From office, pipeline, and refining facilities in Tuscaloosa, Hunt Refining Company produces and markets high-quality petroleum products in five southeastern states and New Jersey.

Hunt is one of Alabama's largest suppliers of diesel fuel, the largest seller of paving asphalt, and is estimated to be the leader in asphalt sales to roofing companies in the southeast.

Hunt Refining also sells high-quality unleaded gasoline in three separate grades to private brand retailers, as well as through

Hunt markets high quality gasoline through its Parade retail outlets in Alabama and Mississippi.

PARADE branded convenience store and gas station outlets in approximately 75 locations in Alabama and Mississippi. In addition, the company also markets jet fuel for use in U.S. military aircraft, and petroleum coke which is used for fuel.

In the New Jersey market, Hunt has a significant presence in the home heating oil and diesel supply business. The heating oil and diesel fuel are shipped to New Jersey via the Colonial Pipeline, which runs from Houston to the East Coast, supplying petroleum products to major population centers.

All of Hunt Refining's finished petroleum products are shipped locally in truck-load quantities, in barges, railcars, or through interstate pipelines. The capacity at the Hunt refinery in Tuscaloosa is approximately 40,000 barrels a day or about 1,680,000 gallons each day and operates 24 hours, 365 days per year.

Aside from its major, 240-acre supply facility in Tuscaloosa, Hunt Refining services bulk terminal outlets in Mobile and Decatur, Alabama; and Newark and Carteret in New Jersey. Hunt employs about 250 people.

The crude oil and raw materials refined at Hunt facilities originate from both domestic and foreign sources. Crude oil from Mexico, Venezuela, and the Mideast and, domestically, from south Alabama and Mississippi, flows into the Tuscaloosa refinery via pipeline, barge, or truck.

A wholly owned subsidiary of Hunt Capital Corporation, Hunt Refining Company was founded in 1946 by the legendary businessman and oil millionaire H. L. Hunt, Jr. Hunt left his Illinois home at the age of 15 to wander the country, taking odd jobs. By age 22, he owned an Arkansas cotton farm near

Hunt Refining can process 40,000 barrels of oil a day at its facility in Tuscaloosa.

the Mississippi River. Through land speculation and wildcat oil exploration, he built a fortune in the ensuing decades.

In 1944, Hunt discovered oil in Choctaw County, Alabama, in what became known as the Gilbertown Field, the first commercial oil production development in the state. Hunt's crude oil find in Alabama could most effectively be utilized and marketed as asphalt, and so the decision was made in 1946 to build a refining facility in Tuscaloosa to produce asphalt. Initial production at the refinery was 3,500 barrels per day.

Through the years, numerous improvements have been made to Hunt Refining facilities including a $65 million Coker complex investment in 1981 that expanded production to its current level and improved product quality, and a $5 million pipeline constructed in 1984 to connect with the Houston to New York Colonial Pipeline. More recently, in 1993, a $25 million diesel desulfurization unit was brought on line and a $2 million Research and Quality Assurance Laboratory was constructed.

All of the expansions and product improvements at Hunt Refining are made with one overriding thought in mind: to enhance the company's status as a major regional supplier of energy. ❖

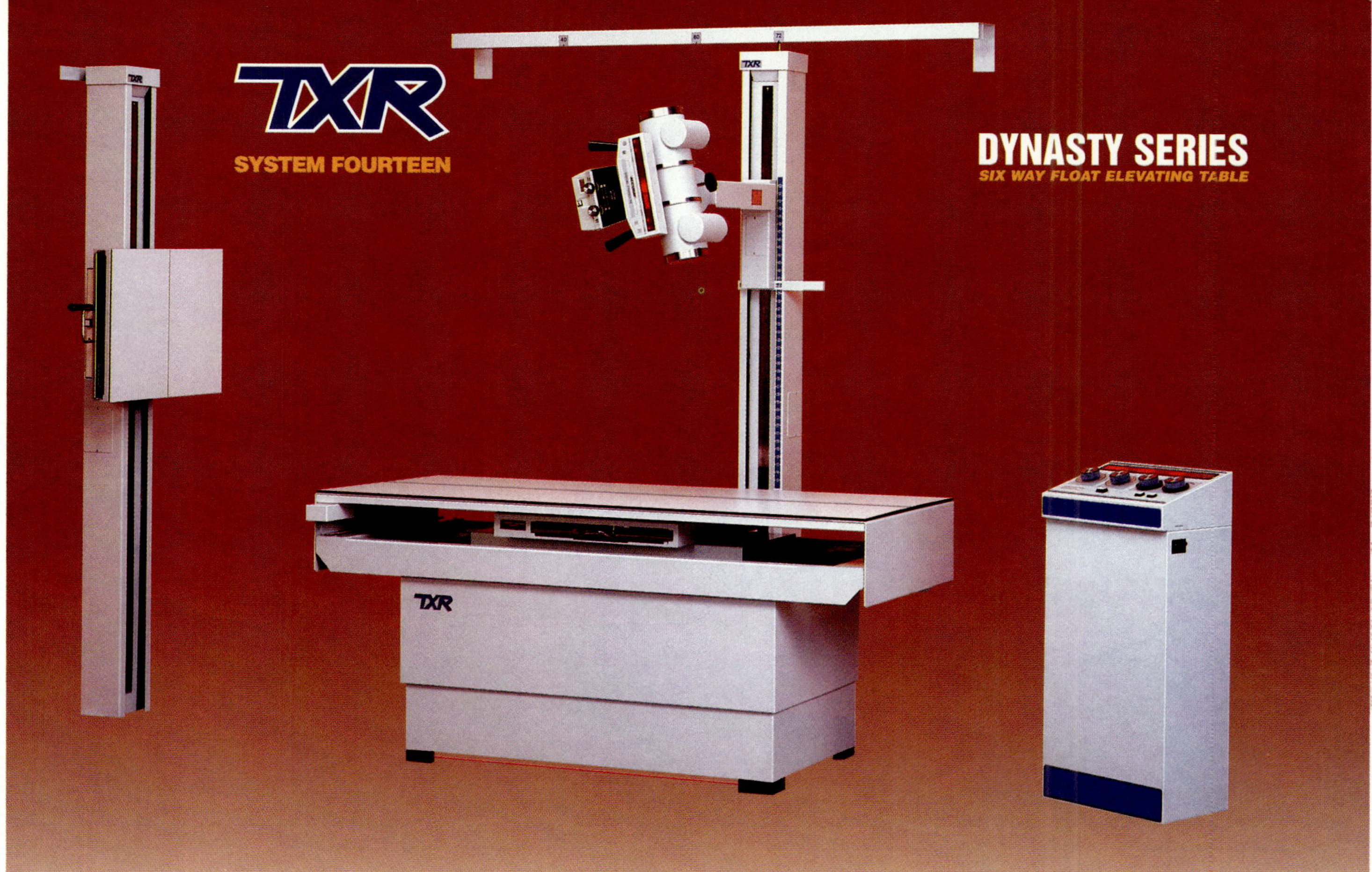

Tingle X-Ray Products, Inc.

One of the only independently owned x-ray equipment manufacturers in the United States, Tingle X-Ray Products, Inc. has built a worldwide reputation for design and product excellence.

Headquartered in Vance in Tuscaloosa County, Tingle X-Ray or TXR is a world-class company that competes head to head with foreign and domestic medical equipment makers. Using some of the finest sub-contractor parts producers in the United States, enables it to produce top quality x-ray equipment and systems. Though small, when compared to some, TXR is an industry trendsetter in terms of innovation, engineering, and product design.

Founded more than 15 years ago by Jerry Tingle, the company has evolved from manufacturing three basic x-ray devices—Tube Stand, Bucky Stands and X-ray Tables—to designing, manufacturing, and assembling complete digital x-ray systems.

All TXR products are designed to be easy to install, use, and maintain. That's good for the customers of TXR, who enjoy a partnership with the company that extends far beyond the initial sale and installation. The warranties offered by TXR—including 100 percent quality assurance and ETL product safety testing compliance—are the best in the business, and the service given to customers is second to none. Consistent performance and product safety are ensured by our "Total Quality System" approach and is the foundation of every TXR product. The key to TXR's success is its long term commitment to its customers' needs.

TXR designs 18 core systems of x-ray equipment that can be customized to fit the diagnostic needs of a wide variety of health care professionals. From basic devices to orthopedic x-ray systems, the company has sold its products throughout the world: the United States, Canada, Mexico, Central America, and the Middle East. The easy-to-use and impeccably designed systems improve the productivity of TXR's customers and sharpen their competitive edge.

Research and development are the keys to the future growth of the company and its place in an ever-expanding world of medical diagnostic equipment. For example, specialists at the company are working on the development of a modulated, high frequency x-ray generator that will require only a small amount of floor space yet deliver more power for diagnostic purposes. On some of its research and development projects, TXR works in concert with the Industrial Engineering Design Clinics at the University of Alabama.

The future for TXR will bring still more product innovations, equipment that will offer greater cost efficiency in the field, and high-speed data transmission for expert medical diagnosis. At Tingle X-ray Products, Inc., exemplary customer service, innovation, and setting trends for the rest of the industry to follow is an everyday part of the business. ❖

Jerry Tingle, President of Tingle X-Ray Products, Inc.

Tuscaloosa Vending Company

In 1951, Dr. Joe Phifer, a practicing veterinarian, initiated a small business venture by placing two coin operated coffee brewers in the local B.F. Goodrich tire plant. Rudimentary by today's standards, the machines operated mechanically, using instant coffee blended with cream or sugar to taste and served in a paper cup.

Today, forty-three years later, Tuscaloosa Vending markets an extensive variety of full-line vending products at Goodrich. Using state-of-the-art equipment while providing personal and prompt service, Tuscaloosa Vending has grown from two machines serving a single plant, to over sixteen hundred machines serving customers in hundreds of manufacturing, institutional, and service-type businesses—large and small—throughout the community.

Tuscaloosa Vending believes the key to vending success begins with close customer contact. Attentively serving customer needs and making certain individual product requests are met, merchandise is fresh, and machines are well maintained, all form the foundation of Tuscaloosa Vending's service philosophy. The use of high quality, name-brand products, the company's devotion to service, and the attitude displayed toward customers have all facilitated the continued growth of Tuscaloosa Vending.

Dr. Phifer continued to practice veterinary medicine for eighteen years after founding Tuscaloosa Vending, running the business as a one-man operation before adding his first employees in 1960. Today, the company employs a second generation of the Phifer family, along with some 65 other people in three service divisions: 1) vending and foods, the backbone of the business, 2) institutional and office coffee and tea, and 3) coin-operated amusements.

Tuscaloosa Vending's customers are all located within West Central Alabama and are serviced by regularly scheduled route drivers. The company warehouses products, stocks and maintains the machines, and collects all monies. Tuscaloosa Vending provides all equipment free of charge and customers are either paid a commission for locating machines on their property, or receive savings in the form of lower prices.

One of the major advances in the vending industry has been the ever-increasing variety

Tuscaloosa Vending has grown from two machines to over sixteen hundred machines throughout the community.

Tuscaloosa Vending's customers are all located within West Central Alabama and serviced by regularly scheduled route drivers.

of products available. Today, Tuscaloosa Vending's machines offer everything from low-fat snacks and fresh pastry to sandwiches, soft drinks, sports beverages, milk, and fresh-ground, gourmet coffee and cappuccino. Consumer demands for variety, health, and convenience dictate the ever-changing vending market.

Since personal service means customer satisfaction, Tuscaloosa Vending strives to ensure customers remain satisfied and that their individual needs are continually met. For example, as an independent marketer of all major label soft drinks, a drink machine can be customized to carry any combination of brands with the mix determined by the customers and not the guidelines of the soft drink bottlers.

Tuscaloosa Vending also operates their own commissary where sandwiches, salads and buttermilk biscuits are made fresh every day. All transportation vehicles and food service facilities meet the highest standards of the Health Department. Answering services for emergency maintenance or other calls are maintained 24 hours per day, 7 days per week while the company has a complete machine repair and restoration shop with a full technical staff. It is company policy to respond to all out-of-order calls in minimum time.

Tuscaloosa Vending has kept pace with technical advances in the ever changing vending market through active participation in the programs of the National Automatic Merchandising Association. Company personnel have also served on the Board of Directors and as past President of the Alabama Vending Association. Through the years the Phifers' family business has grown and developed while earning a reputation as an excellent home-grown, community-minded, and service-oriented business. ❖

Mercedes-Benz

As part of its globalization strategy, Mercedes-Benz AG chose Tuscaloosa County as the home of the German automaker's first U.S. passenger vehicle production facility, a $300 million plant near Vance, Alabama.

Mercedes-Benz Project, Inc., an independent subsidiary company formed in 1993, is headquartered in Tuscaloosa and responsible for the design, development, manufacturing, and worldwide marketing of Mercedes' new four-wheel drive, all activity vehicle.

The first vehicles roll off the production line in 1997, and will be produced at a rate of about 65,000 vehicles a year. Half of that volume will be sold in the United States, with the other half exported throughout the world. The plant will provide approximately 1,500 highly trained jobs. Thousands more will be employed at the auto industry suppliers and related businesses that locate in the Tuscaloosa/Birmingham region to meet the Just-In-Time delivery needs and sophisticated service requirements of a modern assembly plant.

The decision by Mercedes-Benz to build a passenger vehicle manufacturing facility in the United States was a strategic, market-driven one, based on a number of important business factors: A plant in this country puts Mercedes in the largest customer base for four-wheel drive passenger vehicles in the world. Because of the strong U.S. automotive supplier network, Mercedes knew it could build the highest quality product in the United States at a competitive cost. A U.S. facility also helps the company to avoid debilitating currency fluctuations.

The search for a site for the Mercedes plant began in April, 1993, and lasted six months. From an initial list of 150 sites and existing

The first vehicles will roll off the production line in January 1997.

facilities, the field was narrowed to six sites, then pared again to just three sites—in Alabama, South Carolina, and North Carolina. The main search criteria was the availability of a quality work force, a strong business climate, good transportation infrastructure, easy proximity to a supplier network, and a strong university presence.

In the end, Tuscaloosa County was chosen because it represented the best combination of criteria Mercedes was seeking, because of the strong commitment by the state and local communities, and because of the partnership that was forged between Mercedes and those in Alabama.

The location of a Mercedes auto plant in the United States is a giant step towards realization of a company goal to become fully immersed in the global economy. Mercedes parent company, Daimler-Benz AG, was listed in 1993 on the New York Stock Exchange as part of this same strategy. Daimler-Benz AG is the largest industrial group in Europe.

The newest member of the Daimler-Benz family in North America is Mercedes-Benz Project, Inc. in Tuscaloosa County. The vehicle manufacturing company will contain assembly, body and paint facilities, a training

Mercedes-Benz AG chose Tuscaloosa County as the home of the German automaker's first U.S. passenger vehicle manufacturing facility.

center, and a customer center. Plant and support facilities encompass 1 million square feet on a 966-acre Tuscaloosa County site near Vance, about 20 miles east of Tuscaloosa along Interstate 20/59.

There the company plans to set a world-class example in the quality of the vehicle produced, in its role as a good corporate citizen, with minority involvement, and in work force training programs that will have a positive impact on the whole region.

In conjunction with the state of Alabama and area colleges, Mercedes is developing training programs that will create for all area employers a top-caliber labor force with skills that will enhance the economy and business prospects of the entire region.

With skillful teamwork, enterprise, and entrepreneurship, Mercedes-Benz will combine the latest in automation with old-fashioned craftsmanship to create a world-class product—made by Mercedes and the hands of Alabamians—for the global marketplace. ❖

Chapter

13

Business & Finance

Southland National Insurance Corporation

"Service Southland Style" equals satisfaction for the customers of Southland National Insurance Corporation, a life insurance company that relies on a flair for personal service and niche marketing to compete effectively in a tough industry. The slogan is not only a reflection of the strong regional roots of the company and its gracious Southern heritage, it's a concise description of the personal touch Southland brings to the life insurance business.

Southland National Insurance Corporation operates as a general agency insurance business utilizing a network of independent agents in the company's marketing region. Licensed in six southeastern states—Alabama, Mississippi, Tennessee, Louisiana, Georgia, and Florida—Southland is a public company traded on the Over-the-Counter market. A widely held issue, no individual owns more than 5 percent of Southland's stock.

The insurance industry is complex and on the national and international level dominated by corporate behemoths. For a relatively small company like Southland National, the key to success is the all-important niche and the way in which a well-managed company locates and fills those niches. For Southland, effective niche marketing and high-quality customer service are the keys to success.

Southland does offer traditional life insurance products such as universal life, but in recent years has not been active in the term insurance market or in annuities. It has never been involved in the property or casualty insurance markets. But the company has found great success in the specialized niches of the pre-need and senior insurance markets.

Licensed in six southeastern states, Southland National Insurance Corporation utilizes a network of independent agents in the company's marketing region. Photo by Barry Fikes.

The pre-need market is served by an insurance product that funds pre-arranged funerals for funeral home customers. Instead of being placed in a trust by the funeral home, individuals can purchase a Southland policy, which is used as a funding instrument for the pre-arranged funeral. Funeral home owners and employees act as agents in selling these Southland policies, one of the few that offers a guaranteed rate of growth on the face amount of the policy.

Another insurance business niche filled by Southland is the senior market, typically defined as people 50 years old or older. Southland has developed and markets a supplemental policy that carries a relatively small face amount of generally between $3,000 and $5,000. This type of policy has proven to be very attractive and useful to individuals in late middle age and in their Golden Years.

Southland has also worked to develop a relatively new insurance product that has been on the drawing board and looks like a winner. Called the Increasing Benefit Term Policy, this innovative product is funded by the typical fixed premium of a term insurance policy. The unique advantage this product holds for policyholders is a death benefit which doubles every 10 years.

In addition to these niche products, Southland operates a wholly owned subsidiary founded in 1983, the Southern Insurance Management Association, frequently known by its acronym, SIMA. The subsidiary is a third-party administrator for the health plans of self-insured companies. As a third-party administrator for self-insured companies, SIMA completes all the clerical and administrative duties associated with managing a company health plan, including the paying of claims.

While Southland restricts itself to a six-state southeastern region in marketing its insurance policies, SIMA is able to solicit business from companies in nearly all 50 states.

The key to success in all of these different avenues of business is service with an emphasis on a personal and speedy response. The phones at Southland are answered by real people, not faceless voice mail. And statistics show that the response time at Southland in addressing customer claims and needs is quicker than average for the American insurance industry.

The folks at Southland are convinced that for a small company to win an advantage in the marketplace, the principle of quality customer service must be observed. That's why the company specializes in fast, personal service, taking a one-on-one approach with customers. Southland always tells customers that they are as close as the telephone.

Southland National Insurance is headquartered in Tuscaloosa. All clerical, customer service, claims, underwriting, accounting, marketing, and management functions are conducted from the home office. Two field marketing consultants work in the six-state region, recruiting, training, and servicing the approximately 300 independent agents that sell Southland products.

Southland National Insurance is something of a commercial landmark in downtown Tuscaloosa, and its principals and employees are active and progressive proponents of growth and improvement for the Tuscaloosa area. William H. Lanford, the president and CEO of Southland, has been very involved over the years in the business and community life of Tuscaloosa. On a national level, Mr. Lanford has served as president of the University of Alabama National Alumni Association. He served as the president pro-term of the Tuscaloosa City Council from 1985 through 1993, vice chairman of the West Alabama Planning and Development Council, and is a past vice president of the Tuscaloosa Chamber of Commerce and a past member and chairman of the Tuscaloosa City Board of Education. He has held local leadership positions with United Way, the YMCA, Girl Scouts, Boy Scouts, United Negro College Fund, Heart Fund, and Cancer Fund.

That level of involvement indicates Southland's deep roots in the community. The company was founded by Judge Lecil Gray. Gray was the probate judge in Walker County before moving to Tuscaloosa and entering the insurance business with Cotton States Insurance. As an executive with Cotton States, he directed the marketing efforts of the company.

In 1965, Judge Gray resigned his position with Cotton States to form his own insurance company, initially concentrating on the direct mail market. By 1969, the company—then known as the New Southland National Insurance Company—had met the capital requirements to do business as a legal reserve

insurance company. Lanford—who had worked with Gray at Cotton States and moved to Southland—became president of the company in 1976. Other members of the top management of the company—including Vice President Dennis Painter—have a similar long association with the insurance business in the Tuscaloosa area.

Throughout its history, Southland has enjoyed slow but steady development—to many minds the perfect way for an insurance company to grow. Over the decades, the management has been able to identify and serve niche markets that have reaped benefits for employees, shareholders, and customers. Through hard work, honesty, and perseverance, Southland National Insurance Corporation has delivered quality products and service to its customers. ❖

(seated) William H. Lanford, president and CEO; (standing) Dennis E. Painter, vice president. Photo by Barry Fikes.

Interior of Southland National Insurance headquarters in Tuscaloosa. Photo by Barry Fikes.

The Chamber of Commerce of West Alabama

Since the turn of the century, The Chamber of Commerce of West Alabama—though it has been known by different names over the years—has stood for progress, business growth, and an ever-improving quality of life for the residents of the Tuscaloosa area.

A private-sector, volunteer organization, the mission of The Chamber is to provide leadership and coordination for the advancement of economic vitality and an enhanced quality of life for the total community throughout Tuscaloosa County and West Alabama. In carrying out that mission, members of The Chamber always have strived to demonstrate sensitivity and responsiveness to the needs and concerns of the people of the whole region.

Supported and funded through membership investments of a wide-range of businesses, industrial and professional members, institutions, and individuals, The Chamber brings together a diverse constituency of citizens who find themselves with a commitment to improve the economy, business climate, and lifestyle in the Tuscaloosa-Northport metropolitan area and the surrounding West Alabama region.

The Chamber is a volunteer-driven organization that utilizes the tremendous talent of Tuscaloosa County's business, educational, and professional communities; and puts it to work daily on a wide variety of important initiatives that bring positive results. Efforts of Chamber volunteers are supported and given organizational form and direction by The Chamber's top professional staff operating out of a progressive, functional operations center in Downtown Tuscaloosa.

Because of the quality of its programming and its broad-based representation—with virtualy all major industries and businesses counted among the membership—The Chamber of Commerce of West Alabama has earned a reputation as an aggressive and effective voice of business.

Chamber volunteers are organized in a variety of task forces and committees to focus on and achieve progress in areas of concern of the business community as well as the community-at- large. These task forces have made significant impact over the years through The Chamber's major divisions of Business Development, Education, Community Relations, Governmental Affairs, and Membership Services.

Despite the breadth of expertise and abilities Chamber members bring to a particular challenge or opportunity, The Chamber excels at building coalitions and partnerships to achieve the kind of success for which the organization has become so well known and respected. These initiatives may include the highly- successful Adopt-A-School Program or other eductional reform efforts; or it might be a development program for area small businesses or retailers; or even pulling together a diverse group to meet particular community needs, such as a Clean Community Commission, a Sister City, or a Crime Stoppers initiative.

With over 1,900 members, The Chamber lends credibility and impact to many broad programs designed to enhance The Chamber's mission of providing leadership to meet community needs and economic expansion.

The Chamber is an action-oriented organization that touches the life of the community and its citizens daily. Chamber members, as well as the community-at-large, can be involved in Coffee Club, Business After Five, small business training workshops, legislative briefings, the popular Chamber In Session, and Market Place, which has become West Alabama's largest small business trade show.

Chamber events and activities are always informative, often fun, and represent a real opportunity for members and the community to work together and network to achieve substantive successes individually and as a community. And these activities are supported daily by effective communication vehicles including "The Chamber Channel," a

The Chamber serves the community from a professional, functional center of operations developed under the administrations of two Past Chairmen--Dr. Roger Sayers, who was the first President of the University of Alabama to serve as a Chairman of The Chamber, and Verta Barr, the first woman Chairman.

The Chamber's growing membership and volunteer-led initiatives and broad-based programming are served and supported by a top-level, dedicated professional staff.

24-hour, daily TV bulletin board; "To The Point," a weekly half-hour issues TV show; monthly newsletters and legislative alerts; and a variety of other communication tools.

While Chamber members are working for the good of the community, they are also realizing some gains of their own. The many activities of The Chamber represent tremendous and meaningful opportunities to network and obtain key contacts, meet new clients, and develop opportunities for business development.

Even from the earliest days, the organization that would become The Chamber of today was instrumental in the economic, cultural, and lifestyle progress of Tuscaloosa.

The date was June 1, 1900. In a city with few paved streets, mule-drawn trolleys, and a fledgling industrial and institutional base; a handful of local business leaders began to meet as the Commercial Club. Perhaps one of their most important accomplishments during these early years was in 1907, when they succeeded in having the Warrior River placed on the federal government's water transportation development program.

In June, 1909, a decade after its founding, the Commercial Club voted to change its name to the Tuscaloosa Board of Trade. Its first Chairman, F.G. Blair, played an instrumental role in business development

in Tuscaloosa for many years through the Board.

In 1920, the organization's name was changed again, this time to the Tuscaloosa Chamber of Commerce. Among early accomplishments included recruitment of various major firms to the community including Alabama Power Company in 1923, Gulf States Paper Corporation in 1929, the Veterans Affairs Medical Center, and numerous other development initiatives over the years such as B.F. Goodrich Tire Company, Hunt Refining, and other major employers.

The Tuscaloosa Chamber was at the forefront of much of the business development and progress enjoyed by Tuscaloosa. From development efforts involving the airport, state park, highways, tourism, and business recruitment; the Tuscaloosa Chamber was effective in contributing to a better community.

In order to bring the business and industrial community to Tuscaloosa County and West Alabama in a more cohesive and effective force, a merger was consummated on January 1, 1984 between the Greater Tuscaloosa Chamber of Commerce and the Northport Chamber of Commerce. Under the leadership of Charles Land, The Chamber of Commerce of West Alabama was formed.

Perhaps one of the most significant steps forward, the unity achieved through The "New" Chamber has provided a key to the organization's success and effectiveness today. The Chamber of Commerce of West

Alabama has become the largest private-sector, business organization in West Alabama, almost tripling in membership, budget, and programming since the merger was achieved.

The Chamber has become a bold advocate and progressive voice on behalf of the business community of West Alabama while at the same time contributing to the overall development of Tuscaloosa County's exceptional quality of life.

Whether through Leadership Tuscaloosa or the Adopt-A-School program—transportation development, retail promotion, or small business support and assistance—legislative and public policy initiatives, education reform, or improved community and human relations efforts—or simply working daily to create the ideal home for business, The Chamber is making a positive difference in Tuscaloosa County.

Almost a century after its first days as the Commercial Club, the leadership of today's Chamber is still leading the way towards a

Johnnie Aycock, Executive Vice President of the Chamber of Commerce of West Alabama.

community that is consistently improving as an ideal place to live, work, and grow—and a community that cherishes its traditions, takes pride in its spirit and diversity, and has a vision of an even brighter future. ❖

Harco Drug

From a single, classically "Main Street" drugstore in downtown Tuscaloosa more than half a century ago, Harco Drug has built a tremendously successful chain of self-service, discount drugstores with additional corporate divisions operating in home health care and auto parts retailing.

A true family business—now in its third generation of family management—Harco has been one of the shining examples of growth and progress in the drug retailing industry. In fact, in the mid-1980s, the trade publication Drug Store News named Harco the outstanding small drug store chain in America. In 1990, CEO Jim Harrison, Jr. was named Chain Drug Retailer of the Decade. The company's 12 Gold Link Awards for Excellence in advertising are the highest honors presented by the professional association that serves the retail drug business.

Harco's 50-plus-year journey from the Main Street days of soda fountains and quiet small towns has brought the company to the modern era with more than 136 Harco Super Drug stores serving the everyday needs of busy families in communities across three southeastern states. The story of Harco has been an inspiring saga of a family of savvy business people who created an enterprise that has brought tremendous service and value to customers and a livelihood to thousands in an extended family of associates.

One of the maxims the Harrison family has lived by in building the business of Harco is that success flows from an ability to attract and keep good people. The company has been blessed with associates who have been a part of the company from the very beginning. Much of the company's management and leadership are long time Harco associates.

The creation of a multi-state chain with 136 stores wasn't the likely outcome when James I. Harrison, Sr. and his wife, Elizabeth,

purchased Central Drug Store, a Tuscaloosa commercial landmark, in 1941. James Harrison, Sr. had operated a drugstore that failed in the Great Depression. He went to work as a pharmacist, and to make additional money James and Elizabeth made and sold sandwiches to students at the University of Alabama. The income they made from that enterprise served as seed money for purchasing Central Drug. Although it took him several years, James I. Harrison, Sr. was able to pay back all of the creditors he could locate from his earlier bankruptcy. The young business owners did whatever they had to do— endured long hours and the stress of ownership—for the opportunity to build something of lasting value for their family. James and Elizabeth Harrison and their sons, Jim Jr. and Ben, worked hard at their American dream.

The store blossomed into a successful family enterprise for the Harrisons. By 1955, they decided on a small expansion. The Harrisons purchased Druid Drug on Tuscaloosa's University Boulevard for their son and current Harco CEO, Jim Harrison, Jr., to operate following his graduation from the School of

In 1990, CEO Jim Harrison, Jr. was named Chain Drug Retailer of the Decade. Photo by Barry Fikes.

Pharmacy at Howard College (now Samford University). Following this first acquisition, a few more stores in the Tuscaloosa area were gradually added to the company.

By the late 1960s, the idea of multiple store chains began taking hold in the retail drug industry. What had been for Harco an expansion policy based on availability,

TotalCare is the home health care division of the Harco company.

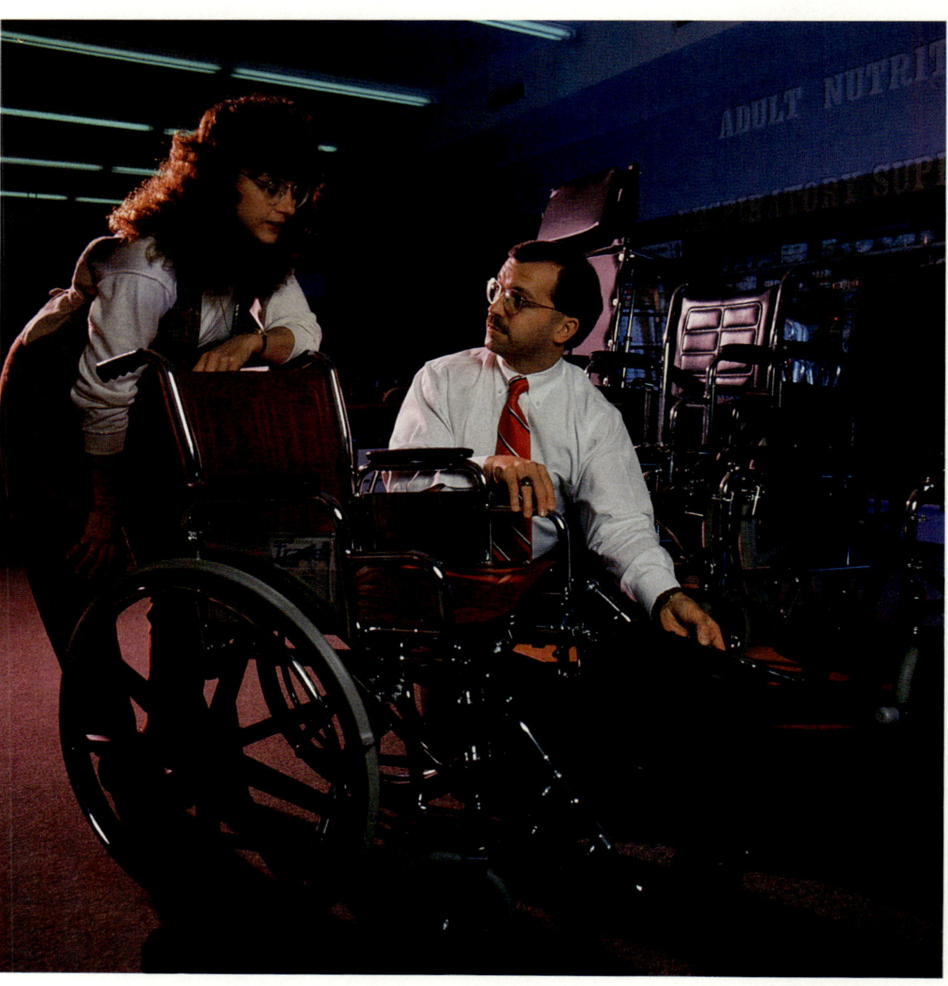

The Carport, an auto parts retail chain with more than 45 stores, is operated by a second division of Harco.

business qualities, and potential of individual stores gradually became a more controlled and well-planned series of acquisitions designed to build a company for the future. In 1969, Harco opened its fifth store—its first completely new one—in Northport. It sported a new logo for Harco Super Drug and was the company's first self-service drugstore in a strip shopping center.

The self-service concept was the new format that would fuel Harco's expansion outside of the Tuscaloosa area. The company's management—Jim, Jr. would soon trade his stewardship of Druid Drug to take over management for all stores—purchased a store in Talladega and converted it to the new format, and constructed a store in Clanton. These early successes gave the company the impetus to undertake an ambitious expansion program. A 30-year veteran of a Mid-Atlantic states chain, Albert Zepresko, was hired to give the company expertise in large-scale merchandising. The other important aspect of the company's success was a respect for the value of employees and the importance of a corporation's people.

That sense of value runs deep at Harco. The company's corporate mission statement reads: "To be the best retail company in the nation for the people who work here and the people who shop here." With this kind of deeply held belief at its bedrock, Harco has grown into a major regional retail chain with more than 2,400 employees and a payroll in excess of $32 million. The family members, management, and employees of Harco come together in a caring company, a family-owned business that puts customers first.

The 1980s were good to Harco. The company grew significantly. The space in its corporate headquarters in Tuscaloosa doubled to include a 250,000-square-foot distribution center and a large office complex. The lobby area of the office is decorated to call to mind the furnishings and memorabilia of an early 20th century drugstore and soda fountain.

Harco's largest acquisitions to date took place in the 1990s with the purchases of 8 SuperX stores, 19 Eckerd Drug Stores, and 12 Revco Drug outlets.

In recent years, the corporate structure of Harco has also undergone some major expansion. Harco TotalCare, the home health care division of the company brought into being in 1978, now ranks as the largest supplier of durable goods products in the state of Alabama. The division also developed Stim-U-Care, which provides physical therapy rehabilitation and home intravenous therapy.

The Carport, an auto parts retail chain with more than 45 stores, is operated by a second division of Harco. This division was formed in 1983, and has been experiencing steady growth ever since. The additional retail businesses of Harco are operated with the same drive for customer satisfaction and corporate quality as the drugstore business.

The corporate management of Harco always keep their eyes glued on that original prize of customer service and business growth. Strong family ties no doubt help the corporate focus to stay clear. The children of CEO Jim, Jr. and his wife Peggy are all active in the company. Peggy is so active in community and charitable affairs she might be called Harco's goodwill ambassador. The Harrison's sons, Jim III, Ronnie, and Kie, are in corporate management, as are their daughter, Cheri, and their two son-in-laws, John Sisson and David Fuhrman. David manages the Carport division.

Jim Harrison, Jr. likes to say that the family of Harco associates has—through their talent, energy, and hard work—built a company that is a great source of pride.

From the Harrison family through the extended family of employees to the families who turn to Harco for quality products and great service, Harco is a company that has built a reputation for caring and quality, and realized a dream of impressive growth and business success. ❖

AmSouth Bank of Tuskaloosa

AmSouth Bank of Tuskaloosa has a history rich in tradition—from its philanthropic founding in 1871, to its merger into the AmSouth family in 1986, to its present status as the premier financial institution in West Alabama with 10 banking locations in Tuscaloosa County.

Full service banking and building rewarding relationships with customers are the hallmarks of AmSouth.

AmSouth Bank of Tuskaloosa began its institutional life as First National Bank of Tuskaloosa. Both the bank and the city of Tuscaloosa were named for the great Indian chief Tushkalusa. In the interest of historical accuracy, the bank chose to retain the letter "k" used in the original Native American spelling. Meanwhile AmSouth had its beginnings as National Bank of Birmingham, then First National Bank of Birmingham.

Along with the similarity of its origins, the two financial institutions shared another characteristic, a common bond that made the transition from First National of Tuskaloosa to AmSouth a natural process. This common thread was a deep commitment to the community served. Each bank was very involved in supporting the kind of worthwhile civic endeavors and organizations that helped the community to prosper and grow.

The circumstances surrounding the birth of First National Bank of Tuskaloosa would be an indication of its philosophy for years to come. In 1871, money was scarce in the South. A wake of destruction was left behind in the aftermath of the War Between the States. Southerners were dispirited and so were the people of Tuscaloosa. There was no money to rebuild homes, farms, and businesses.

That's why, on July 5, 1871, nine men and women met in the office of Judge Washington Moody to establish the First National Bank of Tuskaloosa. The bank's founders risked all in order to give the people of West Alabama the resources they needed to rebuild their shattered lives.

One year later, in 1872, AmSouth opened for business as National Bank of Birmingham. The economy was in a tailspin at the bank's opening and many predicted doom for the institution. In 1882, the bank was renamed the First National Bank of Birmingham.

A century later, a decision was made to form a statewide affiliation of banking institutions, and First National Bank of Birmingham became the first affiliate bank of the new holding company, Alabama Bancorporation. Affiliations in Mobile and Decatur followed and strategic acquisitions throughout the state continued. In 1981, Alabama Bancorporation became AmSouth Bancorporation.

In 1986, AmSouth and First National Bank of Tuskaloosa merged, bringing two great banking traditions together as one. Each brought unique qualities to the new relationship, enhancing the quality of financial relationships for the people of Tuscaloosa.

Today, AmSouth continues the tradition, led by the bank's Tuskaloosa City President and Area Executive, Carl W. Albright, together with a broad base Board of Directors and effective management team. AmSouth is consistently first in bringing the newest innovations in banking to the good people of West Alabama. Perhaps the best thing of all about the relationship with Tuscaloosa area customers is AmSouth's commitment to be a part of the community. To help the people who live here realize their dreams. To foster economic progress and contribute to organizations that enhance the quality of life in West Alabama—for example the advances in education created by the AmSouth Educational Grant Fund. It's been a longstanding policy for AmSouth Bank of Tuskaloosa employees to be active in progressive community organizations.

That's a lot to live up to, but that's the way AmSouth likes it. The standards of service and community involvement set over a century ago are high standards, and the challenge of meeting them is great. But then, that's what being a great bank is all about. ❖

Crafton & Company

Crafton & Company has been finding insurance solutions for business and individual clients in Tuscaloosa and the surrounding area since 1959. It primarily functions as a Brokerage General Agency for many highly ranked Life and Disability companies, with Principal Financial Group being its "Flagship" insurer.

Most of Crafton & Company's commercial insurance business is written for small to medium-sized, closely held corporations. Those business relationships, built up over many years of service and customer contact, are marked by Crafton & Company's well-known reputation for integrity and quality.

For commercial clients, the company offers high-quality policies for business insurance such as Key-Man and Buy-Sell situations. Employee benefit programs such as Group Life, Group Health, and Group Disability, as well as Qualified and Nonqualified Retirement Plans, including Pension, Profit Sharing, and 401K are a major area of focus.

For individuals, Crafton & Company develops programs of life insurance for estate planning, income replacement, college funding, retirement income, and funding for estate taxes.

The company, and particularly principal Gene Crafton, is also immensely proud of Tuscaloosa. That sense of pride was a big factor in Crafton's building of the company's new signature headquarters building, Tavern Place.

Opened in May 1993, Tavern Place was constructed to beautifully occupy its historic site next to the Old Tavern at the west end of University Boulevard on the edge of Capitol Park. Tavern Place is unique. Built to closely resemble the landmark Gorgas House on the campus of the University of Alabama and to complement its next door neighbor, the historic Old Tavern, Tavern Place is Gene Crafton's attempt to help perpetuate Southern heritage in historic Capitol Park.

While the building is new, many of its architectural details would be right at home in most any historic building. The classic old brick came from the Old Raymons Department Store building in downtown Tuscaloosa and the exterior custom crafted shutters came from "The Villa," a Phillip Schutze designed apartment building south of the Buckhead area of Atlanta. The six inch hardwood floors in the building, along with door facings and corner blocks, salvaged from old local homes, are more than 100 years old. The four front exterior doors with unusual horizontal mortise locks, dating from the latter half of the 19th century, were salvaged from an 18th-century London ale-house. Interior conference room doors are from 19th-century Belgium. The beautiful fluted columns on the front facade and the posts on the back balcony are from 19th-century plantation homes in south Georgia. Most of the architectural artifacts that add such character to the structure were provided by Architectural Accents, an architectural design firm in Atlanta, Georgia.

Crafton & Company's pride in Tuscaloosa and Alabama clearly shows in this wonderfully new "old" building, which is the company's third home in Tuscaloosa.

After graduation from the University of Alabama's School of Commerce and Business Administration in 1953, Gene was working with Stockham Valve in Chicago when he decided in 1959 to go into the insurance business. "When Coach Bryant came back to Alabama in 1958, I figured it was time for me and my family to come home too." He opened for business in Birmingham, but shortly thereafter moved to Tuscaloosa, opening offices in the First National Bank Building. Later, the company outgrew that space and moved to Capitol Park Center which Crafton and a partner had developed in 1978.

Crafton & Company employs three support staff members and is associated with five highly qualified salespeople. Company President Gene Crafton is a Qualifying member of the Quarter Century Club of the Million Dollar Roundtable, having qualified for the honor for 27 consecutive years, and in addition is currently a member of the 1994 "Court of the Table." Crafton's son Scott, is now with the firm and represents a second generation providing continued quality insurance services to Tuscaloosa area companies and individuals.

In its more than three decades of providing quality service, the business built by the people of Crafton & Company has become a model of insurance know-how and integrity. ❖

Tavern Place is Crafton & Company's new office at Capitol Park.

Looking from the foyer into Crafton's conference room in the Tavern Place headquarters.

SouthTrust Bank of Tuscaloosa County

With corporate ties to a large regional bank holding company, SouthTrust Bank of Tuscaloosa County, N.A. offers the best of both worlds as a "super community bank." With local management and a local board of directors, the bank makes 98 percent of customer decisions in Tuscaloosa County including approval of loans, setting of rates, and the fees the bank charges customers. Yet its affiliation with the SouthTrust Corporation (founded in 1887) offers customers the stability and resources of one of the largest bank holding companies in the Southeast with 40 affiliated banks in six states. As of December 31, 1993, SouthTrust Corporation had achieved a 10 year total return to shareholders of 583 percent, one of the best records in the country.

SouthTrust Bank of Tuscaloosa County, N.A. is a full-service bank offering customers everything from trust services to checking. The bank is an aggressive and growing financial institution that in recent years has

SouthTrust has a variety of real estate loan products to suit every financing need.

enjoyed growth averaging 15 percent annually. The management team is young, energetic, and well prepared for the future. In fact, one of the most important strengths of the bank is its personnel. The bank hires good people and then trains them well to focus on the needs of customers.

As those needs change in the years to come, SouthTrust Bank of Tuscaloosa County, N.A. will be prepared to change along with them. The management of the bank sees growth opportunity in providing financial services to the senior market, minority market, small business market, as well as to the executive or professional customer. In the future, the bank will also be moving more forcefully into offering investment services, such as a full line of mutual funds. Trust services also will very likely be a growth area for the bank.

Growth plans call for SouthTrust Bank of Tuscaloosa County, N.A. to be a $200 million financial institution by the late 1990s. Expansion plans will focus on serving the bank's declared market area of Tuscaloosa County. An affiliate, SouthTrust Mortgage Company, also has aggressive plans for expansion in its customer base.

The growth will come, just as it has in the past, through careful planning and an extreme dedication to customer service. That, after all, is how SouthTrust Bank of Tuscaloosa County, N.A. has grown from the very beginning. Originally opened in December, 1979, as Citizens Bank of Northport, SouthTrust Corporation acquired the bank in April, 1982, and the name change to SouthTrust Bank of Tuscaloosa County

SouthTrust's main office is located at 1427 Greensboro Avenue, Tuscaloosa.

was officially finalized later that same year. In the years to come, the bank gained its national bank charter and grew into the third largest bank in the county with six branch locations at Northport, Bama Mall, Five Points, downtown Tuscaloosa, Indian Hills, and Skyland Promenade. The headquarters of the bank is located in Tuscaloosa where the city's oldest house, the McGuire-Strickland House (circa 1820), once stood.

The one constant throughout the bank's years of operation has been the paramount position the customer holds within the corporate culture of SouthTrust. SouthTrust Bank of Tuscaloosa County, N.A. is absolutely committed to top-quality service. Just witness the bank's Quality Service Guarantee Program. If a customer is not treated to top-notch service, money comes out of the company's own pocket. For example, SouthTrust pays customers for less than courteous service, a bank statement error, for waiting longer than 5 minutes in a teller line, or for a malfunctioning automatic teller machine.

At SouthTrust Bank of Tuscaloosa County, N.A., quality service is a guarantee. And so is service to the community. Employees are encouraged to make a positive impact in the community, pitching in to help with economic development initiatives, educational needs, and social services. ❖

First State Bank of Tuscaloosa

Established in 1968, First State Bank of Tuscaloosa has combined service to its customers with a strong commitment to the community to become one of Tuscaloosa's most reliable financial institutions.

Offering a full range of banking services and providing customers with access to trust services, mutual fund and annuity investments, and mortgage lending, First State prides itself on being flexible enough to work with its customers, whatever their banking needs.

More than 40 staffers—from customer service representatives, to account advisors, to lending professionals, and bank officers—serve the greater Tuscaloosa area through

First State's downtown headquarters and through its branches at University Mall and in Northport, both of which offer customers the flexibility of Saturday banking . . . expanded service hours that are in addition to what are already the area's best weekday banking hours: 8:30 a.m. to 5:00 p.m. Monday through Thursday, and 8:30 to 6:00 on Fridays.

Competing with the state's banking giants, First State has carved out its competitive niche based on its greatest strengths, flexibility and commitment. It's commitment to work with residential construction companies and small businesses has given First State a special rapport with this vital segment of the Tuscaloosa business community.

And, through construction financing, commercial checking, corporate credit cards, merchant processing, and working capital lines of credit—all customized to meet the need of growing small businesses and contractors—First State continues to play an important role in Tuscaloosa's growth and prosperity.

First State Bank Directors include: (L-R) Thomas P. Hester, J. Mike Richardson, A.H. Bean, Terry DeWitte, William J. Strickland, Clyde Price, and Tom Tarleton.

Executive Vice President Terry DeWitte and President Tommy Hester.

But First State's commitment to the community extends beyond successful service to its customers. Involvement in community programs is a priority among the bank's staff and officers. Bank personnel work with service associations, community development organizations, and with school and church groups.

First State has placed a particular emphasis on the Adopt-A- School initiative, which the bank supports financially and which bank employees support by giving of their time. First State's adopted school is Northington Elementary where a number of employees serve as role models, mentors, and friends to students, especially those who are troubled or considered at-risk.

It is that type of commitment that personifies First State Bank of Tuscaloosa's approach to the business of banking. Looking out for the needs of others, taking the time to smile, worrying about your community, and your customers . . . and putting people first.

First State is a bank where people know your name and where it's as easy to go in and talk about a loan as it is to talk about last week's ball game. It's also a bank that is as professional in its approach to service as it is friendly in delivering that service.

First State President Tommy Hester, has a long and distinguished career in banking and is one of the most respected bankers in the Tuscaloosa area. First State Chairman of the Board and successful local contractor and developer Lloyd Wood, is a highly respected Tuscaloosa professional who understands the value of delivering effective banking service to individuals and businesses alike. The entire staff at First State places one goal above all others: quality service to each and every customer.

Committed, caring, and professional. That's First State of Tuscaloosa. ❖

First Alabama Bank/ Tuscaloosa

First Alabama Bank/Tuscaloosa strives to be the bank of choice for today's families, fulfilling a widely varied need for financial services and offering customers the security of a financial institution that has won industry accolades as one of the strongest banks in America.

The consistency of the banking experience at First Alabama Bank/Tuscaloosa is one of the primary benefits customers enjoy. First Alabama's employees care and that attitude comes through with every transaction. Customer receipts bear the bank's pledge: "to provide you with a positive, pleasant experience with First Alabama Bank at every possible opportunity." That pledge is more than just words. At First Alabama Bank/ Tuscaloosa, devotion to customer service is the philosophy that drives the employees to give their best every day.

First Alabama, which overall serves one in four households in the state, offers a full line

First Alabama Bank serves one in four households in the state.

of financial products, priced competitively to give customers great banking value.

The needs of every sort of customer can be met at First Alabama. The bank offers a variety of checking accounts and such services as trust, brokerage, investments, and financial planning. Business and personal lines of credit, installment loans, home mortgages, student loans, and major credit cards meet the credit needs of customers. First Alabama offers 24-hour convenience with numerous ATMs and telephone banking.

With about 150 employees working in eight offices in Tuscaloosa County—in the cities of Tuscaloosa, Brookwood, and Northport—First Alabama Bank is a financial institution that can be counted on today and tomorrow.

As for its history, First Alabama/ Tuscaloosa is the oldest bank in West Alabama. Founded in 1865 by James Harris Fitts, in its earlier days the bank was known as J.H. Fitts and Company. One of the first employees, W.P.G. Harding, later became governor of the Federal Reserve Board. A later bank president, George LeMaistre became director and chairman of the Federal Deposit Insurance Corporation.

The young financial institution was renamed City National Bank in 1902. A white marble building at 23rd and Broad Streets in Tuscaloosa became the bank's impressive home in 1922. In 1967, the

First Alabama Bank/Tuscaloosa offers a full line of services including trust, brokerage, investments, and financial planning.

main office of City National was moved to a new headquarters building on 9th Street. The old main office building was donated to the University of Alabama in 1981.

Just as it had in the 19th century, the bank continued to grow and prosper through the middle decades of the 20th century. In 1955, City National opened its first branch office on the University of Alabama campus. Four years later, stock in the bank, until then held by only a few families, became more widely circulated.

City National joined the state's first, multi-bank holding company, First Alabama Bancshares, Inc., at the end of 1973, linking it with a broad network of banking offices and the capital strength of a large financial institution. In 1994, First Alabama Bancshares, Inc. changed its name to Regions Financial Corporation which more accurately described its position as a full financial service company for the southeastern United States.

First Alabama has established a tradition that supports economic growth and quality of life in Tuscaloosa County. The bank's officers serve as volunteers for the area's many charities and in leadership roles in organizations such as the Chamber of Commerce of West Alabama and the Tuscaloosa County Industrial Development Authority. All of these activities relate to the bank's mission of serving both customers and the community it calls home. ❖

The Bank of Tuscaloosa

Modeled after the classic operating philosophies of the old-line community bank, The Bank of Tuscaloosa strives to offer innovative financial products and the best in personal service to the citizens and businesses of Tuscaloosa County.

The twin benefits of being associated with a true community bank are substantial (1) depositor money stays in Tuscaloosa where it can do the most good for the community, and (2) decisions on loans and other financial matters rest with local people who intimately understand local market conditions and potential.

The bank's board of directors is made up of local business leaders who understand the needs of businesses and individuals in the community and who have a financial stake in a strong Tuscaloosa County. That's just one more aspect of the value of a home-grown bank.

The track record of The Bank of Tuscaloosa since its inception in 1988 certainly attests to the continued importance of local community banks. In its first six years, the bank has grown from a fledgling start-up with $5 million in capital and 13 employees into a financial institution with more than $100 million in assets, 54 employees, and a legal lending limit exceeding $1 million. With that kind of record, The Bank of Tuscaloosa has been the fastest growing bank in West Alabama.

The management of The Bank of Tuscaloosa makes banking personal and friendly, convenient and uncomplicated. There is a total of five banking offices in Tuscaloosa County. All branches are situated with an eye towards convenience and the potential for growth. The main office of the bank is located on the first floor of the renovated Stafford Plaza, long the site of Tuscaloosa's finest hotel and still one of the city's best-known landmarks.

Employees at The Bank of Tuscaloosa are encouraged to become actively involved in the community. They can be found participating in a variety of community programs including Chamber of Commerce functions and events, the United Way, various service organizations, and helping school kids through the Adopt-A-School program. Employee involvement simply underscores the deep commitment The Bank of Tuscaloosa has for the community which it serves.

The Bank of Tuscaloosa is an affiliate of Synovus Financial Corporation, a regional bank holding company headquartered in Columbus, Georgia. Synovus has a total of 31 affiliate banks, including five in Alabama cities: Tuscaloosa, Jasper, Birmingham, Montgomery, and Huntsville. Synovus provides its affiliate banks with significant resources through its $476 million capital base. Total assets for Synovus are in excess of $5 billion. One of the guiding principles of Synovus is the company's belief in independent local management for each of its 31 affiliates.

Because of this philosophy, The Bank of Tuscaloosa and its customers experience the best of two worlds: the advantages of the time-honored tradition of the strong, knowledgeable, and active community bank, and access to the financial resources of one of the nation's finest bank holding companies. ❖

The Bank of Tuscaloosa strives to offer innovative financial products and the best in personal service.

Chapter

Professions

Phelps, Jenkins, Gibson & Fowler

A major regional law firm in Alabama, Phelps, Jenkins, Gibson & Fowler of Tuscaloosa operates a broad legal practice providing clients with counsel and service.

The firm was officially organized in 1968 by senior partner Sam M. Phelps, as a successor to the Mize, Spiro & Phelps firm that was founded in 1940. Historically a strong litigation firm with an emphasis on defense, the Phelps firm has expanded its practice and services in recent years to include a business, tax, and corporate practice.

Clients of Phelps, Jenkins can be found throughout the West Alabama region—stretching from the Shoals Area south to just north of Mobile and eastward into the middle of the state. The firm serves an ever-widening base of individual, corporate, and institutional clients.

As one of the largest and oldest firms in West Alabama, the Phelps firm has successfully established a well-balanced mix between the attorneys in the firm who practice mainly in litigation and those engaged primarily in business, tax, and corporate law.

The firm's business, tax and corporate division includes several experienced partners and associates who hold master's degrees in taxation from some of the country's most prestigious graduate tax programs. Attorneys in the firm practicing in this division are engaged in banking, business formation, bonds and tax-exempt financing, securities, estate planning and administration, trusts, sales and acquisitions of businesses, business financing, real estate development, condominium law, commercial transactions, health care law, employee benefits and retirement plans, creditors rights, environmental law, trademark and copyright, labor/employment, and tax procedure and litigation.

Attorneys in the litigation division try cases in both state and federal court. The trial practice is primarily in the state courts of Tuscaloosa, Jefferson, Bibb, Choctaw, Clarke, Fayette, Greene, Hale, Lamar, Marengo, Marion, Pickens, Sumter, and Walker counties and the Northern, Middle, and Southern Districts of the federal court system in Alabama. Appellate work is handled in the Alabama Court of Civil Appeals and the Alabama Supreme Court, as well as the Fifth and Eleventh Circuits of the United States Court of Appeals and the United States Supreme Court.

Most of the firm's litigation attorneys are engaged in a general litigation practice involving employment discrimination, medical malpractice defense, product liability, workers compensation, school law, family law, real estate law, local government law, and business, tax, and corporate related litigation matters. Most of the firm's litigation is defense oriented, although about a third of the civil litigation and the general business and commercial litigation work is undertaken on behalf of plaintiffs.

Phelps, Jenkins, Gibson & Fowler is small enough to be a hands-on law firm with senior partners directly involved in a great percentage of cases, yet the firm is also large enough to allow access to a broad variety of legal expertise.

The firm represents several banking and financial institutions, advises both new and

The office space and design are patterned after a 1763 landmark Wythe House in Virginia.

The partners of Phelps, Jenkins, Gibson & Fowler are: (seated) Sam M. Phelps, (L to R back row) Michael S. Burroughs, Randolph M. Fowler, J. Russell Gibson, Farley A. Poellnitz, C. Barton Adcox, James J. Jenkins.

established local businesses, and serves as local counsel for many national companies. At the same time, the firm provides prompt, personal service to the business or individual needing advice on only one legal matter.

The Phelps firm is housed in its own 14,000-square-foot building—patterned after a 1763 landmark Wythe House in Virginia. The offices stand on oak tree-lined Greensboro Avenue, which is one of the most picturesque and historic of the broad avenues in downtown Tuscaloosa.

Attorneys of the Phelps firm assume leadership roles in the community at large. Members of the firm serve on the governing bodies of their churches and are active as officers, board members, and attorneys for a

number of commercial, governmental, and charitable organizations. These organizations include several banks, the Tuscaloosa County Industrial Development Authority, the Tuscaloosa City School System, the Civil Service Board for the City of Tuscaloosa, The Chamber of Commerce of West Alabama, the DCH Regional Medical Center and the DCH Foundation, the Junior League of Tuscaloosa, the Tuscaloosa Children's Center, and the Boys' and Girls' Club of West Alabama. The firm is frequently a leader in fund-raising drives undertaken to finance community projects.

In its geographic service area in Alabama and with its legal expertise—Phelps, Jenkins, Gibson & Fowler is a law firm with a clear and important mission: to provide clients with the very best in legal advice, counsel, and service. ❖

The firm has a well-balanced mix of attorneys with different areas of expertise.

No representation is made that the quality of the legal services to be performed is greater than the quality of legal services performed by other lawyers.

The firm is housed in its own beautiful 14,000 square-foot building.

Jamison, Money, Farmer & Co., P.C.

Seated: Harold E. Phillips; left to right: Carl T. Jamison, George H. Jones, Richard E. Gibson, Richard E. Kirkpatrick.

In business since 1920, the Certified Public Accounting firm of Jamison, Money, Farmer & Co., P.C. (JMF) brings high-quality service and an impressive depth of professional expertise to a broad range of business and individual clients.

The Tuscaloosa-based company—with approximately 40 accountants on a total staff of 65 and with offices in Tuscaloosa and Birmingham—is one of the oldest, largest, and most respected accounting firms in the state of Alabama.

One of the major strengths of the firm is the combined years of experience and diverse expertise of its professional practitioners. Jamison, Money, Farmer & Co., P.C. is a firm large enough to offer the broad

Left to right: Bryan R. Chandler, Charles F. Horton, William D. "Billy" Jamison, T. Jerry Humber, Ernest E. "Dick" Miles, D.S. "Buddy" Burton, Jr.

experience that brings outstanding service to clients while maintaining a personal touch and hands-on service from even the most senior members of the staff.

Jamison, Money, Farmer & Co., P.C. is committed to quality and participates fully in voluntary peer review as a member of the SEC and Private Companies Practice Sections of the American Institute of Certified Public Accountants Division for Firms.

From construction and manufacturing companies to businesses involved in international trade, JMF has the resources, including full computerization and an excellent support services staff, to serve its wide range of clients.

The services provided by the firm are varied and include the complete range of accounting functions. Estate planning and estate tax return preparation are particularly strong suits of the firm. In addition to traditional accounting services such as auditing, tax accounting, and financial statements, JMF also provides assistance in personal financial planning; projections/forecasts; estate and gift planning; trusts; business acquisitions, mergers, expansions, sales, and valuations; oil and gas, pension plans; personnel matters; business planning; retirement plans; and systems design, selection, and implementation. There are also other services offered by the firm.

Over the years, Jamison, Money, Farmer & Co., P.C. has worked extensively in industries such as health care, banking, real estate, government, manufacturing, lumber, farming, and nonprofit organizations.

The firm was founded in 1920 by the late Carl C. Jamison, one of the first Certified Public Accountants in the state of Alabama. He developed accounting systems for such local institutions as the City of Tuscaloosa, Stillman College, *The Tuscaloosa News*, and Druid City Hospital, and assisted with the system designed for the State of Alabama. Jamison's son, William D. "Billy" Jamison, is a senior shareholder at JMF today. Jamison's grandson, Carl T. Jamison, became a partner in 1987 making Jamison, Money, Farmer & Co., P.C. one of the first public accounting firms in Alabama to have three generations of family ownership.

James E. Money joined the firm in 1948, leading it until his retirement in 1974. Hugh W. Farmer became a part of the firm in 1953 and was instrumental in developing its computerized accounting procedures.

The current shareholders are William D. "Billy" Jamsion, Charles F. Horton, Ernest E. "Dick" Miles, Davis S. "Buddy" Burton, Jr. Harold E. Phillips, T. Jerry Humber, Carl T. Jamison, Richard E. Gibson, Bryan R. Chandler, Richard E. Kirkpatrick, and George H. Jones.

The firm's shareholders and staff fill leadership roles in numerous Tuscaloosa area civic and professional organizations.

With a strong foundation built on the firm's storied history, excellent performance and expertise, JMF enthusiastically looks forward to the future. ❖

Tom Joiner & Associates, Inc.

Tom Joiner & Associates, Inc. is a geological and engineering consulting firm specializing in providing professional services in oil and gas, geology, hydrology, and environmental disciplines. The well-trained scientific professionals employed by the firm are as committed to serving the needs of clients as they are expert in their respective fields.

Clients of Tom Joiner & Associates, Inc. are treated to the highest quality service and the very best in professional standards of geological and engineering consulting services. The capabilities of the company's professional staff are broad and far reaching because the firm serves a diverse and growing clientele. The staff includes individuals who are fully knowledgeable and familiar with the latest regulations and technologies. The scientific disciplines of the staff members include geology, hydrology, geography, petroleum engineering, environmental engineering, and civil engineering. They offer clients a combined total of more than 150 years of experience in the oil and gas industry, geology, and environmental studies in the United States and abroad.

The staff's ability to work with all types of clients is a real company strength. Excellent communication and management skills assure effective and efficient working relationships with clientele which includes large corporations, small businesses, governmental agencies, bankers, attorneys, and others.

Tom Joiner & Associates, Inc. is carefully structured and strategically positioned to

Joiner has developed a well-balanced, successful firm by surrounding himself with talented professionals.

work at peak efficiency for clients. Two separate divisions—the Oil and Gas Division and the Geologic, Hydrologic, and Environmental Division—meet the technological needs of clients.

The engineers, petroleum geologists, technicians, and support personnel of the Oil and Gas Division work for major and independent oil and gas companies, landowners, attorneys, and estates. Services offered by the Division include comprehensive oil and gas exploration, permitting, reservoir analysis, coalbed degasification studies, property valuation, and expert legal and regulatory testimony.

The Geologic, Hydrologic, and Environmental Division services include mineral resources evaluation, geologic mapping, regulatory permitting, soil and groundwater assessments, contamination monitoring and clean up, environmental audits and assessments, and storage tank assessments and closures. The Division specializes in producing comprehensive studies in geology, hydrology, environmental compliance, and waste management for clients throughout Alabama and the Southeast.

Company founder, Tom Joiner, began the consulting firm in 1981, after leaving his position as Alabama State Geologist and State Oil & Gas Board Supervisor. By surrounding himself with talented professionals, he has built Tom Joiner & Associates, Inc. into a well-balanced and successful firm.

The people at Tom Joiner & Associates, Inc. make the difference in delivering top-quality services to clients. Not only are the staff members of Tom Joiner & Associates, Inc. active in professional societies and

associations but the company strives to make an impact on the community as well. Staff members give a significant number of volunteer hours in service to the community. For example, Tom Joiner serves on the board of directors of AmSouth Bank in Tuscaloosa, the Tuscaloosa Industrial Development Authority, the DCH Foundation Board, and the Governor's Environmental Advisory Board. Other members of the firm are active in the Adopt-A-School program, the Chamber of Commerce, church activities, and other civic organizations.

The personal touch and care that Tom Joiner & Associates, Inc. brings to each client relationship, along with the staff's top-flight professional abilities, are the root reasons behind the past and future success of this engineering and geology firm. The people make the difference. ❖

Tom Joiner (right) began the consulting firm in 1981, after leaving his position as Alabama State Geologist and State Oil & Gas Board Supervisor.

Watson, Harrison & deGraffenried

The strength of the Tuscaloosa law firm of Watson, Harrison & deGraffenried lies in the abilities and expertise of its well-known and respected attorneys. The firm has a practice with a statewide and regional base of clients.

Watson, Harrison & deGraffenried is active in the fields of oil, gas and minerals, corporate law, criminal defense, matters of estates and probate, and all legal issues having to do with real property.

The firm was formed in 1978 on the strength of its expertise in the legal issues that surround the oil, gas, and mining industries. In the 1970s, partner Tom Watson was an assistant attorney general of Alabama and counsel for the State Oil and Gas Board and the Geological Survey. Steve Harrison was his law clerk. Later, after Watson moved into private practice and Harrison graduated from law school, the two formed a law partnership, and soon thereafter Thomas W. Holley joined the firm.

Tom Watson, born in Selma, Alabama, was admitted to the bar in 1970. Steve Harrison, born in Birmingham, was admitted to the bar in 1978, and Tommy Holley, also a Birmingham native, was admitted to the bar in 1977. All three received their JD degree from the University of Alabama, and are members of the Tuscaloosa County and American Bar Associations and the Alabama State Bar.

Early on the firm specialized in oil, gas, and mineral law concentrating on such things as land title searches, pre-drilling legalities, and regulatory work. Over the years, the firm grew to seven attorneys.

In 1992, the oil and gas exploration industry experienced a severe nationwide downturn, and in order to maintain its pattern of growth, the law firm began moving towards a

Seated, Michael C. Cornwell; Standing, Steven F. Harrison

more general practice of law with the addition in July, 1993, of Ryan deGraffenried as a partner and counselor.

Ryan deGraffenried, a trial lawyer, has served in the Alabama Senate since 1978. He was admitted to the bar in 1976 following his graduation as president of his class at the Cumberland School of Law at Samford University. He has served as President Pro Tem of the Senate for successive four-year terms. Senator deGraffenreid, one of the state's major legislative leaders, has also served as president of the senate.

Watson, Harrison & deGraffenried now maintains a strong practice in criminal defense, estate and probate matters, and all the many legal issues related to real property. In addition, the firm continues to offer clients—particularly in Mobile Bay and southwest Alabama—its special knowledge of oil, gas, and mineral law.

The strengths of the firm include its familiarity with the regulatory environment related to oil and gas development and production, mining, and the environment. Watson, Harrison & deGraffenried also maintains a strong reputation in corporate and commercial law and the practice of real estate law.

The firm is small, so clients enjoy the added advantage of most often dealing directly with a senior attorney. And though small, the firm employs an adequate staff of support personnel to get the job done, and provides its clients with the very best in legal services. ❖

Seated, Ryan deGraffenried, William T. Watson; Standing, Steven F. Harrison, Thomas W. Holley

Hubbard, Smith, McIlwain & Brakefield, P.C.

Among the oldest and most established law practices in Tuscaloosa, the law firm of Hubbard, Smith, McIlwain & Brakefield offers litigation and commercial law services to a formidable group of top-flight clients.

Originating nearly fifty years ago, Hubbard, Smith, McIlwain & Brakefield, P.C., a professional corporation, has continued to be one of the well established and most successful firms in Tuscaloosa. The firm's long list of past partners includes such noted attorneys as Walter P. Gewin, who served on the United States Fifth Circuit Court of Appeals; and George LeMaistre, past-chairman of the United States Federal Deposit Insurance Corporation.

Hubbard, Smith, McIlwain & Brakefield, P.C., maintains a sophisticated practice comparable to larger firms in neighboring cities. The firm provides the expertise and quality work product of a large firm without the negatives normally associated with such firms. The firm's size allows prompt personal service to clients' individual needs without the high costs usually associated with such attention.

The firm has a diverse and extensive general practice including litigation, insurance, corporate, commercial, employment, and real estate matters.

The firm's litigation practice, in federal and state courts, includes general insurance; coverage issues; personal injury and wrongful death defense; fire and casualty; surety and fidelity bonds; subrogation; automobile; life, health, and disability insurance; building and construction; commercial matters (detailed below), and an appellate practice.

The firm's commercial practice includes transactions and litigation involving banking; bankruptcy and reorganizations; creditors' rights; commercial and consumer collections; commercial real estate transactions and closings; commercial and consumer loans; commercial and asset-based financing; trouble loan workouts; and lender liability. The firm is an agent of Commonwealth Land-Title Insurance Company and writes title insurance for both commercial and consumer real estate transactions. The firm also provides counsel in general corporate and business matters. The firm's employment law practice includes Title VII defense, civil rights defense, co-employee torts defense, and employer-employee relations.

While the majority of its practice is focused on the West Alabama region, the firm serves the legal needs of clients throughout the state and represents their interests all over the nation.

With three partners, four associates, and a staff of about 20 employees, the firm provides quality service while retaining the intimacy of the attorney-client relationship. Clients of

Located in downtown Tuscaloosa, the offices of Hubbard, Smith, McIlwain & Brakefield are convenient to courts, businesses, and financial institutions.

Hubbard, Smith, McIlwain & Brakefield receive the hands-on expertise of senior lawyers as a matter of course due to the leanness and efficiency of the firm. When it comes to working for clients in the most efficient and effective manner, the firm's size is often a distinct advantage.

All of the firm's attorneys are graduates of the University of Alabama School of Law. The firm's partners and shareholders are Mike Smith, Chris McIlwain, and Marc Brakefield. Associate attorneys are Ken Aycock, Cooper Shattuck, Chip Bankston, and Scott Dulaney.

From offices in downtown Tuscaloosa—convenient to courts, businesses, and financial institutions—the attorneys and support personnel of Hubbard, Smith, McIlwain & Brakefield conduct a first-rate practice of law. ❖

No representation is made that the quality of the legal services to be performed is greater than the quality of legal services performed by other lawyers.

With three partners, four associates, and a staff of about 20 employees, Hubbard, Smith, McIlwain & Brakefield serves clients throughout the state and their interests across the nation.

McGiffert and Associates

A civil engineering firm, McGiffert and Associates has for almost half a century played an integral role in the development of West Alabama.

As a first-rate engineering firm, McGiffert and Associates lays an excellent foundation for successful projects and satisfied clients by adhering closely to the time-honored principle of providing the sort of personal service that assures success.

McGiffert and Associates is a small enough firm to offer clients hands-on attention from the most senior members of the staff; yet, at the same time, the firm is large enough to encompass a wealth of talent and resources.

Tuscaloosa County Industrial Park - McGiffert and Associates, Inc. provided Design, & Construction Services for Access Roads, Railroad Spur, Utilities & Site Plan Preparation for several of the Industries shown.

A number of the firm's employees has worked for McGiffert for many years, which adds to the stability of the firm and the comfort level of clients. After all, day to day, the clients of McGiffert and Associates are dealing with very experienced people.

The firm employs 37 people in a central office in Tuscaloosa, including professional engineers, staff engineers, professional land surveyors, computer/CADD operators, surveying crew personnel, construction inspectors, and a clerical and accounting staff.

Civil engineering is the branch of the profession that is concerned with water systems, natural gas systems, sanitary and storm sewers, roads, bridges, railroads, and the like. The business interests of McGiffert and Associates are similarly broad-based.

The firm's work encompasses civil engineering work on residential subdivisions (which dates back to the earliest days of the company) and commercial land development throughout West Alabama. Industrial-site work for major manufacturing and processing plants is also a major part of the firm's workload. McGiffert is also very active in road projects, construction of access roads, and street improvements.

Environmental engineering and drainage projects—including the improvement of existing drainage systems for municipalities—also keep the firm busy. In addition, McGiffert and Associates provides engineering services for distribution, storage, and treatment for 26 water systems for rural areas and small towns that serve anywhere from 200 to 3,000 customers, as well as projects for the City of Tuscaloosa Water and Sewer Department.

For the coalbed methane industry in West Alabama, which extracts natural gas from coal layers, McGiffert and Associates offers engineering and surveying services such as environ-

Wastewater Treatment & Compression Facility for Methane Gas Industry - McGiffert and Associates, Inc. provided Site Plan Design, Water Treatment Facility Design which includes Tanks, Pipelines, Sludge Drying Facilities, Pumps and Construction Services.

mental engineering, pipeline design, water treatment, and regulatory permitting.

The antecedent companies of McGiffert and Associates were founded in the late 1940s by W.H. Nicol and his son Thomas Nicol. David G. McGiffert, after becoming a partner with Thomas H. Nichol, bought out his partner and formed McGiffert Engineering Company, which was later incorporated as McGiffert and Associates in 1965.

Today, David G. McGiffert's sons, David and Allen, are the firm's top management and principal stockholders. Their father, David G., is still active with the company in a limited way.

The longevity of the firm has placed McGiffert and Associates in the unique position of renovating or expanding some of the same structures for which the company completed the original engineering work many years before. That gives the firm an even clearer sense of having participated in the development of Tuscaloosa County and other parts of West Alabama.

With the entire area poised for continued growth in the years to come, McGiffert and Associates looks forward to many more opportunities to help put structure and form to growth and development in West Alabama. ❖

Almon Associates, Inc.

Almon Associates specializes in planning and designing the infrastructure systems which make our modern lifestyle possible and enhance the convenience, health, and safety of our society. These systems are necessary for progress and environmental protection in government, commerce, and industry.

Almon Associates offers clients planning, study, and design services in the multi-faceted disciplines of engineering, surveying, and architecture. Some of the specific areas of Almon's practice include civil, environmental, and structural engineering; water supply and treatment; wastewater collection and treatment; traffic and transportation planning and engineering; all types of surveying and mapping; and general architecture.

For nearly 40 years, the firm has continuously developed by offering its services through highly skilled and professional associates, specializing in various disciplines. These associates direct and manage all projects with the support of an experienced staff of engineers, surveyors, architects, and other technical and administrative personnel.

The firm's varied client base includes municipalities, industries, local, state and federal agencies, institutions, and commercial enterprises. The broad scope of work Almon completes for its clients includes feasibility studies, preliminary design, permitting, site evaluation and development, design and analysis, contract documents, cost estimating, construction review and administration, and assistance in start-up operations.

Whether the project is a large multimillion-dollar public works project or a survey for title or an environmental assessment, Almon works closely with clients to be certain that services are performed in a professional, timely, and economical manner. Project values vary from a few thousand to more than $30 million. Almon Associates realizes the importance of contract administration and construction overview. These are critical services which help ensure the quality and intent of the design and, thus, the value of the project is realized for the client.

In all dealings with projects, Almon Associates is guided by an overriding concern for quality and integrity. Stated simply, the company's philosophy is **"do it right while you're doing it."** Accomplishing this philosophy requires skill, experience, patience, and confidence. Those are the qualities of the professionals at Almon Associates.

Strict adherence to the importance of professionalism has been the hallmark of Almon Associates throughout its history. The firm was initially founded as the Alsey C. Parker & Son Engineering Company in 1956. Current company president, Robert N. Almon, went to work for the firm two years later in 1958. A massive project of the 1960s, managed by Mr. Almon which established the firm's reputation, was the design and construction of Lake Tuscaloosa and the North River Water Supply Project. This project will serve

Associates: (Seated) Calvin Cassady; Tom Hughes, Secretary; Bob Almon, President; and Rex Veron. (Standing) Bob Evans; Jeff Wood, VP; Mike Williams; Jim Ezell; Russ Nevin; and Phillip Guin.

Tuscaloosa and surrounding areas far into the next century.

In 1969, Robert Almon purchased the firm from the Parker estate and continues expanding the company's capabilities and building its professional stature. Through the years, there were many more projects, large and small, all undertaken with the highest degree of professionalism and commitment.

Today, that stature as a highly professional design firm is secure. The success of Almon Associates lies in its excellent record of designing infrastructure and providing service and true value, those essential elements in the success of a business venture, industrial enterprise, or community. ❖

Chapter

15

Building Greater Tuscaloosa

S.T. Bunn Construction, 160;
Tuscaloosa Title Company, 161;
RaCON, Inc., 162

S. T. Bunn Construction

ST. Bunn Construction Company is one of the oldest, family-owned construction businesses in the state of Alabama. Bunn specializes in highway and commercial asphalt construction work.

Founded in 1939, S. T. Bunn Construction is said to have paved or re-paved every street in Tuscaloosa at least once over the years. S. T. Bunn, Sr. began the business with just two trucks and an overriding belief in the promise of the American free enterprise system.

In the early days, S. T. Bunn Construction hauled asphalt for other construction companies; the company even did some hauling of defense materials during the war years. Gradually, Bunn moved resolutely into the asphalt business, and it became a specialty of the company.

Bunn Construction has grown steadily and intelligently over the years, adding people, facilities, and equipment as the demand for its quality-conscious work grew. The company has become a fixture in the area's construction business and has been responsible for a

Reconstructing city streets Tuscaloosa, Alabama.

majority of the highway construction on the west side of Alabama, from Butler to Hamilton.

The construction work that Bunn undertakes entails site preparation, basing, and paving. While highway construction is certainly a mainstay of the company, Bunn is also involved in commercial projects such as paving the parking lots of shopping centers and malls and the streets and roadways of residential subdivisions and office parks.

The quality of Bunn's work has been well documented over the years. In 1991, the company won the Alabama Highway Department Quality Pavement Award for the best paving work for a stretch of roadway constructed on Interstate 59 in Sumter County.

In 1981, brothers Sonny and Terry Bunn—who had been working for their father from the time they were quite young—purchased the construction business from S. T. Bunn, Sr. Sonny is a civil engineering graduate of the University of Alabama, while Terry received a business degree from Livingston University. Both men have been past presidents of the Alabama Asphalt Pavement Association. Terry also serves on the board of trustees of Livingston University.

Sonny is the president of the company and Terry serves as the vice president. Both men enjoy big game hunting; the trophy animals displayed in their offices in Tuscaloosa attest to their skills.

Today the company employs about 130 people. Aside from the actual construction of

Resurfacing I-59 in Tuscaloosa County.

roadways and pavement, Bunn operates three asphalt plants in West Alabama, in the towns of Fayette, Tuscaloosa, and Epes. The new $1.2 million asphalt plant in Tuscaloosa came on line in 1994; it is one of the largest in the state and employs the most modern design and technology.

In its asphalt manufacturing processes, Bunn takes the raw materials—sand and gravel—washes and crushes the materials, and produces the finished asphalt. While Bunn Construction utilizes most of the production of their asphalt plants in their own construction jobs, they also market some of the asphalt to other companies.

Bunn has been fortunate over the years to operate in a state that believes strongly in the value of a good, comprehensive program of road and highway construction. The company has responded in kind by strict adherence to the codes of exemplary business conduct and the utilization of the highest quality construction materials and processes.

The result of Bunn's approach to quality paving construction is visible for all to see on the excellent interstates, roads, and parking lots of West Alabama. ❖

Tuscaloosa Title Company

In its 96th year of operation, Tuscaloosa Title Company, Inc. has expanded from a small local abstract company to a multiple service regional firm serving residential, commercial, industrial, and governmental customers.

Exclusive agents for Lawyers Title Insurance Corporation, Tuscaloosa Title Company offers a broad range of services: title insurance; real estate transactions, including loan closings; title searches; and oil, gas, and mineral abstracts.

Tuscaloosa Title Company has a long and distinguished history. Founded in 1898 by abstractor Walter Smith, the firm quickly became a respected part of the Tuscaloosa business community. Purchased in 1936 by Joe Duckworth and John Pearson, the company was owned and operated by family members and associates until 1974, when it was sold to Richard and Annette Shelby who retain ownership today.

The firm has had several locations in its illustrious history, including the Old Masonic Building, a building on Seventh Street, and a

Tuscaloosa Title Company's office staff is committed to efficient, quality service.

Pam Blackwell reviews HUD-1 settlement with purchasers.

suite in the First Federal Building. The company is currently located at 2210 Eighth Street in Tuscaloosa.

Tuscaloosa Title Company's commitment to efficient, quality service has assured its place as the premier title company in West Alabama. That reputation has been built and maintained by a dedicated staff led by Pamela B. Blackwell, president of the firm and chief operating officer. A native of Tuscaloosa County, Pam has been with the company since 1974.

Pam Blackwell is an active member of numerous community and business organizations in West Alabama including the Chamber of Commerce of West Alabama, Tuscaloosa Board of Realtors, American Land Title Association, Dixie Land Title Association, Homebuilders Association of Tuscaloosa, Realtors Land Institute, and Women's Council of Realtors.

Tuscaloosa Title Company is an approved closing agent for every lending institution including AmSouth Mortgage Company, Inc.; AmSouth Bank, N.A.; The Bank of Moundville; The Bank of Tuscaloosa; BancBoston Mortgage Corporation; B.F. Goodrich Employees Federal Credit Union; CTX Mortgage Company; Compass Bank; Compass Mortgage Corporation; Collateral Mortgage, Ltd; Colonial Mortgage Company; Citicorp Mortgage, Inc.; Farmers Home Administration; First Alabama Bank; First Federal Bank; First National Bank of Pickens County; First State Bank of Tuscaloosa; PHH US Mortgage Corporation; Real Estate Financing, Inc.; SouthTrust Mortgage Corporation; SouthTrust Bank of Tuscaloosa County, N.A.; Standard Mortgage Corporation of Georgia; TFE Credit Union; West Alabama Bank & Trust.

A hardworking staff of 14 people keep these Tuscaloosa Title clients satisfied. The staff is dedicated to making this distinguished and longtime Tuscaloosa business work. ❖

RaCON, INC.

Well known for getting the job done—doing it right and on time—RaCON, INC. has built a business that enjoys an excellent reputation, particularly in highway construction circles.

Professional. Careful. Efficient. RaCON, INC. is a company that knows what it is doing and hustles to meet the needs of its customers.

RaCON shines in the arena of workplace safety, an especially important part of the efficiency of a construction firm. The company is very safety conscious and strives hard to create a good, drug-free, and safe place to work.

About 70 percent of RaCON's business is in highway construction—building highways, roads, and some city streets for Departments of Transportation in states, counties, and municipalities. Typically, RaCON will receive a contract to clear and grade a section of roadway (road contracts are typically let in three- to five-mile segments). The company completes all road construction tasks short of actual paving and overpass construction. RaCON also frequently becomes invoived in roadway repair work.

The balance of RaCON's work—about 30 percent—revolves around the preparation of industrial sites, a very important part of the company's work load. Projects such as the site work for the JVC plant, facilities for Hunt Refining Company, and the huge Mercedes-Benz plant in Vance, Alabama, are but a few examples of the industrial site work completed by RaCON.

In short, RaCON can take a simple cow pasture or a section of woodland and turn it into a productive industrial site. Such projects are frequently large undertakings. For example, at the Mercedes project, 4 1/2 million yards of earth were moved. RaCON also works with customers on a project basis, making site repairs or developing additional land for industrial use. The type of work completed by RaCON at the typical industrial site includes clearing of land, excavation, pad preparation, sub-surface drainage systems, and developing soil base layers prior to paving.

RaCON, INC. is hard at work on the massive Mercedes-Benz site development project.

At the height of its work season, RaCON employs a total of about 200 people. The company has 125 permanent employees and operates 150 pieces of equipment, from trucks to large earth- moving machinery. Projects are administered under a superintendent/project management format so there is plenty of management hands-on control.

RaCON typically completes about six to eight major projects a year, working within a 200-mile radius of Tuscaloosa County.

Engineers, administrative personnel, safety coordinators, and clerical employees—in all about a dozen people—work at company headquarters on Highway 69 in Northport. Project superintendents work from mobile offices right at the work sites.

Up until 1983, RaCON used a renovated house, circa 1899, as its company headquarters. The current building was first occupied in 1988.

Company President Ramona Andrews founded the company as R.M. Andrews Construction Co. in 1979. An accomplished woman who worked toward a doctorate in pharmacognosy, she began working in her husband's construction office when Benton Andrews was managing projects for Southeast Contractors. After gaining administrative expertise and construction experience, Ramona decided to open a small construction company in 1979.

The company's first contract was as a sub to a Dothan contractor on $1 million worth of work on U.S. Highway 82 in Reform in West Alabama. With a handful of equipment and a good deal of know-how (Benton Andrews brings 30 years of construction experience to the company), they built that first job and have gone on from there. The company incorporated as RaCON in 1981. Son, Keith, joined the firm early on and is now vice president.

Together, the family operates a business that pursues excellence as it completes projects. ❖

Chapter

16

Education & Quality of Life

The University of Alabama

I n 1818, one year before Alabama became a state, the Congress of the United States granted land in the territory to create a "seminary of learning." The University of Alabama welcomed its first students to Tuscaloosa in 1831. It became coeducational in 1893 and opened to students of all races in 1963. Today, the 1,000-acre campus by the Black Warrior River draws scholarly and research talent from around the world to its twelve academic and professional colleges and schools. Students come from 53 states and territories, with 72 percent from Alabama. A University-wide honors program involves hundreds of undergraduate scholars each year in accelerated curricula in several disciplines. A separate Computer-Based Honors Program has been recognized for innovative teaching for a quarter century.

The University's Department of Civil and Environmental Engineering prepares students for the expanding and essential field of environmental engineering.

Undergraduates at The University of Alabama were the first at a major Southern university to complete a mandatory core curriculum ensuring exposure to many fields of learning. Through the core curriculum, the University seeks to produce well-rounded students able to think and act productively on the many interwoven issues that characterize contemporary life. The responsibility is one the University also accepts for itself. Participating fully in the life of its community, state, and nation, the University strives to model the citizenship it fosters in its students. "We are a place," says 27th University president Dr. Roger Sayers, "where young men and women learn to think beyond the present and to invent the future; where, working alongside a faculty with national and international reputations, they learn to solve problems at a pace that permits reflection."

Undergirding all its activities is the University's threefold mission of teaching, research, and service. A concern for high-quality teaching and learning is foremost. About 19,000 undergraduate and graduate students attend UA. Teaching them is the institution's primary responsibility, and effective teaching is the threshold requirement for tenure. The award-winning faculty strive to use the latest knowledge and technology to make the classroom experience an invigorating and lasting one. Their research—whether

The President's Mansion is one of four original campus buildings that survived the burning of the University by Union troops in 1865.

in the humanities, commerce, nutrition, telecommunication, or other fields—fuels this effort. Students gain when they learn from the world's top limnologist, or most prolific accounting scholar, or nationally respected historian. Such pioneering teacher-researchers are found throughout the University.

Their professors' energetic teaching and scholarly achievement inspire students: More than a dozen Rhodes Scholars are among the University's alumni, along with a half-dozen Pulitzer Prize winners and the only person to win both the Pulitzer and the National Medal of Science. The University literary magazine *Black Warrior Review*, produced by graduate students, is counted in the nation's twenty most influential literary publications. The UA program in clinical psychology has a strong reputation nationally for graduating fine therapists and researchers. The College of Engineering was chosen recently by the National Science Foundation to join a select national coalition reshaping undergraduate engineering study to accommodate a rapidly changing industry.

Helping students reach their academic goals is a central focus of the UA Center for Teaching and Learning. The center staff equips new students with study skills that can make them successful; tutors students grappling with challenging subject matter; and maintains a library of video-taped lectures and an extensive assortment of self-paced learning materials. They help teaching assistants assess and improve their classroom

Crimson Tide football enjoys a championship tradition and legions of loyal fans.

Graduate fellows in engineering and management work full-time with the Harrison Division of General Motors in Tuscaloosa while pursuing advanced degrees at The University of Alabama.

skills and offer a special program through which learning-disabled individuals achieve equal access to University education.

Interpreting broadly its mission to "advance the intellectual and social condition of all the people of the state," the University is also committed to the state's economic development. In two decades the institution has offered direct development assistance to one-third of Alabama counties, resulting in nearly twelve thousand newly created jobs and an announced capital investment of more than $1.3 billion by 1992. Workforce-training programs of the University—and the quality of life in Tuscaloosa, to which the University contributes—were key factors in the Mercedes-Benz company's decision in 1993 to locate its first international plant in Tuscaloosa County. Through partnerships with firms like General Motors, the University has helped increase the state's productivity, drawing a new image of Alabama for the corporate world.

Several University of Alabama centers apply the academic quest for knowledge to the immediate needs of Alabama's citizens. The University's Small Business Development Center (SBDC) guides up-and-coming entrepreneurs toward successful business practices. Providing the most basic level of information transfer from the University to the business community, the center serves eight counties, reaching hundreds of clients each year through publications, seminars, and counseling.

Like the SBDC, the Alabama International Trade Center shares University resources with Alabama businesses interested in new markets. The trade center helps firms with international potential investigate their overseas options. The center staff meets companies' needs with practical market information to help them discover where to sell a product, who to sell it to, how to ship it, and how to find local trade partners. The trade center's periodic seminars, workshops, and trade missions abroad encourage successful international ventures by Alabama companies large and small.

Industrial clients exploring new products and manufacturing processes turn to the Bevill Center for Advanced Manufacturing Technology, located in Gadsden, Alabama. The Bevill Center teams UA and other resources to develop the sophisticated machinery and processes that lead to cost-effective manufacturing, and to create a workforce educated to run them. The center enjoys support from city and federal governments and agencies statewide; in return it enables Alabama companies to try out technologies and compete for bids that require more equipment and resources than they currently own. The Bevill Center is the flagship of the state's Centers of Technical Excellence network, which was created to provide a technology assistance base for state businesses, to provide education and training, and to generate jobs through entrepreneurial stimulation and support of industrial recruitment.

The Alabama Productivity Center, part of the College of Commerce and Business Administration, shares the Bevill Center's goal of helping Alabama firms improve their competitive position. The center addresses challenging productivity and quality problems that businesses may not have the time or internal resources to solve themselves. Through on-site research projects that bring UA faculty and students into the client companies, new techniques of productivity and quality improvement and management have reduced operating costs, improved product/process designs, and generated further knowledge.

While a steadily expanding industrial base makes up ever more of Alabama's economy, portions of the state remain rural and need resources to maintain their viability. Helping rural communities identify strengths they can use to secure their future is the UA Program for Rural Services and Research (PRSR). The program emphasizes all-around community development. University students involved in the program's rural health mission have built playgrounds, produced town histories, and conducted citizen surveys. Their activities have led to the creation of a dozen rural clinics and have helped communities win government support for health-enhancing projects like the modernizing of water systems. In addition to its healthcare efforts, the PRSR spurs local schools to an active role in rural redevelopment and independence. Its "Better Schools Building Better Communities" program, conducted with the Ford Foundation, has gained international notice while teaching skills for twentieth-century rural life, from running a combine to running a computer.

Urban and rural communities alike face a need to give youngsters the basic skills that are the foundation of all higher learning. Acting on a belief that education for the twenty-first century must be a seamless web from kindergarten to college and beyond, The University of Alabama today is enhancing its reputation as the "Capstone" of public education in Alabama. Student success at the University rests squarely on the learning experience provided by the public schools, so the institution's commitment to improving those schools is a natural outgrowth of its teaching mission.

Faculty of the UA College of Education lead the way, fostering excellence in new generations of K-12 teachers; developing new classroom technologies and strategies; providing *pro bono* consulting services to school districts; offering veteran teachers opportunities for professional growth; and participating fully in teacher-education and school-funding reform efforts. The Center for Communication and Educational Technology (CCET) is the newest UA division to reach out to public-

The University of Alabama's Capstone College of Nursing provides an excellent undergraduate education for the professional practice of nursing.

The University's faculty in aquatic biology is world renowned.

school students. CCET enriches middle- and high-school education with pioneering "distance learning" programs. Through the "Integrated Science" program, for instance, televised lessons featuring energetic and appealing teachers instill youth in 15 states and Canada with excitement about chemistry, physics, and other natural sciences. More than 300 schools and 75,000 students participate.

CCET also uses interactive video technology to offer rural high-school students unprecedented courses in anatomy, physiology, advanced geography, and Japanese language. Nearly 60 schools and their students have participated, and lives have been shaped by the expanded horizons the curricula provide. Other Alabama high school students have broadened their interests and knowledge by studying in summer honors programs or attending various

summer workshops and camps organized by the University.

Today's students need access to an emerging global marketplace. The University offers numerous pathways, from extensive language instruction, to international specialization in the undergraduate business degree, to overseas placement of student-teachers, to foreign exchange programs in 13 countries. A bachelor's degree in international studies and master's program in Latin American studies are offered; the University's research and training partnerships with Japanese and German industry create further opportunities for students. Hosting international students from some 70 nations, the University encourages an awareness of the world's great diversity.

The University of Alabama's seven libraries contain nearly three million volumes, as well as the latest information technologies. All parts of the campus are being linked to a broadband network through which students and staff have quick access to each other, to research resources, and to international computer networks, from their dorms, offices, even off-campus sites. In such information networking—as in its curricula, facilities, and student life—the University is steadily preparing for a new century whose realities will demand a campus that is flexible, efficient, and results-oriented. ❖

The Paul W. Bryant Conference Center

The Bryant Conference Center on the campus of The University of Alabama is one of the South's finest and most modern conference environments, and indeed, one of the finest university-owned and operated conference centers in the country. It is the ideal environment for conferences and meetings of all types.

The adjoining Sheraton Inn Capstone, Paul W. Bryant Museum, and Alumni Hall place The University of Alabama at the top of the list nationally for conference locations. Since its opening in 1987, the Bryant Center has experienced outstanding success in fulfilling its mission of enhancing academic and public service opportunities for both the University and community at large. The Center has been host to numerous local, state, regional, national and international meetings extending the resources of the University to an ever widening constituency.

The Sheraton Inn Capstone offers 152 spacious, elegantly furnished guest rooms. Each room is equipped with study space and a closed-circuit television link from the conference center that can be used for pre-conference information or a live feed during the actual conference.

The Paul W. Bryant Museum of football traces the Alabama tradition through its roster of legendary coaches—Wallace Wade, Frank Thomas, and Paul "Bear" Bryant—then chronicles the contemporary careers of Ray Perkins, Bill Curry, and Gene Stallings. Photographs, memorabilia, and audio-visual displays put you in touch with the Alabama men who "writ her name in crimson flame."

Designed for adult continuing education and public service, the Bryant Center offers both university and community groups an ideal meeting environment within a university setting. The Bryant Center features advanced media facilities and equipment to enhance the learning experience. Staffed with full-time media technicians, the media center offers conference audio-taping and high-speed duplication, video-taping and editing, down-link audio- and video-teleconferencing, closed-circuit television distribution, in addition to the more traditional audio-visual meeting needs.

Meeting rooms are designed with the utmost in flexibility and variety. The Center has a total of fourteen meeting rooms including luxurious executive boardrooms, tiered seminar rooms, spacious classrooms, and a 10,000 square feet multi-purpose auditorium with the capacity to accommodate up to 1,200 conferees.

The interior environment is especially conducive to support the conference experience. Special care has been taken in selecting public and conference room furniture for comfort and design. The conference rooms feature natural as well as both incandescent and fluorescent lighting. All rooms feature individual climate controls, acoustic wall treatment, white marker boards, electronic projection screens, voice reinforcement, and ring-down communication to the conference concierge. Public space includes registration areas, spacious lobbies, and ample hallways.

The Bryant Center offers full conference management support with a team of professionals equipped to handle all aspects of conference and meeting management. The staff is keenly aware of the need for attention to detail in planning and conducting your conference or meeting. No task is too big, no detail too small to merit their attention. ❖

The Paul W. Bryant Conference Center and the adjoining Sheraton Inn Capstone provide an ideal environment for meetings for up to 1,200 conferees.

The Bryant Conference Center's fourteen meeting rooms range in size and scope from executive board rooms to tiered seminar rooms to a 10,000 sq. ft. multi-purpose auditorium.

Stillman College

"**S**ervice to students" is the motto that governs the activities and programs at Stillman College, a historically black, four-year, liberal arts college in the heart of Tuscaloosa.

With a student/teacher ratio of about 15-to-1, the approximately 1,000 students at Stillman College enjoy a healthy measure of personalized attention. The focus is very much on the individual, and the college tries hard to maintain the sense that a student's time at Stillman is, in essence, a personal journey of discovery and enrichment.

In keeping with the attention to quality seen in many American businesses and orga-

nizations, Stillman College employs the Continuous Quality Improvement system as a model for the entire college community to live by—with students, the college's primary customers, being the main beneficiary of a value system that strives always for the best.

"At Stillman College, learning is neither the storing up of a reservoir of knowledge nor the passive submission to the ministration of a faculty. It is, instead, an active and immensely difficult undertaking by each individual. It aims at the maximum development of certain intellectual skills, certain survival skills, certain social skills, certain spiritual skills, which are known to us and the world over as the liberal arts."

"It aims as well at the acquisition of certain understandings for which men have sought in all ages. These are the fundamental understandings of self. First of all and above all, it aims to help you know yourself and to gain an understanding of your fellowman, the global world around us, and the sovereign God who guides our destinies."

Those are the words of Stillman College President Dr. Cordell Wynn. Along with his duties at the college, Dr. Wynn has also been,

for concurrent terms, Chairman of the National Association for Equal Opportunity in Higher Education and Chairman of the Presidents of Member Institutions of the United Negro College Fund. In those positions, Dr. Wynn has served at the head of two of the most prominent black organizations in the world. The United Negro College Fund supports 41 private, predominately black institutions. The goals of the National Association for Equal Opportunity in Higher Education, a nonprofit organization representing the interests of 117 historically and predominately black colleges and universities, call for growth in student enrollment at historically black colleges, an increase in African Americans with doctoral degrees, increased cultural diversity, and more awareness and support of black institutions.

But Dr. Wynn has had his greatest success at the helm of Tuscaloosa's Stillman College. Enrollment is up. The faculty and staff are first-rate. And the students have a clear sense that here is a college that understands its mission is to educate and enrich lives.

Stillman College is in the front ranks of America's historically black colleges and universities. A four-year, fully accredited, co-educational liberal arts institution, Stillman is accredited by the Southern Association of Colleges and Schools, and the Alabama State

Stillman College is a historically black, four-year, liberal arts college in the heart of Tuscaloosa.

Dr. Cordell Wynn is a native of Eatonton, Georgia. Under his leadership, Stillman has prospered and continues to see growth in all areas of campus life.

Department of Education, and affiliated with The Presbyterian Church (U.S.A.).

Founded by Dr. Charles A. Stillman in 1876, with the guiding motto "Enter to learn and depart to serve," Stillman College has had a varied and fascinating institutional history. The founder, Dr. Stillman, became pastor of the First Presbyterian Church in Tuscaloosa in 1870. He later founded the Tuscaloosa Institute, a school that educated young blacks interested in entering the ministry. For 17 years he served as superintendent of the institute, and in 1895, the Presbyterian Church honored him by renaming the school Stillman Institute. Later still its name was changed to Stillman College.

Over the decades, Stillman has been, in turn, a seminary, high school, farming operation, junior college, trade school, and school of nursing. It became a four-year liberal arts college in 1949, and was first accredited four years later in 1953.

Today, 17 tradition-rich buildings dot the 100-acre campus. About 52 full-time and 11 part-time instructors teach the diverse and motivated student body.

A student who matriculates at Stillman can choose from a broad range of major areas of study. These include biology; business; chemistry; communications; computer science; elementary education; English; health, physical education, and recreation; history; international studies; mathematics; music; physics; recreation management; religion and philosophy; and sociology. The communications program has experienced plenty of growth at the college in recent years, but the largest enrollment is made up of students pursuing degrees in business administration.

Students interested in following a professional career path can choose from the following pre-professional programs at Stillman: engineering, law, medicine, ministry, and social work. For specialized interests, there's even a certificate program in gerontology.

In order to extend the academic reach of the institution, Stillman College has also entered into cooperative agreements with other colleges and universities. With the University of Alabama, Stillman has cooperative programs in engineering, nursing, ROTC, social work, and other disciplines. Allied health courses are offered in cooperation with the University of Alabama at Birmingham. Other programs are offered in medicine (Meharry Medical School, Nashville); law (St. John's University School of Law, Jamaica, New York), Student Exchange (Alma College, Alma, Michigan); the Faculty Resources Network (New York University, New York); and through the Black College Telecommunications Network.

Another special program at Stillman College is the Stillman Management Institute, a program of study followed by adult working students age 25 years or older. Unlike other nontraditional student programs, students in the institute are grouped together as a real class. People begin the 17-month program as a unit and graduate as a unit, which leads to a deeper bond among students and a more well-rounded academic experience.

Stillman is a residential college with 85 to 90 percent of students coming from the state of Alabama. In the 1993 freshman class, students originated from a total of 22 different states, though Alabama had the lion's share of the representation. The college has active alumni chapters in cities such as Atlanta, Chicago, and Washington, D.C. These chapters serve as excellent recruitment centers for out-of-state students.

Wherever the students come from, there is a tangible bond that develops among the people—students, faculty, and staff—that make up Stillman College. This sense of belonging to a family of like-minded and similarly inspired individuals, the Stillman College Family, has led to tremendous growth and development in the past and wonderful promise for the future of the college. ❖

Each year, Stillman gives its new students a formal welcome to the campus, with its matriculation convocation and formal opening.

Students at Stillman can choose from a broad range of major areas of study.

Shelton State Community College

Shelton State offers exceptional training in a wide variety of occupational fields and academic disciplines including health care and sciences.

A two-year educational institution that focuses on the needs of students in order to lead them to academic or career success, Shelton State Community College has an exemplary record of providing excellent academic learning and superior business training.

Shelton State has been progressive in the development of a number of educational advances such as Distance Learning and Training for Business and Industry. Enrollment at Shelton State tops 7,000 students, and the school is the largest feeder institution of any two-year college to the student body of The University of Alabama.

The components of Shelton State are the Academic Services and Technical/ Occupational Services Divisions, which coordinate all certificate, diploma, and transfer education; the Alabama State Fire College, which trains Alabama's fire fighters for municipalities and volunteer agencies; the C.A. Fredd Campus, a traditionally black college that merged with Shelton State and expanded Shelton's technical/occupational programs; and the Alabama Water Resources Training Center, which trains water and wastewater treatment operators.

Over seventy different programs of study are offered by Shelton State. A majority of those program areas prepare students for jobs in a technical, trade, or service industry in today's workplace. The balance of the programs of study are designed to prepare students for the academic requirements that will follow their transfer to a four-year institution.

Shelton State offers exceptional training in a wide variety of occupational fields and academic disciplines. Programs of study include nursing; technical careers in fields such as air conditioning and refrigeration, electronics, machine tool technology, and fire science; trades such as automotive mechanics, truck driving, landscaping, cabinetmaking, cosmetology, and commercial art; health careers in such fields as wellness and fitness management; allied health careers such as emergency medical technician; office careers such as office administration, and management and supervision, and numerous others.

Examples of Shelton's cutting edge philosophy of developing programs that speak to real-world concerns and opportunities are easy to identify. Shelton's Machine Technology Program trains students in computer-aided manufacturing, preparing them for the modern production facility. A computer-assisted instructional lab provides a state-of-the-art learning environment for students in the Electronics Technology Program; the latest AutoCad software enhances the lab options for students in the Drafting Program.

Established by the Alabama State Board of Education on January 1, 1979, Shelton State Community College was created by combining two existing institutions: Shelton State Technical College, which was established in 1952, and the Tuscaloosa branch of Brewer State Junior College, which, though headquartered in Fayette County, began operating a branch school in Tuscaloosa back in 1972.

Over the years, Shelton State has developed an excellent rapport with the community, which has led to its large and growing enrollment. It also maintains excellent relations with its major four-year college neighbor, The University of Alabama. Shelton maintains a close working relationship with the University through curriculum coordination and academic connections. The core

A computer-assisted instructional lab provides a state-of-the-art learning environment to prepare students for modern production facilities.

An Alabama Fire College instructor prepares student fire fighters before attacking a flammable liquids fire. As a division of Shelton State Community College, the Fire College provides a variety of training courses for Alabama's 30,000 municipal, industrial and volunteer fire fighters. Classes are held at the Fire College facilities in Tuscaloosa and throughout the state.

curriculum offered at Shelton makes it very efficient for students to get an excellent start and a strong college academic base. When Shelton students move on to a four- year college, they are well prepared. In fact, Shelton State students who transfer to The University of Alabama graduate at a greater frequency rate and with a higher grade point average than four-year students who enter the university as freshmen.

A major innovation at Shelton State has been the development of Distance Learning, an important program that involves the microwave or telephone transmission of a teacher-led class to a remote site far from the Tuscaloosa campus. Although the class may be taking place in the normal classroom on campus, students at off-campus locations can technologically tune-in and gain the same knowledge and insight into the material as traditional students. Distance learning is a creative use of technology put to work in education for the good of students. Many experts believe this type of learning is part of the answer to the need for quality education in economically deprived, rural areas.

Shelton plans to expand its distance learning applications into surrounding counties, including Bibb County High School and the soon to be constructed Bibb County Correctional Facility. In fact, building plans for this facility include designated space for at least seven Distance Learning Classrooms and six computer labs. Currently, classes are beamed to a site at a housing project in a town over thirty miles away from the main campus. Shelton State is the second institution of higher learning in the United States to offer courses off-campus at sites in a federally funded housing project.

Another important aspect of learning at Shelton State Community College is the institution's much-admired program of Training for Business and Industry. The school works with area businesses to develop tailor-made training programs for the company's personnel. Again, many experts in the fields of education, workplace training, and business productivity and competitiveness believe these kinds of partnerships between educational institutions and businesses are key in realizing greater work productivity and enhanced job abilities.

The Training for Business and Industry group might develop training programs for companies based on any one of a number of different needs. For example, a program on management skills might be offered to one client company. Or the focus might be placed on learning how to build teams in the work environment. Or the training might take place on a more remedial level with a basic reading program for workers.

Shelton State's Training for Business and Industry Program is highly regarded in the business and economic development community; in fact, it was named as part of the consortium of institutions identified to provide training or retraining for the work force at the new Mercedes-Benz plant to be located in nearby Vance, Alabama.

Shelton State offers opportunities for customized training for business and industry.

While the school is a complex and growing institution, all of the many varied educational programs at Shelton State are designed with one purpose in mind: to offer the West Alabama area the very best in community college learning.

The most exciting news for the coming years is that Shelton State Community College will begin construction of a new comprehensive community college campus four miles south of the city of Tuscaloosa. All the different educational functions will be combined at the site of the new campus. This state-of-the-art facility will be the first new two-year college constructed in Alabama in over two decades. The new campus will feature the latest in learning technology and offer the citizens of West Alabama the very best in learning environments. ❖

Tuscaloosa Convention & Visitors Bureau

Tuscaloosa is a city of exciting fairs, festivals, and theatrical flair. Courtesy of Convention Bureau.

The marketing arm for the City of Tuscaloosa, the award winning Tuscaloosa Convention & Visitors Bureau creates marketing and business opportunities for the city's visitor industry.

Area hotels, motels, restaurants, retail stores, tourist attractions, and recreational facilities benefit from the work done by the Convention & Visitors Bureau. The bureau's job is to attract visitors. Conventioneers, tourists, outdoors enthusiasts, and group tours are all targets for the bureau's diverse marketing efforts.

The bureau is housed in the gracefully restored Jemison-Van de Graaff Mansion on Tuscaloosa's Greensboro Avenue, which serves as an elegant reminder of Tuscaloosa's past. That past is one of the things that people come to Tuscaloosa to experience. There are 22 antebellum homes in the area. Still the traditions, architecture, and history of the American South is only part of the attractions people visiting Tuscaloosa can enjoy. The Jemison-Van de Graaff Mansion will house the Tuscaloosa Visitor Information Center in 1994.

Tuscaloosa is used to visitors. For years the city has hosted major college football teams and their fans for University of Alabama home games. The area's hospitality industry is adept at playing the host. With plenty of hotel rooms, good restaurants, and exciting nightlife, Tuscaloosa is a city tailor-made for visitors to enjoy. It's a safe community with plenty of opportunities for wholesome family fun. The rural parts of the county are a wonderland for hunters and hikers alike. The area's lakes and rivers hold the promise of glorious times on the water for anglers and boaters alike.

Outdoor attractions such as Lake Lurleen State Park, Deerlick Creek Campground, and Tannehill Historical State Park are wonderful places for families and campers.

Moundville Archaeological Park is an ancient place of beauty and mystery, a prehistoric Indian settlement that had more than 3,000 inhabitants between 1000 and 1500 A.D. It is famous for the quality of its artifacts and the cultural importance of its ceremonial mounds.

Museums in Tuscaloosa are extraordinary and extraordinarily diverse. The Paul W. Bryant Museum brings to life the accomplishments of college football's greatest coach and over 100 years of football history. Kentuck Museum in Northport exhibits contemporary and traditional crafts, fine art, and folk art. A third major museum in Tuscaloosa is the Alabama State Museum of Natural History located in a 1909 Classical Revival building on the University of Alabama campus. Right downtown in Tuscaloosa is the Children's Hands-On Museum where every exhibit is a fascinating learning experience for children.

In addition to terrific museums, Tuscaloosa is home to impressive art collections: The Warner Collection at the National Headquarters of Gulf States Paper Corporation is renowned as one of the finest collections of art in the United States Additional works in the Warner Collection are on display at the Mildred Warner House. Other cultural attractions include the Garland Hall Art Gallery at the University of Alabama, Artists' Alley in downtown Northport, and the Frank Moody Music Building on campus.

The city has also preserved the city's African-American heritage with sites like Stillman College, founded in 1876 to educate black ministers; Murphy-Collins Home, one of the city's greatest black leader's home; and Greenwood Cemetery, the resting place of many of Tuscaloosa's important African-American citizens.

For sports-minded visitors, the biggest game in town is the football team of the University of Alabama, frequently the NCAA national champion; the women's gymnastics team is also a national champ. Outside the realm of the NCAA, the city has also hosted two national bass fishing championships. Greyhound racing takes place at nearby Greenetrack.

Tuscaloosa is a city of festivals including a major southern arts and crafts show at Kentuck Festival, the annual Cityfest in the fall, Heritage Week in the spring, and a celebration of Japan in the Sakura Festival.

But whether or not there is a special event, Tuscaloosa is a great place to visit. A message that the Tuscaloosa Convention & Visitors Bureau spreads with style and marketing savvy. ❖

The restored Jemison-Van de Graaff Mansion will serve as the future Visitor Information Center. Courtesy of Convention Bureau.

Tuscaloosa Academy

An independent, college-preparatory, coed day school, Tuscaloosa Academy offers the premier private educational experience in the Tuscaloosa area.

Tuscaloosa Academy prepares students—from pre-school through the 12th grade—for success in academics and in the world beyond through a well-rounded curriculum, top-flight instructors, and a strong institutional belief in the importance of a quality education.

Located on a beautiful 33-acre site just north of the Black Warrior River in one of Tuscaloosa's finest residential areas, Tuscaloosa Academy enrolls approximately 500 students. When the school was opened in 1966, enrollment was 113 students. The academy's budget in 1967 was $100,000; today the school operates on a budget in excess of $1 million a year. Over the years, almost 100 percent of Tuscaloosa Academy graduates have attended college.

Physically the school's campus is an attractive collection of buildings, playing fields, and beautiful wooded areas.

Fully accredited by the Southern Association of Colleges and Schools, Tuscaloosa Academy educates a diverse student body which enjoys a 12-to-1 student/teacher ratio. An active and involved group of alumni and parents adds to the school's excellent esprit de corps. Many of the instructors hold master's degrees, and the Headmaster has earned his doctorate. Such strong academic credentials and background lead to an unparalleled educational experience for students.

The curriculum is designed to meet the needs of individual students in a college-preparatory environment. In addition, there are advanced-placement classes in many disciplines, offering students academic challenges and a chance to receive college credit.

One unique aspect of the school's curriculum is the academy's strong program in English as a Second Language, which accommodates international students whose parents often work for the University of Alabama or such local international companies as JVC or Mercedes-Benz.

Tuscaloosa Academy is made up of three divisions: the Pre-School, the Lower School, and the Upper School. The Pre-School division, using the best combination of early childhood, child development, and Montessori methods of instruction, develops skills for later academic success along with a sense of discovery and awareness. The Pre-School program is for children aged two and one-half to six years, and parents may choose half-day, full-day, or extended-day curricula. Students are enrolled in multiple-age groupings, though a single-age, five-year-old kindergarten program is also available.

The Lower School at Tuscaloosa Academy consists of students in grades 1 to 6. Academic emphasis is placed on the fundamentals of reading, math, writing, social studies, and science. Students begin studying a foreign language in first grade, and their educational experience is supplemented by courses in computer science, art, music, and physical education.

The Upper School is for students in grades 7 to 12. Students are exposed to a classic liberal arts education with an emphasis on developing independent thinking and communication skills. The small classes and dedication of the instructors allow for a great deal of individualized attention, and the college-preparatory curriculum prepares students for the rigors of university study.

Another important aspect of student life at Tuscaloosa Academy is the athletic and extracurricular activities program. The school has had many successes in athletics over the years; the vast majority of Upper School students are active in sports. Extracurricular activities also afford students the opportunity to explore their talents and interests.

Both the academic curriculum and the tenor of life at Tuscaloosa Academy combine to produce well-rounded students prepared to meet the challenges and opportunities they will face in the world. ❖

Tuscaloosa Academy's college-preparatory curriculum prepares students for the rigors of university study. Photo by Barry Fikes.

Tuscaloosa Academy educates a diverse student body which enjoys a 12-to-1 student/teacher ratio. Photo by Barry Fikes.

Pace Learning Systems

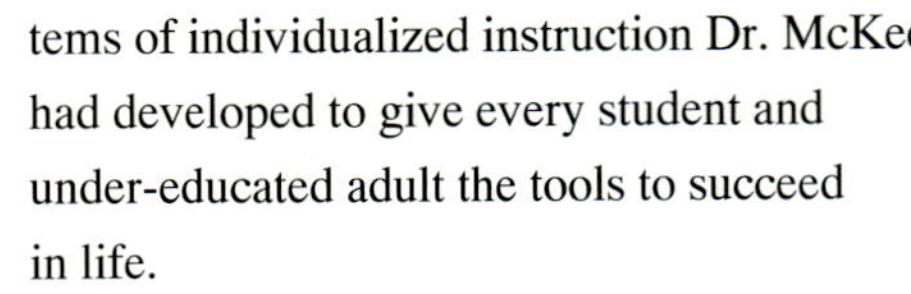

More than 25 years ago the founder of PACE Learning Systems designed the first fully integrated educational/instructional system for efficient, individualized learning. Today, more than a quarter-century later, at-risk young people are finding new hope in school, and adults who have lost hope of meaningful employment are seeing their promise reborn—thanks to PACE.

PACE Learning Systems was founded in 1977 by Dr. John M. McKee, a psychologist who had spent many years studying the root causes of school failure, crime, delinquency, and mental health disorders. The company was created to disseminate the unique systems of individualized instruction Dr. McKee had developed to give every student and under-educated adult the tools to succeed in life.

PACE Learning Systems provides educational institutions nationwide—public schools, adult education programs, training centers, and correctional facilities—with powerfully effective systems to teach basic skills in reading, math, language arts, and employability. While PACE systems—developed at the company's Tuscaloosa headquarters—are in place throughout the nation (the famous California prison at San Quentin uses PACE in its academic and training programs), the primary marketing area is in the southeastern United States.

The hallmarks of the systems are individualized, self-paced learning and instructional materials that are designed and organized to allow for quick mastery of the subject areas. Whether they are high-schoolers who are failing in the traditional classroom setting or adults trying to overcome illiteracy, students utilizing the PACE systems work individually in an academic setting with the teacher or instructor acting as a coach or mentor. All materials are designed to be digested in small increments so that the students have a heightened sense of actually learning and a great deal of positive feedback and frequent reinforcement.

When a student is starting out with a PACE system, the first priority is to determine his or her strengths and weaknesses in each subject area. The system is then tailored to meet the specific needs of each student, so that learning occurs with greater efficiency and ease. PACE Learning Systems is committed to providing "fail-safe learning" for all students. Its materials and products are structured in such a way as to <u>guarantee</u> the success of each and every student who uses them. This philosophy is best typified by the PACE motto . . . "Nothing teaches like success!"

PACE's instructional programs are designed to meet a broad variety of needs within a diverse student population. The programs, both print-based and computerized, include instruction in math, language, and reading from the middle school through the GED level. PACE also makes available an employability program that teaches students how to get a job and succeed in the workplace. Other instructional programs include life skills, applied mathematics for the building and construction trades, and a literacy program to teach non-readers how to read.

Dr. John McKee is now retired from the daily operations of PACE, though he continues to conduct important research into programs to prevent dropouts and school failure. His wife, Dr. Susan McKee, is now company president.

Today, PACE systems are in place in thousands of different educational settings, and they are yielding tremendous success stories. In Ventura County, California, PACE is being utilized in a program for at-risk youths. It is the backbone of the top nonresidential educational center program in the nation—Alabama's Community Intensive Treatment for Youth (C.I.T.Y.)—and improves the self-worth of youthful offenders in South Carolina. And, in an Alabama prison, PACE is teaching inmates to read.

A new learning center is in the works at the company headquarters to showcase to the public the PACE system of learning. The future holds more success stories yet to be written for this Alabama-developed, educational product. ❖

The Individualized Reading Instructional System (IRIS) is a developmental reading program for non-reading adults.

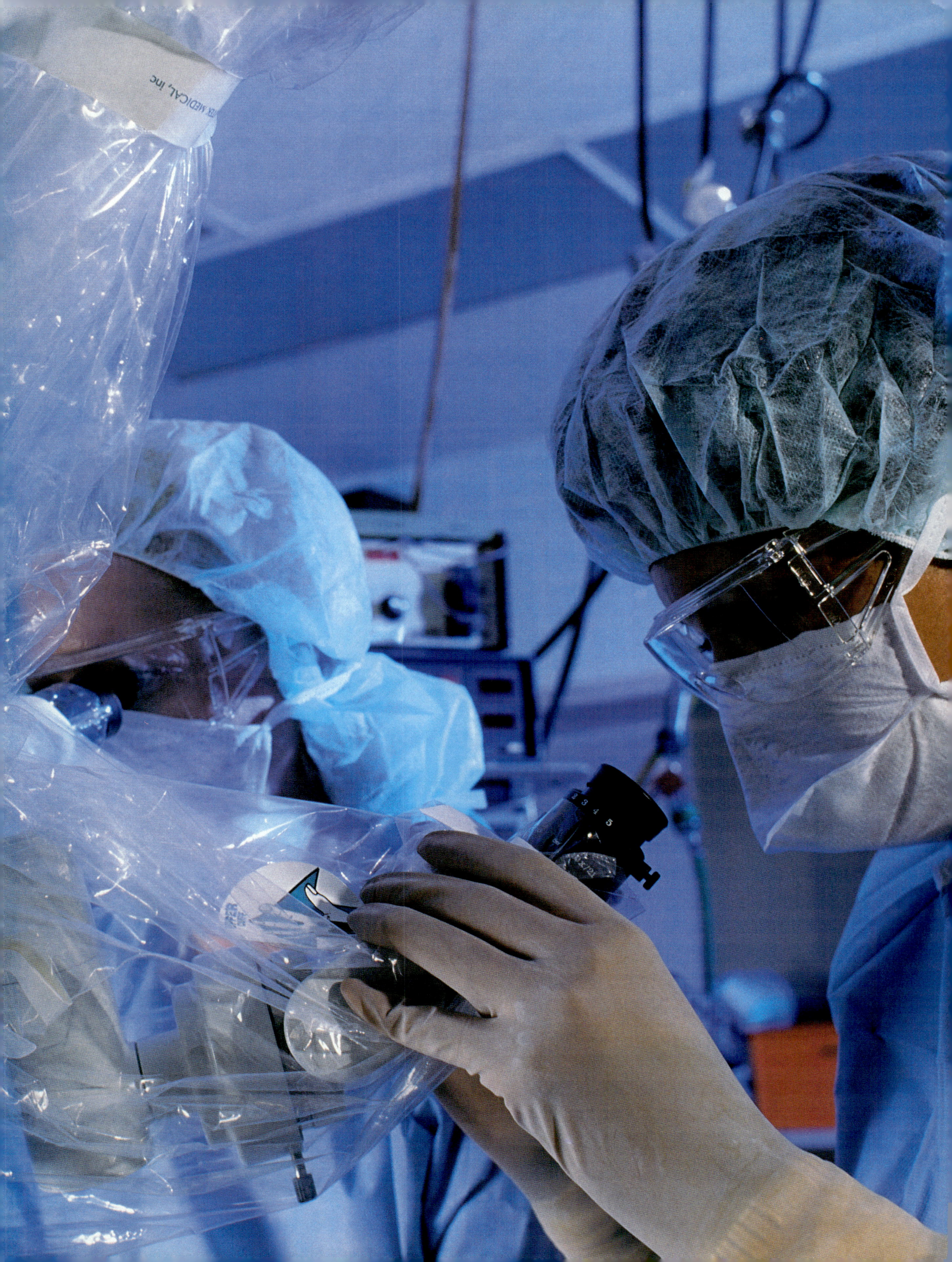

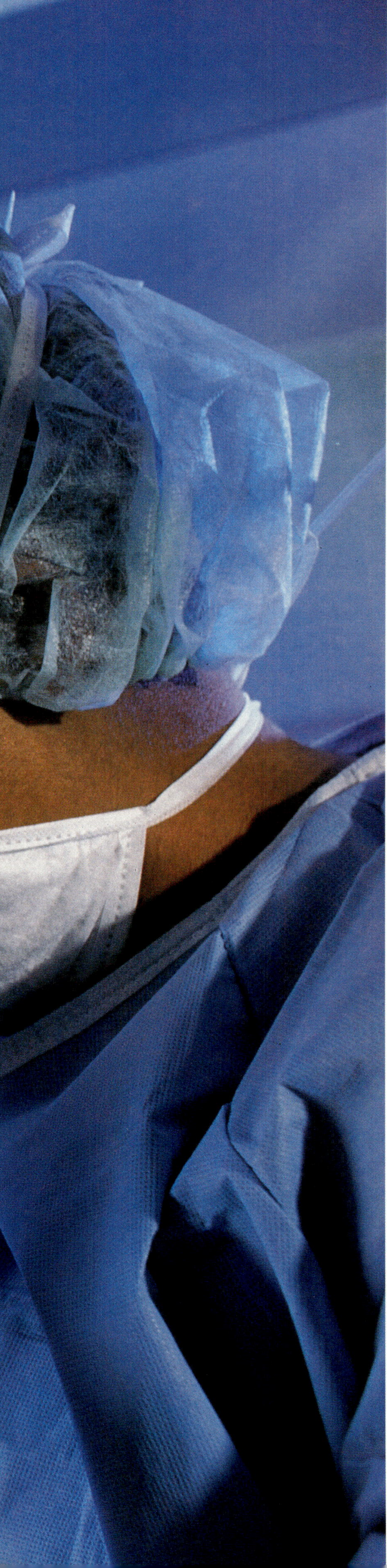

Chapter

Health Care

DCH Healthcare Authority

Under local ownership and leadership, the DCH Healthcare Authority has continually evolved to offer advanced caring to West Alabama.

Tuscaloosa County's locally owned health care system began 70 years ago as a tiny infirmary. The infirmary became a small hospital, which in turn grew into a bustling community hospital. In response to growth in the community and advances in medicine, the hospital expanded its services and its service area to become a regional medical center.

DCH now stands for the DCH Healthcare Authority, a health-care system of several hospitals and health-care services serving a 10-county area of more than 250,000 persons.

The DCH Healthcare Authority is the largest employer in Tuscaloosa County. Its services attract thousands of patients from surrounding counties, boosting the area's economy. But most important, the DCH Healthcare Authority provides a more comprehensive range of services than you'll find in any area of comparable size and population in the South. And DCH provides these services to all those in need, regardless of their ability to pay.

DCH began as a single hospital in the city of Tuscaloosa in 1923. A 12-bed infirmary opened in 1916, but it soon proved inadequate to serve the needs of the growing community. In those days, building and equipping a hospital cost about $100,000—a staggering sum for a small city. But the community pulled together to launch a fund-raising campaign for a new hospital. A bond issue raised $50,000, the public gave an equal amount, and the 50-bed Druid City Hospital opened its doors on March 25, 1923.

In 1950, the community again supported its local hospital by approving a one-cent

The DCH Healthcare Authority continues a tradition of community owned, advance caring.

sales tax to fund construction of a new Druid City Hospital on University Boulevard.

As the community grew and as medicine developed new procedures, DCH grew in size and services to meet the needs of an expanding population. By 1976, Druid City Hospital had 658 beds, making it the third largest hospital in the state.

In 1982, the State of Alabama passed a law to help public hospitals care for uninsured and underinsured citizens and compete with private hospitals. To ensure the viability of publicly owned health care in Tuscaloosa County, the board was restructured under the law as the DCH Healthcare Authority. Shortly thereafter, Druid City Hospital changed its name to DCH Regional Medical Center.

Today, the DCH Healthcare Authority operates a health care system that includes DCH Regional Medical Center, Northport

DCH Regional Medical Center is the third largest hospital in Alabama.

Hospital-DCH, DCH Rehabilitation Pavilion and Fayette County Hospital and Nursing Home.

DCH Regional Medical Center is the cornerstone of the DCH system. The Regional Medical Center has the size, the staff and the scope of services physicians need to serve patients from throughout the region who require acute and specialized care.

Physicians representing every medical specialty and most sub-specialties practice at the Medical Center. As a regional medical center, DCH operates specialty units for pediatrics, orthopaedics, cancer and cardiology, as well as the region's most advanced trauma center and intensive care units. These units are backed by a variety of sophisticated diagnostic equipment, such as computerized tomography and magnetic resonance imaging.

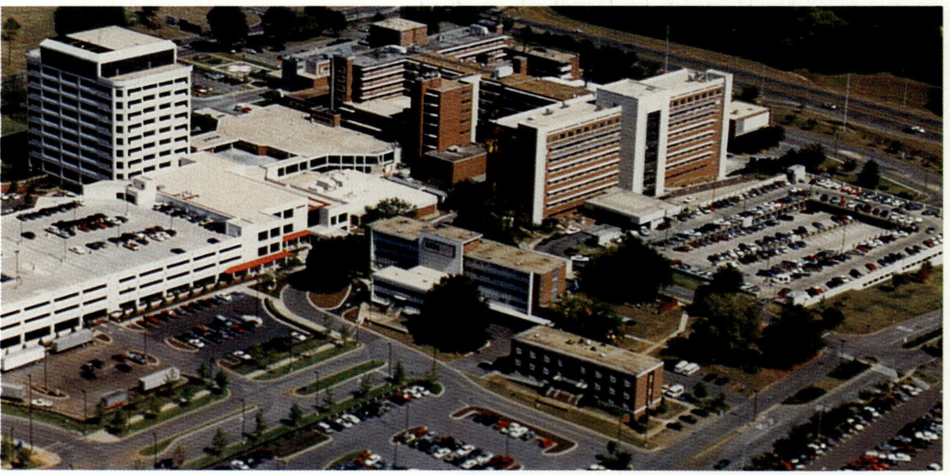

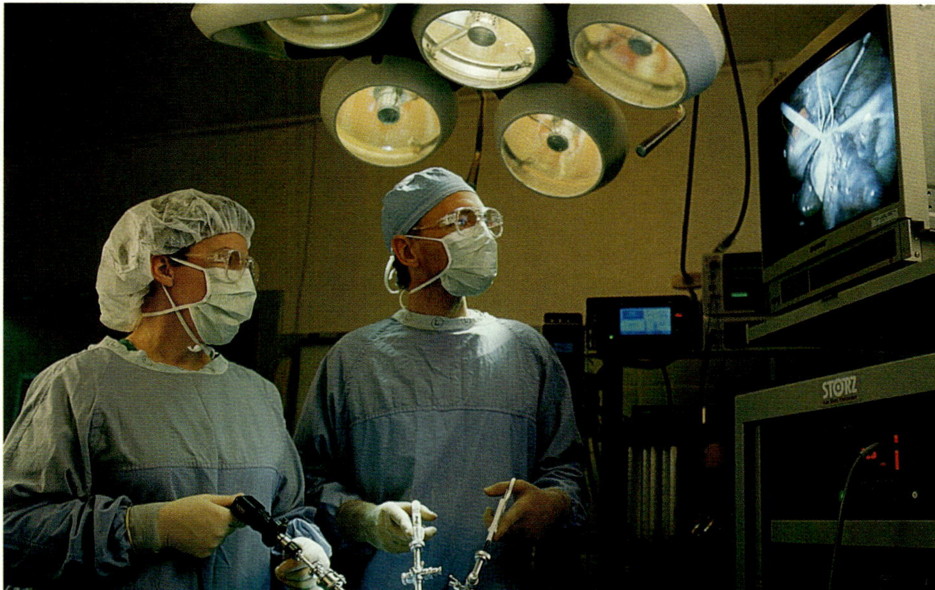

Laparoscopic surgery, performed here at Fayette County Hospital and Nursing Home, is one of the advanced procedures available at DCH Healthcare Authority facilities.

Equipped with an indoor track and pool, the Family Fitness Center at Northport Hospital-DCH features a variety of fitness programs to keep families healthy.

Physicians at DCH use many of the latest surgical techniques, including microsurgery, laser surgery and laparoscopic surgery that requires less recovery time.

From the introduction of open-heart surgery in West Alabama in 1978, to today's development of procedures that can dissolve blood clots without surgery, physicians at DCH Regional Medical Center offer patients many of the latest advances in cardiovascular care. At the DCH Cancer Treatment Center, physician specialists in hematology, medical oncology and radiation oncology lead a dedicated team of nurses and technicians who provide advanced treatment and emotional support.

New parents find a rewarding birthing experience at the Medical Center's Labor and Delivery Unit, along with the peace of mind that comes from knowing that one of Alabama's most advanced neonatal intensive care units is at DCH.

Many procedures that once required an overnight stay in the hospital can now be performed in a single day, saving time and money. The DCH Outpatient Center offers the region's most comprehensive range of services in a private and personalized setting designed for patient convenience.

Other services available through the DCH Healthcare Authority include the Regional Dialysis Center, Home Care Agency of DCH and the DCH Speech and Hearing Clinic.

Northport Hospital-DCH, which joined the DCH system in 1992, is a full-service community hospital with services as diverse and up-to-date as laser surgery and diagnostic computerized tomography. The emergency department serves the community's needs with skilled response to illness and injury, while a dedicated Sports Medicine Center brings together physicians, physical therapists and athletic trainers dedicated to returning every kind of athlete—from scholastic to weekend—to their potential.

A major emphasis at Northport-DCH is the Women's Pavilion, a center of excellence dedicated to the health of women from adolescence through menopause. The hospital's maternity and childbirth facilities are located in the Women's Pavilion, which offers Labor/Delivery/Recovery/Postpartum Rooms where families can enjoy the birth experience in a comfortable, home-like atmosphere. Families are also comforted by the knowledge that the staff offers one-on-one care and each is cross-trained to work in the neonatal intensive care unit if the need arises.

The commitment to families at Northport Hospital-DCH doesn't end with the childbirth experience. The Family Fitness Center, which features an indoor track and pool, offers wellness and aerobics classes, screenings and special programs to keep families fit and healthy.

The DCH Rehabilitation Pavilion uses the latest advances in rehabilitative care to help patients with spinal cord injuries, head injuries, strokes or other neurological or orthopaedic disorders return to independence.

A team approach to rehabilitation has led to a success rate that finds 85 percent of patients returning home with increased independence. This success rate is among the highest of any rehabilitation facility in the country. One reason for this success is Easy Street, a treatment area that simulates various community settings. On Easy Street patients practice skills they'll need when they return to the community. DCH was the second facility in the nation to use this advanced concept.

The Acute Long-Term Care Unit is one of only 120 in the country, and the only one in the state dedicated to working with ventilator-dependent patients until they can breathe on their own and move on to additional levels of rehabilitation.

Fayette County Hospital and Nursing Home is one of the state's most successful rural hospitals. Since it became affiliated with the DCH Healthcare Authority in 1984, Fayette County Hospital has offered the residents of Fayette County sophisticated diagnostic equipment, surgical techniques and specialty clinics. With advanced mammography equipment, computerized tomography, ultrasound and a nuclear medicine department, Fayette County Hospital is as well-equipped as many larger, urban hospitals. Physician specialists regularly come to Fayette County to see local residents. Specialty clinics include oncology, cardiology, urology, neurology, orthopedics, ophthalmology and plastic surgery. The Regional Dialysis Center of DCH also operates a satellite clinic in Fayette. A 100-plus-bed nursing home facility on site is fully accredited and licensed for intermediate and skilled nursing care. Care at the Fayette County facility is augmented by a home health agency that visits more than 1,000 patients a month.

Seventy years ago, the people of Tuscaloosa made a commitment to care for its health care needs with a hospital owned by the people. The DCH Healthcare Authority is proud to continue that tradition of community-owned, advanced caring. ❖

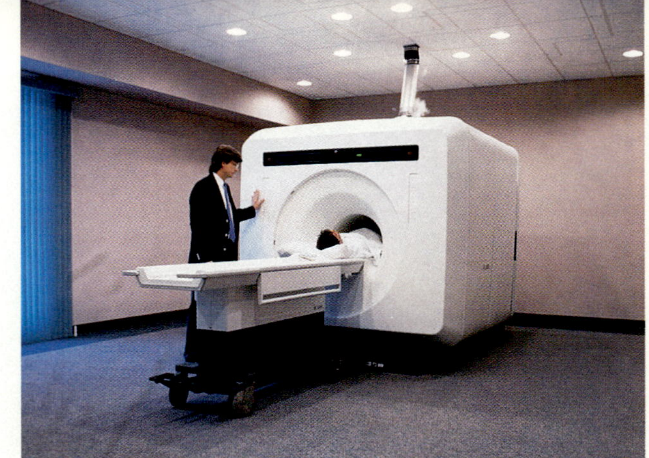

The Radiology Clinic offers a full spectrum of the latest in advanced medical imaging technology.

The Radiology Clinic

Dignity, Privacy, and Confidentiality! These factors were top priorities when the radiologists planned and designed their new radiology facility to serve the Tuscaloosa and West Alabama area. The Radiology Clinic was founded in the 1940s by Dr. William D. Anderson, and the Clinic has continued to provide excellence in medical imaging by certified personnel at reasonable cost for 50 years.

While the mission of The Radiology Clinic has remained constant, the tools at the disposal of the radiologists have become even more advanced and capable. State of the art equipment, medically effective procedures, and highly trained personnel at The Radiology Clinic allow for the detection of medical problems at early stages when intervention and treatment have the best possible chances for success.

The Radiology Clinic offers a **full spectrum** of the latest in advanced medical imaging technology. General diagnostic radiology such as chest x-rays, ultrasounds, noninvasive vascular studies, nuclear medicine studies, computerized tomography (CT), magnetic resonance imaging (MRI), and mammographies are performed at the Clinic.

Mammography is a very important part of The Radiology Clinic. The utmost care was taken in designing the mammography suite at the Clinic. Each woman's privacy and confidentiality are protected by providing a separate waiting area, private examination rooms, and individual and private dressing rooms. The mammography program is certified by the American College of Radiology, the national accrediting organization for radiology. The radiologic technologists who perform mammographies are additionally certified by the American College of Radiology and have more than 60 years of combined experience in patient care. Prompt reporting to each patient's physician is assured so that diagnosis and treatment of any breast disease can begin as early as possible.

The Clinic serves patients from West Alabama. These people are drawn by the reputation of the Clinic's physicians and technologists. Appointments are kept with close attention to the schedules of patients. Reports on diagnostic work are promptly forwarded to attending physicians and the Clinic's administrative staff members are always available and glad to help with insurance forms or billing questions.

The Clinic is easily accessible off McFarland Boulevard, a main Tuscaloosa thoroughfare and is set back from the road to assure a measure of privacy. Separate access roads allow for easy maneuvering away from congested roadways. The Clinic was designed with ample, ground-level parking for easy entry.

Once a patient is inside the building the design of the facility allows easy access to diagnostic areas, to the main lobby, and to exit doors. Separate waiting areas are provided for mammography, general diagnostic studies, CT, and MRI. These separate waiting areas were designed to provide a comfortable and receptive waiting area as opposed to a vast, open lobby or waiting room. Low lighting and soft colors also add to the aura of intimacy to reduce patient stress and anxiety.

From the time a patient enters the Clinic, the registration personnel, technologists, and physicians strive to satisfy the patient's concern for dignity and timeliness. Qualified personnel answer the patient's questions and

The Radiology Clinic was designed with ample, ground-level parking for easy entry.

Low lighting and soft colors reduce patient stress and anxiety.

report to the patient's physicians. In this facility, patients come first, and serving the needs of the people of West Alabama is a top priority.

The radiologists who wholly own, manage, and practice at The Radiology Clinic have been fully trained in their specialty of diagnostic radiology. Each is certified by the American Board of Radiology and has received at least four to six years of specialized training after obtaining Doctor of Medicine degrees.

The radiologic technologists who assist physicians are certified by the American Registry of Radiologic Technologists. Many of them, as well, have obtained special training in mammography, ultrasound, and noninvasive vascular testing.

Of the several types of testing performed at The Radiology Clinic, the newest is **magnetic resonance imaging.** This imaging involves the use of a powerful magnet, radio waves, and a computer to produce a two- or three-dimensional picture of a portion of the body. MRI is especially effective when used in the diagnosis of brain, nervous system, muscular, skeletal, and circulatory difficulties.

All Radiology Clinic personnel strive to satisfy the concerns of patients of all ages.

Another highly sophisticated technology is **computerized axial tomography** (CT scans). This technology uses x-rays to create a two-dimensional image of a cross-section of the body. Studies of a patient's head can ascertain the presence of tumors, blood clots, or other abnormalities while scans of the body are particularly useful in diagnosing problems with inner organs or blood vessels. MRI and CT scans often replace the need for exploratory surgery.

Nuclear Medicine studies involve using traces of radioactive material to produce detailed images of body parts such as the gallbladder, liver, thyroid, and bones. **Ultrasound**, or sonography, has become a very useful tool in diagnosing problems in soft tissues, such as internal organs, and can be useful in diagnosing aneurysms, blood clots, cancer-damaged tissues, and complications of pregnancy.

Noninvasive vascular studies are used to thoroughly examine arteries and veins to determine the root causes and locations of blood clots and poor circulation.

From the earliest days, the mission of the physicians working at The Radiology Clinic has remained the same:

To obtain clear and detailed images of the body, to diagnose diseases and injuries that suggest appropriate treatment philosophies for the referring physician.

This mission has remained constant through the 50 years of existence of The Radiology Clinic, and serving patients is the end-all of The Radiology Clinic. The Radiology Clinic gives patients the opportunity to be examined by a group of highly qualified diagnostic radiologists—physicians adept at unlocking the secrets of the body's ills through the use of technology with a commitment to caring. ❖

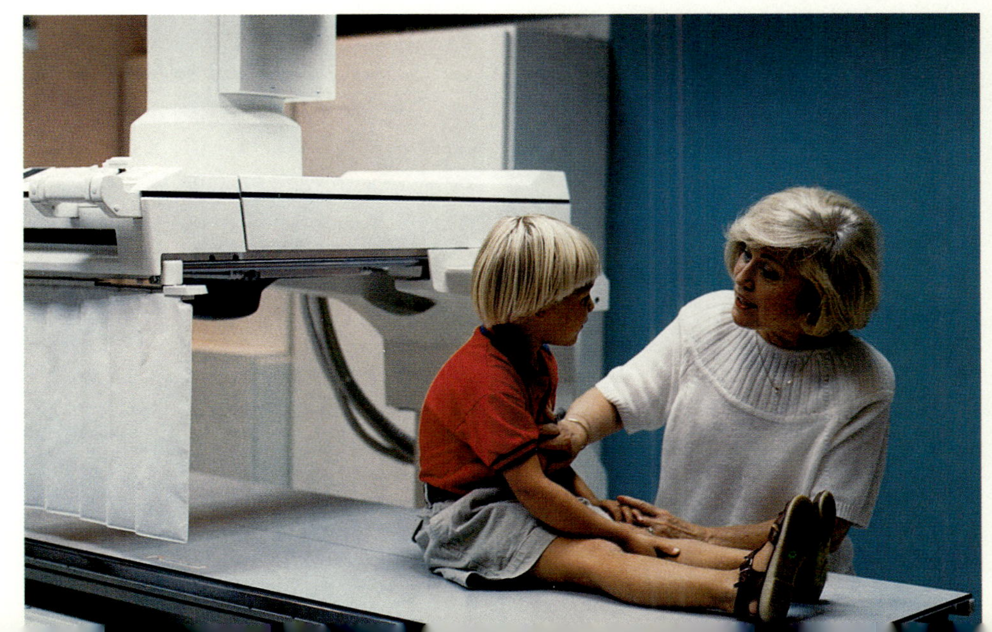

Capstone Medical Center

University of Alabama
School of Medicine-Tuscaloosa

The medical education program at the College of Community Health Sciences at the University of Alabama School of Medicine- Tuscaloosa Program trains physicians—with an emphasis on primary care and developing doctors who will bring the finest in medical care to people in rural communities.

Since its founding in 1972, nearly 300 medical students have completed their clinical training in Tuscaloosa. One hundred and eighty-six Family Practice residents have graduated from the residency program; half have remained in Alabama and of those half are in practice in communities of 25,000 or less.

The Capstone Medical Center is a multi-specialty practice located in Tuscaloosa at The University of Alabama. Faculty member Robert Ireland, M.D., (left) and Dr. Craig Buettner, a family practice physician who is chief resident, take a break from treating patients in CMC clinics.

As a branch campus of the University of Alabama School of Medicine, the College of Community Health Sciences annually trains about 25 third-year medical students, 25 fourth-year medical students, and 36 residents in the discipline of family practice.

DCH Regional Medical Center is the primary hospital utilized in the training of these doctors. The University's Capstone Medical Center serves as the ambulatory care clinic for the program and provides medical care for thousands of people in Tuscaloosa and West Alabama.

The College was established by act of the Alabama Legislature to address a shortage of family practice physicians, particularly in rural areas of the state. The school has had some notable successes in training physicians whose presence in rural Alabama has improved the medical care available in those communities. In order to build on that tradition of success, the College recruits students from rural areas, hoping that they'll want to continue to live a rural lifestyle following graduation; fosters relationships with established, successful rural physicians; and develops managed-care and communications networks to render irrelevant the historical isolation and professional stigma that some have attached to rural practices.

The primary care medical training offered by the College is often cited as one of the key answers to the health care crisis in the United States. The primary care physician is generally the first doctor seen by a patient with a medical need. Fully 95 percent of all the medical problems encountered by people can be treated successfully by a family or primary care physician—at far less cost than more specialized care. For example, continuity of primary care for patients with diabetes or hypertension can forestall significantly or help avoid altogether the expensive dialysis treatment required for advanced renal disease. Primary care can also work wonders in preventing cardiovascular disease and its costly treatment.

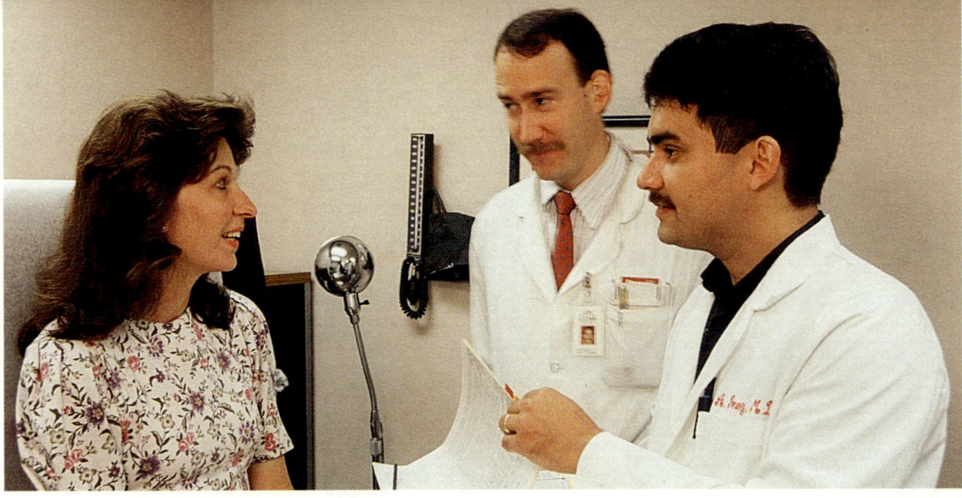

Denis Perez, M.D., (right) Assistant Professor of Obstetrics and Gynecology, and Jeffrey Hopkins, M.D., (center) consult with a patient at Capstone's OB/GYN clinic. Capstone also operates clinics in other specialities and processes laboratory tests on-site.

The curriculum at the College of Community Health Sciences offers the latest training in general internal medicine, general pediatrics, and family practice—all integral components of modern primary care. The College operates three separate facilities in Tuscaloosa: Nott Hall, on the campus quadrangle, houses the school administration as well as the Departments of Psychiatry and Neurology, Internal Medicine, and Behavioral and Community Medicine. The Departments of Pediatrics and Obstetrics and Gynecology are found at the University of Alabama Educational Tower at DCH Regional Medical Center. And the 36,000-square-foot Capstone Medical Center is the ambulatory care center for a group practice consisting of internal medicine, pediatrics, family medicine, psychiatry and neurology, OB/GYN, and occupational medicine.

Faculty, residents, and medical students provide services to hospital patients at DCH and at Tuscaloosa's Veterans Affairs Medical Center. In addition, the school maintains ties with medical practices throughout the state for resident and student training.

Medical care in Tuscaloosa has been enhanced significantly because of the existence of the College. Specialists who might not otherwise practice here are located in Tuscaloosa because of teaching positions at the College, and the opportunities for continuing medical education are enhanced by the school.

Still, the benefits the College brings to Tuscaloosa pale in comparison to the advances in medical care graduates of the College of Community Health Sciences have brought to the people of Alabama for more than two decades. ❖

University Internal Medicine

T he doctors at University Internal Medicine combine personal concern and an intimate knowledge of patients with high-quality and technologically advanced medical treatment to provide the best-possible primary health care for men, women, and adolescents.

"The primary medical care offered by University Internal Medicine is the wave of the future. It is compassionate, high quality, and cost-efficient. It is comprehensive and state-of-the-art, yet in many ways, it harks back to medicine the way it used to be," says practice founder Dr. T. Mark Ricketts.

"Patients are treated with respect. They are listened to and become a partner with the doctor in maintaining their own health. We work hard to develop one-on-one relationships with

Dedicated, compassionate, and caring best describe the physicians at University Internal Medicine.

our patients, really getting to know them as people. So often, physical ailments are really caused by stress factors at home or on the job. To be successful, we have to treat the whole person. We have to understand their environment and what is happening in their lives. Then we can treat the medical problem much more effectively," Dr. Ricketts says.

Internal medicine is the branch of medical care that treats adult illnesses (although the practice begins seeing patients at age 13). Internists are trained extensively to provide primary medical care for ailments ranging from a simple head cold to the management of serious diseases such as diabetes or chronic high blood pressure. The medical knowledge required to care for the many things that can go wrong with the body in adulthood and adolescence is broad-based, and it accounts for the greater training internists must receive before they can begin practicing.

The clinical practice at University Internal Medicine is staffed by four physicians trained in internal medicine and primary care. Two of the four have an additional specialty in infectious diseases. All of the doctors at University Internal Medicine are on the teaching staff of the College of Community Health at the University of Alabama School of Medicine.

Dr. T. Mark Ricketts, a graduate of the University of Alabama School of Medicine,

is an internist and chairman of the Health Care Task Force of the West Alabama Chamber of Commerce. Dr. Keith Collier, a graduate of Wright State University, is a specialist in internal medicine. Dr. Jeffery L.

The staff at University Internal Medicine is dedicated to providing the best-possible primary health care.

Douglas, a graduate of the University of Tennessee, is an internist and a specialist in infectious diseases. Dr. Albert T. White, Jr., a graduate of the University of Liberia, is an internist and a specialist in infectious diseases. Dr. White also specializes in geographic or travel medicine to care for Tuscaloosa-area patients traveling abroad.

The clinical practice at University Internal Medicine was founded in 1991 and is located in the Medical Towers building right in the heart of the DCH Medical Center complex. The location adds to the convenience of patients since advanced testing and diagnostic centers are so close by. The practice draws patients from a 30- to 40-mile radius and employs 13 people.

The health care professionals at University Internal Medicine believe in treating patients as valued customers, and they look after their health needs with sensitivity and respect. ❖

Emergi-Care Clinic, P.C.

Preventive medicine, compassionate and professional care, and the maintenance of a healthy lifestyle. Those are the health care principles followed by Tuscaloosa's Emergi-Care Clinic, P.C. They also happen to be the principles that will likely guide the nation's health care system in the 21st century.

Since its opening in July, 1983, Emergi-Care Clinic, P.C. has been right on the edge of the evolution in modern health care with its reliance on courteous patient service and its devotion to healthy lifestyles and preventative care.

The health care company was founded by Dr. Phillip K. Bobo, who as chief of emergency medical services at DCH Medical Center in Tuscaloosa felt the community needed an alternative to the hospital's emergency department for the treatment of minor injury and illness.

Today Dr. Bobo, who is also state emergency medical services medical director for the Alabama Department of Public Health, co-owns the company with Dr. Pete Weinheimer. In addition,Dr. Bobo owns Gold's Gym in Tuscaloosa with partner Tony Kizzire. The combination of the gym and health club and the primary care clinic is representative of Dr. Bobo's orientation towards total wellness.

Managed care and preventive medicine are the wave of the future, and a big part of the healthy outlook inspired by Dr. Bobo is a strong belief in the ability to change unhealthy lifestyle habits with weight management, stress management, and smoking cessation programs.

Today, with two physicians, nurses (both RNs and LPNs), paramedics, x-ray and lab technicians, and facilities, Emergi-Care offers an extensive array of primary medical care services to patients in Tuscaloosa and the outlying counties. The clinic operates two shifts, employing approximately 25 full and part-time employees. The clinic itself boasts cast rooms, x-ray and lab facilities, treatment rooms, and trauma rooms. A Harco pharmacy operates at the site, a major plus for patient convenience.

Efficiency has always been the key to operations at Emergi-Care. Patients are seen promptly with no appointment necessary. The friendly staff is courteous and professional and devoted to making follow-up calls to be certain advice is being heeded and that patients are making a good recovery. The freestanding primary care clinic really caters to people who work; the professionals understand the needs of working patients and try hard to meet them.

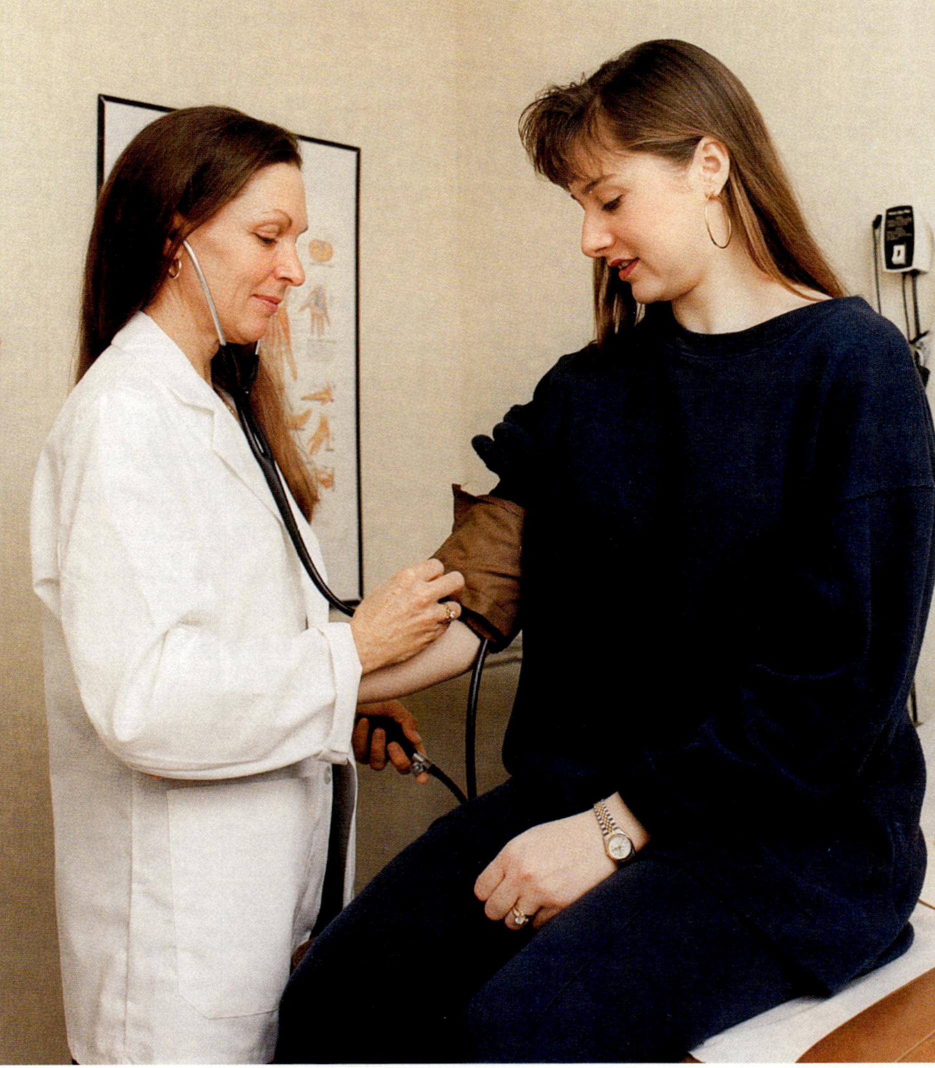

Emergi-Care provides for all of your family's medical needs with professional care.

A growth area within Emergi-Care's business has been the expansion of the company's work in industrial medicine. The company specializes in performing pre-employment and insurance physical examinations, as well as worker's compensation case management.

In treating injured employees, Emergi-Care's goal is to get an individual back to work as soon as possible with a well-developed program of work conditioning. The result is a worker restored to health and a business restored to efficiency.

Efficiency. Good patient relations. Healthy living. Quality medical care. Convenience. Service. Those are the hallmarks of Emergi-Care Clinic and the reason so many trust the clinic's seasoned professionals with their health. ❖

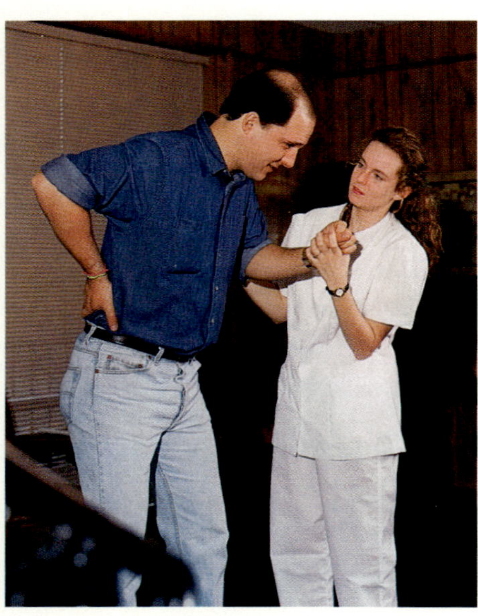

Job related injuries are treated quickly at Emergi-Care by caring professionals.

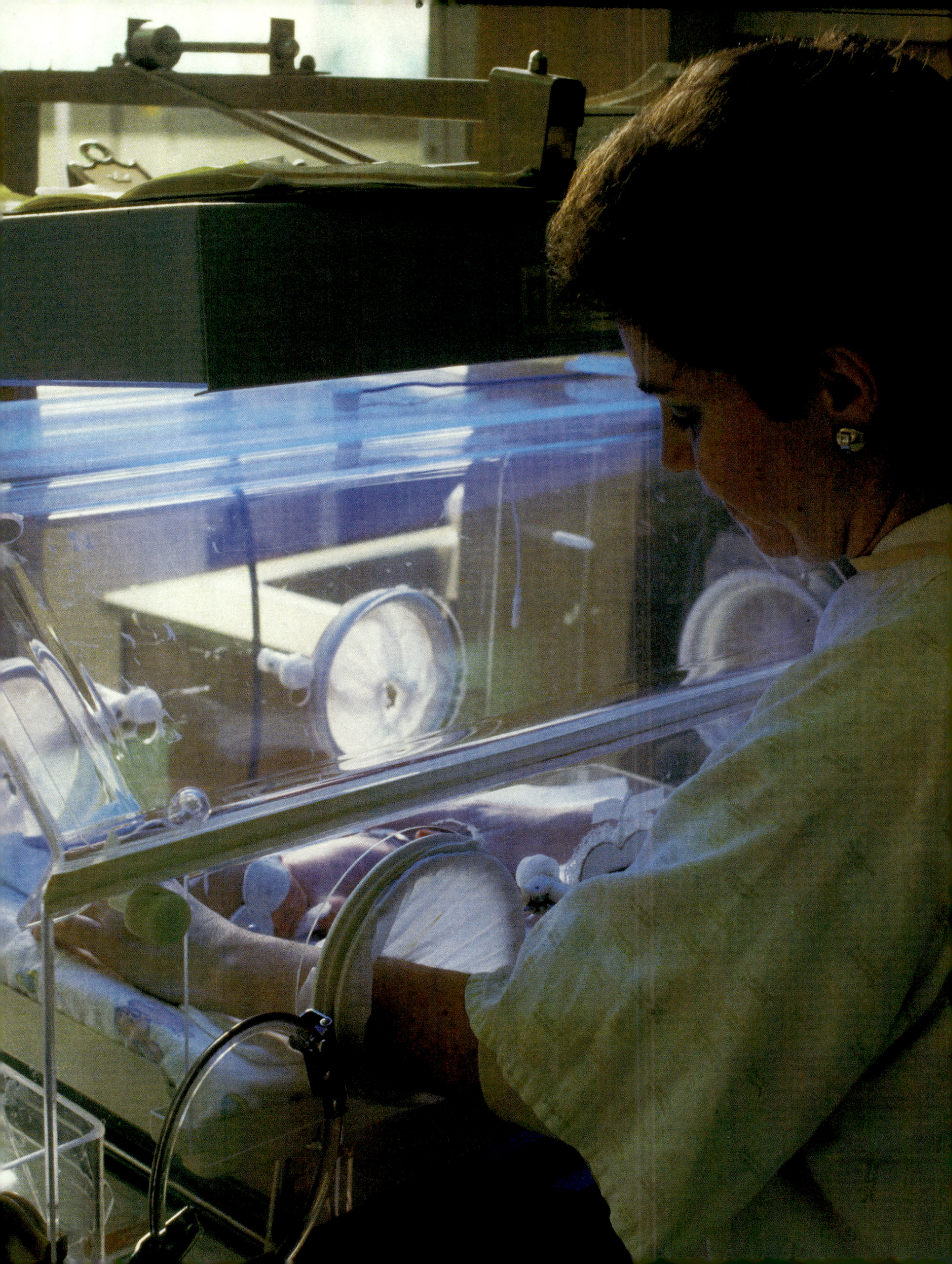

Bibliography

Willis, Kenneth D.; The Harnessing of the Black Warrior River; City of Tuscaloosa, Alabama, 1989.

Hubbs, G. Ward; *Tuscaloosa: A Portrait of An Alabama Community*; Windsor Publications, Inc.; Northridge, California; 1987.

Ball, Marie Shamblin; "Partners in Progress," *Tuscaloosa: A Portrait of An Alabama Community*; Windsor Publications, Inc., Northridge, California, 1987.

Survey of History and Architecture, Tuscaloosa, Alabama; The Heritage Commission of Tuscaloosa County; 1984.

Erlenbach, Peter J., "Transportation Analysis of Major Street Plan;" Community Planning & Development Department, City of Tuscaloosa, Alabama; 1992.

"Report on the Development of Tuscaloosa, Alabama;" Bureau of Business Research, University of Alabama; New Industries Committee of the Greater Tuscaloosa Chamber of Commerce, 1952.

Alabama West Magazine; Alabama West/University of Alabama; George Frangoulis, Publisher & Editor-in-Chief; 1990-1994.

Clark, E. Culpepper; *The Stand In the School House Door: Segregation's Last Stand at The University of Alabama*; Oxford University Press; 1993.

Duke, Drue; *Alabama Tales*; Vision Press; 1994.

Acknowledgements

Special appreciation is extended to all of the individuals and groups that provided materials, thoughts, and ideas to create this publication, many of which are quoted throughout. Your unselfish contributions have made a meaningful impact on the final product.

The following provided specific assistance, support, and encouragement in the development of *Tuscaloosa: The Tradition, The Spirit, The Vision*, for which I am grateful.

Staff, Past and Present of *The Tuscaloosa News*
Kellee Reinhart
Cordell Wynn
Arts Council of Tuscaloosa County
Industrial Development Authority of Tuscaloosa County
Cindy Richardson
The University of Alabama
Dr. Barry Mason

Tuscaloosa's Enterprises Index

Index

This book was set in Times Regular and Frutiger Black at Community Communications, Montgomery, Alabama, and printed on 80lb. Warren Flo Text.